Subotica

Bačka

avonia

•Osijek

lavonski Brod

•Vinkovci

•Novi Sad

Banat

Srijem

•Brčko

a

Bosnia

•Tuzla

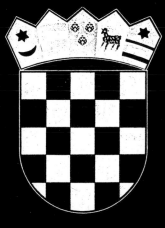

d

• Sarajevo

Herzegovina

• Mostar

Dubrovnik

Kotor

Croatian Cuisine

Croatian Cuisine

Croatian Cuisine
Revised Edition

Ružica Kapetanović & Alojzije Kapetanović

Food Photography by
Ivan Kapetanović

Associated Book Publishers, Inc.
P. O. Box 5657
Scottsdale, AZ 85261-5657
(602) 837-9388

Published by
Associated Book Publishers, Inc.
P.O. Box 5657, Scottsdale, AZ 85261-5657.

This edition is an expansion and revision of *Croatian Cuisine* published by Associated Publishers, San Mateo, CA, copyright © 1978 by Alojzije Kapetanović and Ružica Kapetanović

Library of Congress Catalog Card Number: 92-074953
International Standard Book No. 0-910164-18-5
Printed and bound in the United States of America by Delmar Printing and Publishing.

A note from the publisher: A share of the proceeds earned from the sales of this book will be contributed to the rebuilding of Croatia and Bosnia and Herzegovina.

Dedication

To our parents who taught us to love Croatia and appreciate her culture—our mother, Tereza Dragić Kapetanović, who first intoduced us to the pleasures of Croatian cooking and our father, Ivan Kapetanović, who taught us about Croatia's history and inspired us to learn more.

To all Croatian parents who have instilled a love of their homeland and their culture in their children.

To the brave and determined Croatian people who have persevered through a turbulent and difficult history. To a people who have never lost their pride and identity as a peace-loving, hard-working and progressive nation.

May the ideals of the new Croatian Republic serve future generations to live in peace and harmony with all their neighbors and with the rest of the world.

Acknowledgements

The authors would like to thank Marina Radman for her inspiration, support and encouragement during the revision of this book.

We are especially grateful to Ivanka Kapetanović for her help and support, for designing most of the layouts of the food photographs and for her careful reading and editing of the manuscript.

We are indebted to Vlado Novak for kindly supplying us with many of the photographs for the introduction. Photographs on pages 36, 37, 135, 142, 149, 168 and 175 are courtesy of Alojzije and Emica Kapetanović.

To Dr. Vlado Šakić of the Institute for Applied Social Research at the University of Zagreb we extend our deepest thanks for his support and encouragement. Mr. Stjepan Šterc of the same institute was most generous in reading the introduction and providing many helpful insights and suggestions.

We are grateful to Deborah Draženović for generously giving us her recipe for *breskve*, Mock Peaches and Mary (Marija) Urota Harris for sharing with us her cousin's recipe for *pršunate*, Dalmatian fritters.

We would like to thank all our wonderful friends who have supported our family and stood by us during this difficult past year. A special word of thanks to all our wonderful readers who have waited so patiently for this revision.

Our gratitude is great to all those who have helped in the production of this book, but the authors alone assume responsibility for any possible errors or omissions.

Preface

We are pleased to present a completely revised and expanded version of *Croatian Cuisine*, a book that introduces to the rest of the world the splendid and unique cooking of Croatia. Our intent in writing the original version of *Croatian Cuisine* was to share with the English-speaking world and with the rest of the world this rich area of Croatian culture.

Through his appreciation of Croatian history and culture, Alojzije was inspired to share the rich culinary tradition of Croatia. Seeing a void in the area of Croatian cooking, he conceived the idea of preparing a Croatian cookbook that would also share a little of Croatia's rich history. Ružica enthusiastically accepted the idea and together we authored the original version of *Croatian Cuisine*.

There has been a tremendous demand for *Croatian Cuisine*. We have considered revising the book for some time. The recent tragic history of Croatia, together with her newly established independence have spurned us to make those revisions. We are confident that our readers will agree that the revised edition has been worth waiting for. We have displayed many of the recipes in this book with beautiful color photographs. Not only does this make the book more pleasurable to read, but it offers suggestions for ways of garnishing and serving the food presented in this volume.

No cookbook could possibly include all the foods that are prepared in Croatia and all the variations that one can find. However, we have attempted to give a representational sample of the cooking of the various regions of Croatia. We hope that many of our readers will find recipes that reproduce the wonderful foods prepared by their mothers and grandmothers.

All the recipes in *Croatian Cuisine* have been adapted for the American kitchen. No special foods or utensils are required. However, we would recommend looking for smoked meats at a European specialty store. Many of our recipes lose their very essence if prepared with cured meats. Unless otherwise stated, the recipes in this book will serve six. Eggs are assumed to be large and the butter is unsalted.

There may be small differences in flavor between the foods prepared in Croatia and North America because the basic ingredients used here do not always match those found in Europe. However, you will find that they are delicious none the less. In fact, some American produce results in certain dishes that are even better than the original version!

Finally, we would like to thank our readers who have taken the time to write to us. Please continue to write to us in care of Associated Book Publishers, Inc. We appreciate receiving your ideas and suggestions.

We hope that you will enjoy our work. May you have much success in all your cooking and baking.

The Authors

Table of Contents

Table of Photographs

Croatia is rich in plains, mountains, forests and seashore.

Introduction

Croatia has always been at the crossroads between East and West—historically and culturally a part of the West, but bordering with the East. As a result, many neighboring cultures have left their mark on the Croatian heritage, and particularly her cuisine. This confluence of regional influences is one of the most fascinating features of Croatian cooking, which represents a microcosm of European cooking, but with a distinctly Croatian character. The cuisine of Croatia reflects her complex history and rich tradition. Because of its diversity, it is impossible to isolate one or two distinguishing features that characterize Croatian cooking.

Geographic Location

Croatia's location provides such a diversity of terrains and climates that each region has its own resources from which cooks have improvised for centuries. Croatia's cuisine has distinct regional features. It is often possible to determine the region that a recipe comes from by its ingredients.

Croatia's cultural mosaic spreads across 72,000 square miles from the Adriatic Sea in the west to the border with Slovenia in the northwest, Hungary to the north and the Balkans to the east—the River Drina is the natural and historical border separating Bosnia and Herzegovina from Serbia. For the purposes of discussing Croatian culinary tradition, we refer to all the regions which have historically had a predominantly Croatian population, tradition and cultural heritage as belonging to Croatia.

Croatia is rich in a variety of terrain—rich plains, numerous mountain ranges, lush forests, and a long coastline. In addition to the beautiful blue Adriatic Sea, Croatia boasts many rivers and mountain streams. Rich mineral water springs are abundant throughout the country, and the water is often mixed with wine in a "spritzer."

Geographically, historically and culturally, Croatia can be roughly divided into three major regions—the Pannonian, the Adriatic, and the Dinaric. Northern Croatia, which encompasses the Pannonian plain, is comprised of the regions of Zagorje, Prigorje, Slavonia, and Sriem. Culturally and historically Bačka and Banat also belong to this region. Southern Croatia, the Adriatic region, includes Istria, the Kvarner-Velebit Littoral and Dalmatia, all of which border on the Adriatic Sea. The easternmost region, known as the Dinaric area of the country, includes Lika, Gorski Kotar, and culturally and historically Bosnia, Herzegovina and Sandžak. Each of these regions has developed an individual character and is fiercely proud of its heritage, its culture, and its culinary tradition.

The Pannonian Region

The Pannonian region of Northern Croatia consists largely of vast plains and rich forests, with some hilly regions near the Slovenian border. This area is marked by a continental climate of hot summers and cold winters.

Bačka, Banat, Baranja, Slavonia and Sriem provide a rich agricultural plain with soil that is extremely fertile. The region is naturally irrigated by the Tisa, Sava, Drava and Danube rivers. Because of the rich soil and the year-round rainfall, this area produces a wealth of grains, including wheat, corn, rye, barley and oats.

Croatia is renowned for its excellent wheat. With a high percentage of dextrin, the wheat grown in the area around Subotica, in Bačka, is considered to be the best in Europe. It has always been in high demand for pastry flour. It is obvious why this region is best known for its breads and fine delicate pastries. Croatian housewives have maintained the well-developed art of baking, and much of the baking of pastries continues to be done at home. The quality of these baked goods usually exceeds that of bakery products.

Much of Northern Croatia is fertile agricultural land.

Because grain is a major product of Northern Croatia, the breeding and raising of pork is also very important to the area. Arrays of Slavonian smoked sausages and hams, and huge slabs of smoked bacon are proudly displayed in shop windows. In addition to preserving sausages by smoking, when refrigeration was not available, this region developed an interesting method of storing them in lard in deep crocks.

This gastronomically rich region of Croatia has historically been the wealthiest. The region is characterized by lively tamburitza music, and the love of traditional songs and dances. The national costumes of Slavonia were frequently embroidered with gold thread, those of Bačka with rich silk threads on imported Italian velvet.

Osijek, the capital city of the province of Slavonia, is situated on the Drava river. This region, which borders with Hungary, produces fine fruits and vegetables, grapes and chestnuts. Rich mushroom dishes are characteristic of the region and are made throughout Slavonia. The mushroom yield of the thick forests is dried and exported throughout Europe and the world.

Sriem lies in the picturesque southeast corner of Northern Croatia. The Roman Emperor Probus Marcus Aurelius, a native of this fertile region, ordered the planting of vineyards along the hills of Fruška Gora. During peaceful times, he had soldiers plant the seedlings. This planting was such a success that he also planted vineyards in neighboring regions.

All of Northern Croatia, especially the regions of Medjimurje and Zagorje, are studded with goose farms. The geese are force-fed, with naturally grown corn. This type of feeding makes them exceedingly plump, with tender over-sized livers. The resulting goose livers are recognized as a rare delicacy throughout the world. Other forms of fowl that are very popular and abundant in this area and throughout the country include chickens, turkeys and ducks. During hunting season the repertoire increases to include partridges, pheasants, wild ducks and wild geese. All of these fowl find their way to Croatian tables.

Zagreb, Croatia's capital, is the center of Croatia's political thought and administrative function. The charming city of Zagreb is the pride of Croatia. It embraces the complete character of the national cuisine, north and south, as well as

Photo: J. Bombelles
National costume from the region of Slavonia.

the refinements of international cooking.

In Zagreb, one relives the atmosphere of the continental charm of Old Europe. Strolling through the city in a typical Zagreb promenade, the visitor is surrounded by some of the world's most beautiful Gothic and Baroque architecture.

Zagreb's *slastičarne*, dainty little pastry shops along the city's central squares, offer tempting sweets—trays of pastries stacked high and filled with whipped cream, coffee cream, chocolate cream or any of a number of fruit and jam fillings. These delightful creations are also served with coffee in the quaint little *kavane* and in outdoor cafés that dot the avenues.

It is in these Croatian coffee houses that the country's literary tradition developed and flourished for centuries. The city followed Budapest and Vienna in becoming one of the glorious centers of Western European civilization.

Restaurants in Zagreb provide menus from around the country and from around the world. Certain to be included are the famed *Zagrebački Odresci*, tender veal cutlets stuffed with a thin slice of Trappist cheese and a wafer slice of *pršut* ham, then fried to golden perfection. An excellent accompaniment to this main course is *Zagrebačka Salata*, a delightful salad which combines fresh garden vegetables and is garnished with a vinegar and oil dressing.

Zagreb, the capital city of Croatia.

The entire coast is majestically beautiful.

The Adriatic Region

The breathtaking Croatian Riviera is a popular and sought-after tourist attraction. Subsequently, this is the beautiful region of Croatia with which foreign visitors are most familiar. Croatia boasts Europe's most beautiful island-sprinkled coastline, which stretches from the quaint old towns of the heart-shaped peninsula of Istria in the north to south of Dubrovnik, the medieval Republic of Ragusa.

The entire coast is majestically beautiful, carved into countless peninsulas, coves and inlets. Much of the coast is rocky, and the narrow beaches are generally sandy, especially on the islands and in the south. The water of the Adriatic Sea is incredibly clear, right to the seabed. The utopian climate of the southern coast can hardly be matched anywhere in the world. The temperature averages 75° fahrenheit in the summer, with a full twelve hours of sunshine per day.

In addition to the natural beauty of the Istrian coast, the northern part of the Croatian Riviera offers many splendors of history and art. Every few miles one encounters the remnants of the glory that was once Rome.

The ancient town gate of the city of Zadar.

The highlights include the fresco-covered village churches, the sixth century basilica in Poreč, and the Roman amphitheater in Pula which was built in the first century A.D. The amphitheater is much better preserved than the more famous Roman coliseum. Venice seriously considered dismantling the entire arena and reassembling it in Italy, but never undertook the move. Theatrical productions continue to be staged at the amphitheater after nearly 2000 years.

Rijeka, a bustling port city, is also a crossroad for the many tourists who visit the northern Croatian coast. The city is surrounded by vacation spots such as Opatija and Crikvenica, where summer resorts offer bathing facilities, fishing, aquatic sports and an active night life.

Other coastal cities have for centuries been examples of well-preserved architecture which are cherished national treasures. The ancient city of Zadar which dates from pre-Roman times contains many Roman ruins and many buildings from Venetian times. Holy pilgrims frequently travelled to the city to see the fourteenth century sarcophagus which contains the remains of Saint Simon.

The first-century Roman amphitheater in Pula.

Diocletian's palace, now the center of the Old Town of Split.

Split can be considered Croatia's coastal capital. It is not only a major business center, but an important art and education center. Split is a beautiful old city that blends Gothic, Romanesque and Renaissance architecture. The Emperor Diocletian, a native of the area, built a magnificent palace for his retirement in this coastal city. He had huge granite columns from Egyptian temples and marble columns from Greek temples transported to Split to create this vast palace which covered over 270,000 sq. ft. A black granite sphinx representing the Pharaoh Tutmosis III from the fifteeth century B.C. was also brought from Egypt and lies under the last arch of the Peristyle.

The palace now forms the nucleus of the Old Town with a population of 4,000 people within its ancient walls. In its narrow streets one finds dwellings, boutiques, restaurants and offices, as well as several little squares. The peristyle, the inner court surrounded by columns, makes an excellent outdoor theater where concerts are held and operas are staged during the summer months.

Another example of well-preserved architecture is Sibenik's cathedral of St. Jacob. Its outer walls feature an intriguing frieze by the fifteenth century sculptor and architect Juraj

Frieze on St. Jacob's cathedral in Šibenik.

Dalmatinac. The frieze depicts over 70 citizens of the city, who according to legend, neglected to donate for the building of the cathedral. Some of the faces included in the frieze are said to represent some of the builders of the cathedral.

Over one thousand islands dot the Adriatic Sea along the length of the Croatian Riviera. Many are uninhabited, but some of the larger islands support several towns. Nestled near the Pelješac peninsula lies the pleasantly wooded island of Korčula. This is the famed birthplace of Marco Polo (Polić). A section of the Polić family house still stands on the island today. According to legend, the island was settled by Trojans in the twelfth century B.C., then taken over by the Romans under the leadership of Octavian Augustus. In the ninth century A.D., Croatians settled the island and have inhabited this sunny paradise for over a thousand years.

Like Korčula, Croatia's largest island, Krk, and the longest island, Hvar, offer the visitor a peaceful place to relax and to view some of the world's best preserved ancient architecture.

The long, narrow island of Pag is renowned for its highly prized *Paški sir*. This cheese is a hard, strong variety produced from the milk of sheep that graze the island's sparse grass. The island is also famed for its delicate, intricately worked lace which was once shipped directly to Vienna's imperial court.

The narrow streets of Dubronvik.

Dubrovnik, the pearl of the Adriatic.   Photo: S. Cajzek

The city of Dubrovnik has often been referred to as Europe's crowning jewel. From the unconquered stone wall that surrounds the city to the Rennaissance architecture, Dubrovnik recounts its rich history. For centuries the city has been one of Croatia's major cultural centers with a wealth of contributions to the arts and sciences.

Dubrovnik is certainly Croatia's tourist capital. It has luxurious water, sun and color, is surrounded by villas, hotels, bathing beaches and picturesque and attractive surroundings for excursions. Dubrovnik is not only a trade and navigational center, but also represents a centuries long literary and artistic tradition. Frequently called the pearl of the Adriatic, this enchanting city is considered one of the most beautiful in the world.

Dubrovnik's medieval past is reflected in the independent spirit of the people. An independent state for centuries, Dubrovnik's prosperity allowed her to become the cradle or Croatian art and literature. Her beauty has always atrratcted artists and free spirits, native Croatians and foreigners alike.

Like Venice, the city was an independent republic for many centuries that grew wealthy through trade. Her fearless sailors have long been hailed as Croatia's prolific wanderers, whose merchant vessels traversed the globe, trading between east and west.

The Dinaric Region

From the picturesque coast, one can reach up to the rugged Dinaric mountains which link Coastal Croatia with the inland sections of the country. This verdant limestone mountain range is full of clear streams and excellent wild game. In Lika, at the base of the mountains the streams flow over rocks, yielding a variety of freshwater lobsters which grow to substantial size. The most unique natural phenomenon in this region is the Plitvice Lakes, a chain of sixteen lakes joined by a fantastic succession of waterfalls and rapids against a background of thick, rich forests. Its crystal waters house an abundance of freshwater fish, including the popular trout. It is certainly one of the most magnificent natural landscapes in the world.

Lamb has long been popularly enjoyed in the region of Lika. Like the Bosnians, Ličanins enjoy young lamb roasted over live coals and served with green onions. The region around Gospić, the largest city of Lika, is the birthplace of Nikola Tesla. He immigrated to the United States at the turn of the century where, after leaving the employ of Thomas Alva Edison, he distinguished himself as an inventor in the field of electrical energy. He had over 100 patents issued to him in the United States. As the discoverer of alternating current, he is responsible for the eletricity that we use today.

Even a very simple spit roast can grill a succulent roast pig.

Despite its mountainous terrain, much of Bosnia is heavily wooded. The rich forests are full of wild animal life, from rabbits and red row and fallow deer to wolves, boar and foxes. Here we can also find the brown bear, which is rare elsewhere in Europe. Life in these regions is at times harsh, but Croatians are a hardy people who have outlasted the centuries.

The mountains are rich in minerals and the hard labor performed by the population demanded hearty, substantial dishes. Best known of these hearty dishes are *Bosanski Lonac*, a rich vegetable and meat casserole that won first prize at a Paris International Cooking Competition in the late nineteenth century, and *Hercegovački Duveč*, a baked meat and vegetable casserole.

Bosnia and Herzegovina were under Ottoman subjugation for over four centuries. Mosques with their characteristic minarets are found in most of the major

Plitvice Lakes.   Photo: Vilko Zuber

Photo: S. Cajzek   *The beautiful mountainous regions of Bosnia.*

6

The bašćaršija in the old part of Sarajevo.

cities. *Kavane*, Croatian coffeehouses, serve an important social function as meeting places for relaxation, the exchange of ideas, and discussion of current events. The fascinating contrasts of Bosnia and Herzegovina have enriched Croatia and her cuisine.

Sarajevo, which can be considered Croatia's third cultural capital, reflects an eastern flavor after several centuries of Turkish occupation. The influence of east and west have succeeded each other in this colorful city situated on the Miljacka River.

Sarajevo was an international trading center, attracting caravans from East and West. As a result, many fountains and public baths were built for the convenience of travellers. The view of the city's lovely Moslem houses with latticed windows, and the ornate mosques is truly breathtaking from nearby Mount Trebević. It is not surprising that this picturesque city was called the most beautiful in the Ottoman empire.

The historical commercial center of Sarajevo, called the *bašćaršija*, is a "pedestrians only" maze of narrow streets and alleys. The name derives from Turkish and meant "market place" at the time of Ottoman rule. Around this nucleus were craft centers and streets were named after the various craftsmen and artisans who worked there—coppersmith, cobbler, goldsmith and so on.

Bosnia has given us the famous Croatian Trappist cheese. Trappist monks originally produced the cheese in their monastery of Mariastern. The cheese became a favorite in the entire country. It was carried by the merchant ships of Dubrovnik to ports of call throughout Europe. The

cheese is semisoft and mild in flavor, produced from cow's milk. The French adopted the cheese, which is now being marketed around the world as *Port du Salut*.

The Bosnian town of Travnik is reminiscent of the long Turkish occupation with many fortresses and mosques. Travnik has given its name to another excellent Croatian cheese that originated in the area. *Travnički sir* is a rich, salty cheese made from sheep's milk.

The charming, picturesque city of Mostar is the capital and center of Herzegovina. It lies peacefully on the Neretva River among rugged mountains between Sarajevo and

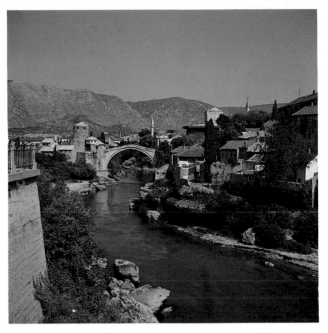

Photo: S. Cajzek   *The ancient town of Mostar in Herzegovina.*

Dubrovnik. Vineyards, tobacco fields and groves of fig trees surround the town. Mostar derives its name from the ancient arched bridge that forms an enchanting frame for the Old Town. It was built in 1566 under the threat of death to the architect if the bridge collapsed as had others before it. The architect is said to have begun digging his own grave upon completion of the project, but his monumental engineering feat has lasted for over 400 years.

Croatian Gastronomy

The Croatian diet is based upon fresh fruits and vegetables, various meats, and assorted dairy products. Casseroles, soups, stews, and stuffed vegetables use a variety of meats. Although preferences vary regionally, pork and lamb can be considered the nation's meat staples. These meats are most popularly grilled, whole for festive occasions, or as *ražnjići* (skewered meats), *ćevapčići* (grilled little meat sausages), or as *pljeskavica* (grilled round meat patties). All can be served sprinkled with chopped onion, or accompanied by a crisp lettuce and onion salad. Spit-roasted meats are extremely popular throughout the country, and many restaurants specialize in outdoor grilled lamb or pork which is often served on outdoor terraces.

The bases for flavoring food vary regionally. Pickled vegetables, especially sauerkraut, are an important staple in the north, serving both as a vegetable and as an important flavoring. Inland, fried smoked bacon, onion, and paprika can be considered the most important bases for flavoring meats, stews and casseroles. Vegetables are layered and alternated with meats to produce savory casseroles.

Olive oil is much more frequently used on the coast and represents an important feature of Istrian and Dalmatian cooking.

Sour cream is a favorite ingredient in Croatian cooking. It is used as a flavoring or additive in soups, sauces, vegetables, stews, meats or desserts. Cheeses, many unnamed, are produced in every part of the country and the variety is seemingly endless. They can be found in cakes, desserts and as flavorings for other foods. Cheeses are most frequently served as appetizers in the inland regions of Croatia, or at the close of a meal, Mediterranean style, on the coast.

Croatia's varied topography and climate are conducive to cultivating a large variety of quality fruits and vegetables. The salt air of the coastal regions, the rich inland soil and the use of natural fertilizers all contribute to the flavor of the produce used in Croatian cooking.

Green, yellow and red peppers have sweet, tender meat and are served fresh in salads, cooked as a vegetable, or stuffed with meat and rice. They also provide an important flavoring for meats, stews, and casseroles. Vine-ripened tomatoes are so sweet that they can almost be eaten as a fruit as well as a vegetable. They, too, are a frequent ingredient in many dishes and serve as a popular vegetable for a variety of salads.

The cucumber, another very popular vegetable, is frequently served with sour cream as a *Croatian Cucumber Salad*. Eggplant, asparagus, zucchini, okra and green beans can be served as a vegetable, but are more popularly stuffed, or served in casseroles and meat stews.

Croatia is Europe's leader in the production of plums, marketing them around the world in the form of fresh plums, as dried prunes, in a rich plum jam known as *pekmez*, and as the fiery *šljivovica*, the famous Croatian plum brandy. Although the center of plum production is Brčko on the Sava River, the fruit is widely cultivated throughout Croatia. Plums are used in desserts, cakes, dumplings and in fish and meat dishes such as **Croatian Trout,** a specialty of baked trout stuffed with prunes and *Dalmatinska Pašticada*, a rich beef pot roast stuffed with prunes.

Other quality fruits are cultivated throughout Croatia. The favorable climatic conditions in Northern Croatia yield a variety of apples, pears, quince, cherries and apricots.

With its Mediterranean climate, the coast is a haven for a variety of fruit trees. Dalmatia and Istria produce almonds, figs, pomegranates, lemons, oranges, dates, carob, olives and the famed Croatian sour cherries. These cherries are most frequently exported in the form of the world renowned Dalmatian maraschino cherries and maraschino liqueur from the region around Maraska.

Croatian cooking utilizes a variety of herbs and spices. Favored seasonings include paprika, bay leaf, marjoram, rosemary, basil, dill, cloves, and parsley. Onions, garlic, shallots, parsley roots, lemon, olive oil and vinegar are also used as flavorings. Unlike Balkan cooking, Croatian cuisine is not overly spiced. It is colorful and varied, blending the individual characteristics of the ingredients. The role of flavorings and spices is to accent the natural flavors of the food—they must not confuse the flavors of the prime ingredients.

Perhaps one of the most charming traditions that lingers in Croatia is her vibrant, early morning open-air food markets. Croatia is one of the European countries where fresh farm produce is still brought daily into the major cities and marketed by the local farmers. Seasonal products from the fertile plains, the Adriatic Sea, and the coast can be purchased at the outdoor stands piled high with fresh produce. These markets are often more than a place to purchase fresh seasonal foods—they are a place to greet neighbors and to exchange the latest news and gossip.

The dazzling blue water of the Adriatic Sea provides an incredible variety of seafood. It is said that there are over 365 varieties of fish, one for every day of the year. Fried or grilled smelts and sardines often make a very simple meal. Bass, tuna, flounder, swordfish, halibut and mackerel are all abundant. Cod is especially popular and may be found fresh or salted. Shellfish such as lobster, crab, oyster, shrimp and mussel find their way into many coastal dishes.

Croatian Wines

Although the coastal regions are the most important wine grape growing areas, one can see vineyards throughout Croatia. Wines are plentiful and with innumerable varieties. Many are exported around the world.

Istria's best known wines are the red wines. *Teran*, a powerful dark wine comes from this region as does *Refoško*, which is lighter in both color and bouquet. *Malvazija*, an excellent white wine, is available either sweet or dry.

Several fine Pinots are also produced in this region.

Dalmatian *Opoli* is a sophisticated rosé of high repute enjoyed by many. *Prošek* is an excellent dessert wine with a distinctive golden brown color, resulting from the fact that it is made from fermented raisins. Between Split and Dubrovnik lies the peninsula of Pelješac where the inhabitants drink *Dingač*, a dark red wine marked by richness and fullness of flavor.

The elongated island of Hvar, famous for its fields of fragrant lavender, and the two neighboring islands of Brač and Vis also produce excellent wines. *Plavac* is a dark wine from Hvar. Vis and Brač produce *Marastina* and *Vugava*, strong golden wines with a delightful flavor. The strong will of the inhabitants of Korčula is reflected in its strong white wine called *Grk*.

Mostarska *Žilavka*, a golden yellow wine of delicate bouquet, has been cultivated and produced in Herzegovina since Roman times. King Tvrtko mentions this wine in a document dating from 1353. In 1866, a winery was founded to supply the royal residence at Vienna with this Croatian wine. *Žilavka* has been exported around the world. Along with the exquisite white wine, Herzegovina prides itself on a dark red wine called *Blatina*.

Sriem produces *Iločki Traminer* which has a marked aroma and is low in acidity, making the sparkling wine pleasantly sweet. *Graševina* and *Iločki Silvaner* are two excellent white wines from this area. The latter was served at the banquet celebrating the coronation of Queen Elizabeth II of England. These fine wines are complemented by an excellent selection of reislings and *rosés*.

In addition, Croatia produces excellent local wines which may not be commercially sold, but are used by the inhabitants of the region producing them.

Croatian Meals

Many Croatians begin the day with the ubiquitous *šljivovica* brandy and a light continental breakfast consisting of coffee, crusty fresh European breakfast rolls (*žemičke*) spread with butter, jam or marmalade. Since this is not a

Grapes are grown throughout Croatia.

very substantial meal, it is often followed by a mid-morning *marenda*. The *marenda* may be as simple as yogurt, a spicy smoked sausage and a roll accompanied by a small bottle of wine; or it may be as elaborate as a formal luncheon meal.

The most popular marenda foods are the smoked meats, sausages, ham, or other products from among the large selection of Croatian *charcuterie*. Egg satarash, or a stuffed vegetable are also popular alternatives, depending upon how much time the individual can afford to indulge on the mid-morning meal.

Ručak, the main meal of the day, is served in mid-afternoon around two or three o'clock. This is usually a family meal with everyone dining from grandparents to little ones. Work schedules often end at this time leaving the rest of the afternoon free for other pursuits. Stores and offices frequently close in the early afternoon, reopening in the evening. *Ručak* is generally a substantial meal including soup, meat, potatoes, rice dumplings or noodles, a cooked vegetable and a fresh salad. Dessert may be fresh fruit, a fruit salad, pastry, or an elegant preparation, depending on the occasion.

Večera, the evening meal, is usually not served until seven or eight o'clock. This light supper is often a simple meal, a main course of stuffed vegetables, *sarma*, eggs, a

An array of Slavonian smoked meats.

salad, smoked meats, hams or a light casserole. This final meal may be followed by fresh fruit, or a light pastry.

Later in the evening, coffee may be served. This is generally Turkish coffee, and is usually served accompanied by a plateful of delicate pastries, a slice of torte, *baklava,* or perhaps a piece of *savijaća.*

Holidays and Festivities

Croatians are a warm, hospitable people who enjoy entertaining. Almost any event can be turned into an occasion for feasting and visiting. Whether the occasion is festive, a simple gathering, or a neighborly visit, guests are highly respected and will always be greeted with a warm, "*dobro nam došli!*" welcome. The hosts will spare no cost or effort in extending themselves to please and satisfy their guests.

A prompt offering of drinks follows a cordial welcome. Glasses of *šljivovica, rakija,* or any one of a number of famed Croatian brandies, will be downed with the Croatian toast *živili.* In Moslem homes, the drink is likely to be a cup of thick, strong *Turska kava* with a sweet Bosnian dessert.

Before a formal meal, drinks may be accompanied by delicate appetizers served on silver, brass or hand-cut crystal serving dishes. These appetizers frequently take the form of arrays of sliced salamis, cheeses, caviar, *pršut,* smoked meats and fish or elegant canapés and patées served on bits of toast or on crackers.

Festive holidays are most frequently associated with one of Croatia's major religions. Most Croatians are Christians, largely Roman Catholic, but a substantial portion of the population adheres to Islam which was introduced the time of the Turkish conquest in the 15th century. Although Islam is more prevalent in Bosnia and Herzegovina, a new mosque and cultural center was recently built in Zagreb to serve the Moslem population of Croatia's capital.

Jewish Croatians are more numerous in the larger cities, but many have blended with the Christian population throughout Croatia. Passover is the most important holiday of the year celebrated by Jews. Included in this collection of recipes is a popular Passover chicken preparation stuffed with matzo and chicken liver. Matzo is the Jewish unleavened "bread of affliction" symbolizing the unleavened dough carried by the Jews during their exodus from Egypt.

The major holiday of Moslem Croatians is Bajram, while the most important Christian holidays are Easter and Christmas. All of these holidays are festive celebrations after a greater or lesser period of fasting.

Easter is most frequently celebrated with ham, although turkey is often substituted in northern Croatia. To the Catholic Croatians, *poklade* is an important event marking the beginning of Lenten fasting. *Pokladnice,* jam filled cakes fried in hot oil, are an important part of the Croatian Shrove Tuesday celebration.

For Croatians, Easter is an important holiday and food plays an integral part in the celebration. Traditionally, bread, often special round Easter breads or Easter braids, were baked on the Saturday before Easter. These breads would be placed with other special foods into handwoven baskets which were taken to church by the lady of the house to be blessed at an early morning Easter mass. In addition to the bread, the baskets would contain smoked ham and sausage, hard cooked eggs, colored and intricately hand-painted Easter eggs, young green onions and horseradish, and would be covered with decorative handmade towels. After the mass, the family would enjoy this special Easter breakfast together.

Christmas would not be complete without *pečenka,* roast suckling piglet and several varieties of small cakes and cookies. Neither would Bajram be complete without a whole roasted lamb. The meat is often grilled outdoors on an open spit.

Decorated Easter eggs.   Photo: Vlado Novak

The Orthodox Christian Croatians celebrate a special holiday marking the family's patron saint. The holiday is known as *Krsna Slava*. The family's friends and relatives join in a celebration that may last for two or three days. The *slava* includes a dinner that ends with a cake made of unmilled wheat, honey, walnuts and raisins, or sweetmeats. This cake, known as *koljivo* or *žito*, is blessed earlier in church and symbolizes life through the grain, and the sweetness of life through the honey.

Historically, an important national holiday celebrated by many Croatians is *Deseti Travanj*—the tenth of April. This day, along with the 30th of May, Croatia's independence day, represents the culmination of the centuries-long aspiration of Croatians for freedom and independence, giving special tribute to all the brave Croatian men and women who have given their lives to assure that the Croatian people will be free and that Croatia will be a sovereign nation. *Pečenka* and spit-roasted lamb are a must, a tradition that Croatians continue to preserve at annual picnics and parties in the United States, Canada and Australia.

Many regional festivals take the form of concerts, drama performances, folk exhibitions, opera, sporting events or folk dancing festivals. Most are traditional and have been held every year for generations. Most festivals are held in the coastal cities and towns, but inland cities also celebrate many local festivals. The national and regional celebrations frequently display traditional Croatian costumes. These richly embroidered, hand-crafted works of art, which could be purchased at markets and in small towns only a few decades ago, are becoming rare collector's items. They vary in style and intricacy of design from town to town, but each is worn with the same pride in Croatia's heritage.

The costumes are displayed at annual folk and musical festivals in many of the major cities and towns, especially on the coast. The largest of these festivals is the annual International Folklore Festival held in Zagreb every summer. Participants come from all over the world to attend this colorful eight-day festival.

Where there is celebration, food, drink and music cannot be too far behind. The tamburitza is the Croatian national instrument. The many Croatians who immigrated to America have maintained the beautiful Croatian tradition of song and dance. Today there may be as many tamburitza orchestras and dance groups in North America as there are in Croatia.

A Brief History of the Croatian People

The Roman Era

The people of Croatia migrated to the shores of the Adriatic in the seventh century A.D. The land has seen the passing of Greek and Roman culture, and the coming of the people who are today known as Croatians. As early as 500 B.C., the Greeks settled Croatia's Adriatic coast and blended with the native Illyrian tribes. The Romans later conquered the region, calling it Illyricum. Much Roman architecture still stands well-preserved in many Croatian coastal cities and many Croatian towns, structures, and monuments are built on Roman foundations.

Settling on the Adriatic Shores

By the seventh century the ancestors of modern Croatians had built an impressive empire known as Greater Croatia, which stretched from Poland to the Ukraine. Its capital was at the site of present-day Cracow. In 626 the Byzantine Emperor Heraclius (610-641) called upon the aid of the Croatians to defeat the Avar tribes who continuously attacked the Eastern Roman Empire. Heraclius made a pact with the Croatians allowing the Croatians to take possession of the lands on the eastern shores of the Adriatic Sea after the Avars had been driven back. The area included the region from Istria in the North to the River Drina in the East and the River Bojana in the South. The ancient Croatians appear to have been a civilized people. They readily accepted the cultural developments of the Romans by applying the refinements of civilization to their own culture.

The arrival of the Croatians on the shore of the Adriatic Sea.
by Oton Iveković   Photo: Vlado Novak

Led by three brothers and two sisters, the Croatians accepted the pact with Emperor Heraclius and settled the area of present-day Croatia. While the Balkan tribes to the east pursued a primitive existence, the people who founded their nation on the shores of the Adriatic were building a heritage that would include the best of classical and modern European culture.

In 679, shortly after settling their new home, the Croatians entered into a pact with Pope Agathon, promising never to attack any nation. The Pope in turn promised that God and St. Peter would defend the Croatians if they were attacked. Croatians can indeed be proud to have signed the first international mutual non-aggression treaty.

It may have been as early as these migratory years that Croatians developed the dried dough product called *tarana* that is still made in Croatia today. *Tarana* is prepared by kneading a paste from flour and eggs. The dough is crumbled into tiny pieces the size of grains of rice. It is from this crumbling action (*trti*) that the cereal product derives its name. The grains are dried in the sun and they may be kept indefinitely. They are cooked like rice in boiling water or used as a soup.

The Kingdom of Croatia

The population voluntarily adopted Christianity and Croatia's democratic tradition began early with the crowning of King Budimir who was selected by the Croatian Sabor. He was crowned in regal splendor with the members of the parliament giving their blessings at Duvno Field in 740 A.D. As Croatia's power grew, she was recognized by the rest of Europe's nobility. In 771, Croatia's royal house was represented at the coronation of Charlemagne.

In an area well suited to growing crops, Croatians were able to provide plenty of food for themselves and for their livestock. The principal source of nourishment during these times must have been a predecessor to *palenta*, a type of porridge made of ground cereal grain. Since corn had not yet been introduced in Europe at this time, it was made from spelt or other wheat. *Palenta* is cooked today much as it was many centuries ago. It can be made soft with milk and honey, or hard, sliced like a cake and served with a sauce, sour cream or bacon fried in its own fat.

The early Croatian settlers made cottage cheese from ewe's milk, raised sheep for food and wool, and produced wine. They had kettles of iron, ceramic and copper. These early cooking utensils enabled these people to cook mutton, or to roast the meat on spits. Vegetables were cultivated and many fruit trees had already been introduced to the region by the ancient Romans.

Bread was introduced with Christianity and it continues to be a staple of the Croatian diet to this day. With the cultivation of wheat, Croatians began to make many new sorts of boiled pastes. These include dumplings, *rezanci* (noodles), *trganci* (a type of noodle that is pinched rather than cut), and others which were cooked in boiling water or added to soups.

Hunting became a sport for nobility and peasants alike. Thick, rich forests provided for great feasts of roast pheasant, duck and wild boar. The plains and marshes abounded in a great variety of wild game and fowl and hunting provided the important addition of meat and game to the simple diet of the population.

The reign of King Trpimir I, the founder of the Trpimirović Dynasty, began a period of history when Croatia grew to her greatest power. At this time the Saracens, a dreaded band of Arabic marauders, were sacking Europe, particularly Italy. Croatia withstood Saracenic attempts at pillage. Dubrovnik was besieged for two years. Again and again the Croatians drove back the hordes. Despite such attacks, Croatia remained a strong world power, respected by Byzantium, Venice and the Holy See under the able leadership of her Kings Domagoj, Branimir and Mutimir.

The most famous of the Croatian royal blood is King Tomislav, who came to power in the year 925 A.D. King Tomislav was crowned at Duvno field, today's town of Tomislav Grad. He was recognized as the first Croatian king by the action of Pope John X, who referred to him as King of the Croatians and listed him among the Kings of Europe.

Tomislav was a great ruler and politician, a courageous knight and warrior who turned back the onslaught of Bulgar and Magyar invaders at the Drava River. He was an enlightened ruler promoting culture and religion. His successors carried on the tradition of a forceful Croatia which had defeated the attacks of the Venetians and for over 150 years exacted tributes from the city for the privilege of navigating the Adriatic Sea.

The Crowning of King Tomislav in A.D. 925.   Josip Horvat-Medimurec
Photo: Vlado Novak

When King Petar Krešimir ascended the throne in the year 1058, he ruled with a deft hand. All foreign place names were replaced with native Croatian names. The Croatian language replaced Latin in church services. This period represents the height of Croatia's power. Croatian territory reached to the Bulgarian town of Vidin along the Danube and to the present-day city of Niš in the south.

Unification with Hungary

After the deaths of King Zvonimir in 1089 and Petar Svačić II in 1091, the Croatian dynasty died out without a male heir. Croatia came into contact with the crown of Hungary through marriage of the royal houses. The treaty of Zagreb of 1102 between the Hungarian crown and the Croatian Sabor accepted King Kolomon of Hungary as the king representing the crown of Croatia. However, Croatia maintained her own Diet (Sabor), her nobility and her independence of any foreign power. The succession of Hungarian kings who had pledged to honor the Croatian-Hungarian dualism disregarded the Croatian law. Much of the Croatian culture and tradition was carried into Hungary at this time, while Croatia was influenced by Hungarian tradition.

Middle Ages

By the year 1300, Croatia's sovereignty and power were declining. The nobility of Croatia began to be appointed instead of following the old pattern of descent from traditional noble bloodlines. At this time, Dubrovnik was expanding its trade line and forming the nucleus of a city-state. Marco Polo's voyages opened a direct route to the Far East. Dubrovnik exploited spice importation, buying the treasured flavorings cheaply and selling them dearly.

With the fall of Constantinople in 1453, the spice route was cut off, but the Arabs from the Near East again supplied the city state with the spices necessary to maintain a profitable trade. Shortly after that time, the Portuguese reached the Spice Islands and Lisbon became the center of European spice trade.

From the 13th to the 16th century, art and culture flourished. Architecture in the Romanesque and Gothic styles was being produced on the coast. Stone was carved with precision and skill, resulting in many buildings of extraordinary beauty and intricacy. Artists such as Juraj Dalmatinac and Andre Buvina created great works of art. The cathedral of Saint Jacob in Šibenik, and the impressive carved doors of the Cathedral of Split, depicting the life of Christ, are monumental works from this period.

Fish was a popular and inexpensive food during the Dark Ages. Christian doctrine imposed meatless days on Fridays, during lent and on numerous other fast days. As a

Photo: S. Cajzek
Trakošćan—a well preserved Medieval castle which is now a museum.

result, meat was forbidden during much of the year. On the feudal estates, the tenant serfs labored from dawn to dusk working the soil. When land changed ownership, the serfs were passed with it. Women worked alongside the men, plowing, sowing, and reaping the fruits, vegetables, and grains. In exchange for their work, they were provided with a small plot of land where they cultivated cereals and vegetables. Their simple meals were eaten from earthenware in contrast to the pewter of the merchant class and the silverware of the nobles.

The household of Medieval nobles had a highly elaborate kitchen. Several chefs directed all aspects of food preparation and service. A complete staff of servants aided the chef in preparing large banquets in which a vast array of decorated showpieces were served. It was popular to make mock fish from vegetables, mock meats from fish, etc.

The Croatian word *blagovati* is derived from *blago*, meaning riches. It was indeed a period of rich dining for the nobles. Dinner was a formal affair which took place to the background of musical serenades provided by the lord's musicians. Stewards served the guests a succession of courses which were presented on intricate silverware. Men and women were segregated, the men sitting at one table, the women at another. A priest, the eldest member of the household, or the most respected, opened the meal with prayer and the succession of food and drink followed.

Monasteries were an important institution during the Middle Ages. They were largely supported by the feudal lords, although the peasants were also required to pay substantial tithes. The monasteries were one of the chief producers of wine, maintaining their own vineyards. Much of the wine was consumed by the clerics and used during Mass. The remainder was sold in the cities. Because transportation was expensive, wine was generally available only to the wealthy. The poor settled for beer, cider, and mead.

The monasteries were self-sustaining communities. They had rooms for baking, brewing, drying and preserving fruit. Various types of livestock were raised, including sheep, pigs, cows, and fowl. Quarters were provided for the coopper, saddler, woodcarver, and shoemaker.

Bosnia had built a strong dynasty of her own with powerful leaders such as King Tvrtko and Duke Vukčić Hrvatinić. In the year 1463, Sultan Mohammed of Turkey invaded Bosnia with a force of 150,000 men. This invasion marked the beginning of over 400 years of repressive Ottoman occupation in Eastern Croatia.

Turkish rule was very repressive, eliminating traditional songs and dances. The Croatians developed new forms of song and dance, including the silent kolo, a circle dance with no musical accompaniment, danced to the beat of the dancer's feet.

The harshest practice of the Turks was the abduction of young boys from throughout Croatia and training these young children as "janissary" soldiers. The janissaries were an elite corps of troops first organized as the sultan's guard, eventually becoming the largest unit in the Turkish army. These soldiers were later sent back to attack their own homeland in the name of the Sultan. As a result of this practice, one finds many Turks with Croatian surnames in present-day Turkey.

Along with the Moslem religion, Turkish rule brought to Croatia eastern art forms and a host of new foods, spices, and methods of food preparation. The exotic new foods and spices were absorbed and transformed by the imagination of the Croatians. They became part of the rural kitchens throughout the country, filtering to the upper classes only decades later.

New varieties of pepper, different from the Spanish pimiento with a milder flavor than cayenne pepper, were introduced at this time. Croatians ground these peppers into a fine powder, introducing Europe to paprika. The name paprika is a diminutive of the Croatian word for pepper, *papar*. The distinctive flavor of the new dried pepper ranges from sweet paprika to fiery hot. The spice quickly found its way into many dishes and casseroles and it soon became common see bunches of paprika peppers turning crimson red in the late summer sun hanging on the porches of village houses.

The most important new food to be introduced was coffee which has become a universal drink. Croatians exported their love of *kava* and the coffee itself to the rest of Europe. A Dalmatian by the name of Pasko opened the first coffeehouse in England in 1652. Although it is not clear that this was the first such establishment in the West, others sprouted quickly in major European cities.

Espresso coffee and capuccino are standards that every cafe will promptly serve. Another popular way of preparing coffee is cold. Iced coffee is served with a scoop of ice cream and whipped cream. However, the favored way of serving coffee is still in the manner known as *Turska Kava*. *Turska Kava* is a strong, thick coffee that is prepared in a long handled copper pot known as a *džezva*, and served in miniature coffee cups.

To make four of the miniature cups of coffee, place four tablespoons of very finely ground coffee into a *džezva*. Pour one cup of boiling water into the *džezva* and bring to a boil until foam rises to the top. Remove from heat and allow the foam to subside. Repeat this procedure two more times. Serve the coffee by first pouring a little foam into each of the cups, and following with the remaining coffee. The coffee is sweetened to taste and is often served with a glass of water.

The light, crisp, flaky dough used for making the eastern desserts of many layered, nut-filled pastries drenched in syrup and honey was adapted by Croatians. They rolled the paper-thin dough around a filling of sweetened cheese, apples, cherries, poppy seeds, walnuts or other fruits.

The quality of the flour helped to make Croatians masters in the art of stretching the pastry dough to semi-transparency. The new creation, known as *savijaće*, became popular in every part of the country. The delicate pastry was quickly adopted by the Austrians and Hungarians where the name was translated to *strudel* and *retes* respectively.

The Austro-Hungarian Empire

With much of the Croatian territory under Turkish rule, the Croatian Sabor selected Ferdinand I of the Habsburg house as King of Croatia in 1527. The alliance with the Habsburgs introduced Croatia to three centuries of interaction with Austria and her court. Vienna benefitted more from this alliance than did Zagreb. Croatia was exploited both economically and politically. Austria wanted to reduce Croatia to the status of a Habsburg province and signed numerous treaties with the Turks to Croatia's detriment.

World-wide exploration by the Spanish, Portuguese and English presented new ingredients to the cuisines of Europe. When the tomato was introduced, it was regarded as the fruit of paradise. It is from the Croatian word *raj*, meaning paradise, that we get the Croatian name for the tomato—*rajčica*.

The Inca civilizations of Mexico provided the Old World with chocolate, squashes, lima, kidney and pinto beans and with the vanilla pod. Croatian sea merchants brought all of these new ingredients back to their native land. They quickly became incorporated into the country's cuisine.

Spanish explorers brought the turkey back to Spain in the holds of their ships. It became so popular that the birds were described to be as numerous as flocks of sheep. The fowl that the Spanish referred to as *gallinas* spread throughout Europe. In Croatia, the *puran* came to be highly respected as a festive bird. It remains a favored roast for holidays and festive occasions.

Another crop from the new world that became extremely popular was corn. It soon became a staple for peasants, replacing other grains for the porridge called *palenta*.

Sweets and desserts at this time became a prominent ending to meals. Such sweets as *palačinke*, yeast cakes filled with fruit, poppy seeds or nuts, and *krempita* were enjoyed by the upper class.

Along with these foods, new spices and herbs found their way into the cities of Europe. Venice and Dubrovnik vied for the lucrative spice trade. Sugar from the Arab lands, cloves from the Moluccas, saffron and ginger from the Far East, pepper from India and coffee from Turkey were spread across Europe through Dubrovnik and Venice.

The first half of the seventeenth century saw the rise of a Croatian national hero to international prominence. He has been heralded throughout Europe. Nikola Zrinski II of the noble house of Zrinski became the Ban of Croatia at the age of 30. He was later awarded the distinction of Duke of the Hungarian nation. For his tremendous military accomplishments against the Ottoman Empire, he was presented with the Golden Fleece of the Spanish empire. He was accepted by the King of France as "Peer of France". He was sent a portrait by the pope and was named Imperial prince by Leopold I of Austria. Despite the international acclaim that he received, Nikola Zrinski frequently expressed pride in his family name and in his Croatian nationality. Aware of the oppressive rule that the Austrians were imposing on Croatia, Zrinski began a movement with the aim of limiting the power of the Austrian emperor.

After his death, Croatia entered a tumultuous period. Nikola's brother Petar Zrinski became the new Ban and the

Petar Zrinski

Krsto Frankopan

leader of the movement. Petar Zrinski and his brother-in-law Christopher Frankopan were aware that Croatians were denied their national rights and they fought ceaselessly for freedom of Croatia from the hegemony of the Habsburg house.

In 1671 Zrinski and Frankopan were invited to Vienna to discuss the Croatian grievances. When they arrived in the city they were immediately arrested and later publicly beheaded. Croatia went into a deep mourning at the loss of these beloved national leaders. The powerful houses of Zrinski and Frankopan were weakened, and their estates were confiscated by the Austrians. Croatians were becoming increasingly disillusioned with the Austro-Hungarian union.

By this time, cooking was becoming increasingly refined. Essays on the fine arts of carving fowl, serving the table and entertaining guests were written. Cooks became chefs, known as gentlemen masters of service and cuisine. Cooking was being transformed into an art. Elegance rather than grandeur became the new standard. Craftsmen created fine porcelain dishware and intricately ornate silverware. The drinking of coffee, tea and chocolate had become *de rigeur* for the middle and upper classes. Fine cooking became so important that military leaders carried small armies of chefs and servants with them on campaigns to keep them well fed.

In Croatia, pastries and tortes of elaborate design were baked in the new pastry shops that became popular in all major cities and towns. Fine crusty rolls were served with tea and *café au lait*, creating the basis of the continental breakfast. Even the working man was beginning to enjoy the hot coffee before his day of labor.

The richness and variety of Croatia's wines became known throughout the Habsburg empire and graced many of Vienna's banquets. This period was the beginning of the restaurant industry, where food of good quality was served at reasonable prices. The people were now exposed to a variety of dishes, which increased their own repertoire.

The Austrian monarchs continued to exploit Croatia well into the first two decades of the twentieth century, using the country as a purely agricultural part of the empire. Because industry was not allowed to develop, agriculture continued to be the major national vocation. The Croatian people fought constantly against the advances of the Hungarians who wanted to "Magyarize" Croatia. A Hungarian was appointed as Ban of Croatia and an attempt was made to impose the Hungarian language in schools and official institutions throughout Croatia.

The military border of Croatia was recognized for the protection it provided Europe. Croatia had won fame for its position as the Austro-Hungarian Empire's best line of defense against the Ottoman Empire. The Croatian fighting man had long been renowned for his courage because he had served with, or next to, most of Europe's armies.

Croatian ships had sailed with the Spanish Armada when it attacked England. Croatians had also served as French mercenaries. These soldiers wore fine colorful ties around their neck as part of their garb. The French nobility was very impressed with this fashion and asked who these soldiers were. Told that they were *Hrvati* or *Croates* in French, they adopted the new fashion, calling the tie *la cravate*, a name it has retained in most languages.

Croatian Rennaissance

When Napoleon came to power at the beginning of the nineteenth century, he overran Croatia and changed the name to the Kingdom of Illyria, referring to the Pre-Roman Illyrian tribes that had at one time inhabited the land. Napoleon and his army brought with them the classical cooking refinements of France, which had a marked effect on both Vienna and Zagreb.

After Napoleon was defeated at Waterloo, his political influence was replaced by that of Prince Von Metternich. The constant struggle between the court of Vienna and Croatia gave rise to the Croatian Renaissance. This movement strove to expel all foreign influences which sought to suppress the Croatian identity and culture, especially from the Magyars and the Austrians.

The movement strove to unify all the Croatian lands, to create a democratic society and to create a sovereign and independent Croatian state. In 1878, the Croatian Party of Rights was established. The party was led by Ante Starčević, who expounded the idea that

Croatians had a historical and natural right to govern themselves. Because he clearly defined the national goals of the Croatian people, Starčević is recognized by Croatians as "The Father of the Homeland."

The newly awakened national consciousness was expressed in the writings and poetry of the period. The patriotism of the Croatians is perhaps best expressed in the words of the country's national anthem which was written at this time—*Mila kuda si nam ravna, mila kuda si planina, mila si nam ti jedina.* (Dear to us across your plains, dear to us across your mountains, you and you alone are dear to us.)

As metropolitantan areas grew larger, farm produce was marketed in specialty shops, and vegetable, meat and cheese stores catering to the needs of the city dwellers. This was a period of Romantic writings and thought. Emotions ran high, especially among national groups, and their was an attempt to transfer these feelings to the cuisine. It was not entirely successful, and the finest qualities of the foreign influences have remained to round out the dishes of Croatia. The *konoba*, a simple gathering place, became the meeting place of the working class. It resembled an English pub—a drinking establishment that also provided food. There was comraderie among the patrons and when not playing cards, they could be observed in heated discussions. All subjects were discussed in this exclusively male atmosphere. Hungarian gypsy bands or Croatian tamburitza orchestras often provided musical entertainment.

Union With Other Slavs

At the end of the first world war, Croatian leaders were embittered by their experience in the Austro-Hungarian Empire. Some leading statesmen believed that they would fare better in a union with other Slavic people. Thus, in 1918 the Kingdom of Serbs, Croats and Slovenes was created without the approval of the Croatian Parliament (Sabor). The decision to join into this union was imposed upon the Croatian people by a self-appointed "Yugoslav Committee" without a referendum and with no popular support.

The Croatian people soon learned that the rule of the Habsburg Monarchs was mild in comparison to the oppressive rule of the Serbian monarchy. The new state was, in effect, a Greater Serbia and Croatian lands were treated as occupied territories by the Serbian rulers.

Stjepan Radić, the leader of the Croatian Peasant Party, became the spokesman

Stjepan Radić

Ante Starčević

for Croatians. He advocated a neutral Croatian State, perhaps within a South Slavic confederation. His attempts at obtaining human rights for the Croatian people were met with cruel violence. He and four colleagues were shot in the Parliament in Belgrade by a Serbian representative. Two died immediately and Radić and two other Croatians were seriously wounded. Radić died of the wounds a short time later.

The Serbian king officially declared a dictatorship, changed the name of the union to Yugoslavia and the terror over the Croatian people intensified.

It is no wonder that under these circumstances Croatians welcomed the fall of Yugoslavia and the creation of the Independent State of Croatia in 1941. Because of circumstances of the Second World War, the centuries-long Croatian dream of freedom and sovereignty was not to last. When the war ended, Croatians were again thrown into a prison—the Socialist Federal Republic of Yugoslavia. The centralized government was again in Belgrade and Croatians were subject to more tyranny.

Millions of Croatians were forced to leave Croatia to look for work elsewhere because Serbs were favored in all job areas. They were a majority in areas of education, the military and the government. Since all major businesses were government-owned, they were also given choice jobs in the areas of business. Many Croatians were forced to leave their homes and their beloved homeland in search of work. They were not denied jobs because of difficult economic times, but because of a calculated plan to resettle their lands. From the very beginning of their union with Serbs, Croatians were forced to live as an enslaved people and their fundamental and human rights were violated.

To compound the misery of the Croatian people, the Serbian-led communist government controlled all areas of the media. With a considerable degree of success, the communist propaganda machine managed to smear the name of the Croatian people in order to justify or cover up its own terrorist policies.

Only now, almost fifty years later, is the truth being written about recent Croatian history, about the mass murders of Croatian men, women and children *after* the Second World War had ended in places such as Bleiburg and Maribor.

Freedom at Last

With the fall of communism in Eastern Europe, Croatians took advantage of the opportunity to establish their national rights. On May 30, 1990, the first democratically elected Parliament in decades convened in Zagreb. This was a time of great joy and anticipation as the Croatian dream was finally being realized.

History does repeat itself. Like Stjepan Radić in the thirties, Franjo Tudjman tried to guarantee the rights of his people within a confederate Yugoslavia as a first step toward complete independence. After a year of failed attempts at even bringing the Serbians to the negotiating table and Serbia's repeated threats to use military force against the unarmed Croatian population, President Tudjman's government held a national referendum regarding the independence of Croatia. Ninety-four percent of the population voted for sovereignty and independence. In accordance with the will of the Croatian people, the Croatian Sabor declared the Independence of the Republic of Croatia on June 26, 1991.

Croatia's declaration of independence was met with brutal violence. The Serbian-controlled Yugoslav army attacked Croatian civilian positions in all parts of the country. Hospitals, churches, day-care centers and schools were frequent targets. Not even the towns of Dubrovnik and Split, which are on UNESCO's list of cultural and natural treasures of the world's heritage, have been spared. They have received extensive damage, even though they had for centuries withheld the onslaught of various adversaries.

The aim of the Serbo-Yugoslav army was to destroy everything that was Croatian. The world was shocked to learn of Serbia's abhorrent policy of "ethnic cleansing" eliminating entire towns and villages through murder or forced expulsions of citizens from their homes and resettling those areas with a Serbian population.

Bosnia and Herzegovina were attacked even more violently and for a longer period. As of this writing the beautiful city of Sarajevo is being savagely shelled every day, and there is almost no building that has not been damaged or destroyed.

We hope that Peace will soon come to Croatia and Bosnia and Herzegovina and that the people of Croatia and Bosnia and Herzegovina will soon be able to rebuild their cities and towns and will be free to pursue happiness and to enjoy the rights which they have finally won—the right to dignity, to freedom, and to happiness. Croatians have honored their pact with Pope Agathon. They have never invaded another nation. Let's hope that no nation will ever invade Croatia again.

The history of Croatia and her cuisine has indeed been turbulent. Through its evolution, it can be traced to a base of fine Croatian natural ingredients. Spiced with a little Turkish influence, peppered with a sprinkle of Hungarian spice, and flavored with a dash of Austrian refinement, Croatian cuisine emerges as one of the richest in all of Europe.

Račići sa Pohanim Lukom
Prawns with Onion Rings

Appetizers

Appetizers are small portions of food that can be served before a meal or as an accompaniment to drinks while entertaining. Appetizers are known as *hors d'oeuvres* in French which means "works of art."

Croatian cooking offers a variety of appetizers, known as *zakusci*, which are visually appealing as well as appetizing. The delicate flavor of the *zakusci* stimulates the appetite and sharpens one's desire for the main course of the dinner.

Simple Croatian appetizers, which often introduce daily meals at home, may include a variety of cheeses, nuts, raw or pickled vegetables, smoked fish or meats and a variety of salamis and smoked sausages. One of the favorites is the renowned Dalmatian ham, *pršut*. It is sliced very thinly and may be offered on a platter of cold cuts, including the savory *Gavrilović salama*.

When entertaining, *zakusci* are often accompanied by *šljivovica*, sweet fruit brandies or other aperitifs. Although generally time-consuming, appetizers need not be difficult to prepare. They offer an opportunity to practice your culinary artistry. Bread is cut into circles, squares and triangles and fried in butter. The shaped toast is spread with various patés and garnished with bits of sliced ham, cheese, tongue, vegetables, egg, olive, smoked fish or caviar. The resulting canapés are complemented with thin slices of *pršut*, an assortment of thinly sliced smoked sausages, dried salamis, olives stuffed with anchovies or other delicacies. The resulting combinations are limited only by your imagination.

Southern Croatia offers a variety of smoked fish, which are considered by many to be among the best appetizers in the world. Smoked sardines, anchovies, and oysters are often served with slices of smoked mackerel, salmon or tuna. Tuna fish is especially popular in appetizers. It is frequently served simply with olive oil, but can also be served with onions on a lettuce leaf. This makes an appetizing first course salad.

Ikra, the roe of the sturgeon, is held in high esteem. The Danubian sturgeon produces the finest black caviar. According to connoisseurs, the finest caviar should be served without any adornment or accompaniment. However, it is frequently sprinkled with fresh lemon juice or served on buttered bits of toast. We have included *Palačinke s Ikrom*, an appetizer of miniature caviar-filled pancakes. If caviar is not obtainable, the roe of other fish may be substituted and garnished with a dab of sour cream.

Small meat and cheese-filled pastries also make excellent appetizers. Cubed veal liver, seasoned simply with salt and pepper and sprinkled with a little paprika, is fried in hot oil and can be served with a sharp mustard sauce and chopped onions. The most enticing liver delicacies are made from goose liver. It is especially appealing as a *paté de fois gras* served with minced onions or eggs.

Palačinke s Ikrom
Caviar Palachinke

¾ c. flour
¾ c. milk
5 tbsp. butter
¼ c. water
2 eggs
½ tsp. salt
½ c. caviar

Combine the eggs, flour, salt, and half the milk in a bowl. Whisk until all ingredients are blended. Add the remaining ingredients, except the caviar and mix well. The batter will be light and thin. Grease a 5" pancake skillet lightly before making the first palachinka. Heat the pan over medium high heat until a drop of water sizzles when placed in the pan. Tilt the pan slightly and pour 2 tbsp. of batter into the pan. Quickly move the pan in a circular motion until the bottom is coated. The thinner the layer, the better the palachinka. Cook for approximately 45 seconds. Turn it over with a spatula. Cook for another 25 seconds. Spread with caviar and roll up into little palachinke. Place on a serving dish and decorate with a little caviar.

Punjene Lignje
Stuffed Squid

2 lbs. squid
¼ c. olive oil
½ c. bread crumbs
½ c. chopped mushrooms
½ c. chopped ham
1 egg
1 tbsp. chopped parsley
5 cloves garlic
salt and pepper to taste

Clean the squid. Gently pull to separate the tube from the head and pull out and discard the long, clear quill. Scoop out and discard anything that may be left in the tube. Pull off and discard the membrane that covers the tube. Rinse well in several waters. Cut the tentacles just below the eyes. Discard the eyes and the material attached to them.

Chop the tentacles and combine them with the bread crumbs, mushrooms, ham, olive oil, egg, parsley, and garlic. Season with salt and pepper. Stuff the tubes with this mixture. Fold the tops into the tubes and secure with a toothpick. Grill on a barbecue or bake, uncovered, in a well-oiled baking pan at 450° for 20-25 minutes until they begin to brown.

Nadjevene Pogačice
Ham-Stuffed Cakes

1 ½ c. flour
½ c. butter
1 c. cottage cheese
1 egg, slightly beaten
½ tsp. salt
2 cakes yeast
1 tsp. sugar
2-3 tbsp. milk, lukewarm

Place the yeast in lukewarm milk. Add the sugar and allow to rise in a warm, draft-free place. Sift the flour into a deep bowl. Cut the butter into the flour to make large crumbs. Add the cheese, salt and yeast to make a soft dough. Roll the dough to a thickness of one half inch. With a round cookie cutter, cut out little cakes. Place them on a clean board and allow to rise until doubled in size. Brush with the beaten egg. Place on a greased baking sheet and bake in a hot oven for about half an hour. Allow the cakes to cool. Cut them in half horizontally. Stuff the cakes with the filling. Replace the tops and serve.

Filling:

½ lb. cooked ham
½ c. chopped pickles
2 hard-cooked eggs
2 tbsp. sour cream

To make the filling, finely chop the ham and eggs. Combine all the ingredients and mix well.

Vruća Srž
Hot Beef Marrow Canapes

3 large boiled beef bones
toast
salt, pepper and paprika to taste

This is a delicacy which can be served on toast as an appetizer or with soup. In either case, the marrow must be hot. Remove the marrow from beef bones which have been cooked in clear beef broth. Spread the marrow on small pieces of toast. Season with salt and a little paprika. Serve immediately.

Pašteta od Sardelica
Anchovy Paté

12 drained anchovy fillets
3 slices white bread
¼ c. sour cream
dark bread or toast

Mince the anchovy fillets. Soak the bread in a little water. Squeeze the bread to drain. Combine the soaked bread with the anchovies. Add the sour cream and stir into a smooth paste. Cut the dark bread or toast into rounds and spread with the anchovy paste. If desired, fry the bread in butter and drain on paper towels before spreading with the anchovy paste.

Kifle sa Šunkom
Ham-Stuffed Crescents

1 c. flour
1 c. butter, melted
2 cakes yeast
2 egg yolks
1 tsp. sugar
½ tsp. salt
1 c. milk, lukewarm
1 tbsp. melted butter
1 egg, slightly beaten
¼ lb. chopped ham
½ c. sour cream

Place the yeast in lukewarm milk. Add the sugar and allow to rise. Sift the flour into a deep bowl. Cut in the butter to form kernels the size of bread crumbs. Add the egg yolks, salt and yeast mixture and beat to form a smooth, elastic dough. Shape the dough into a loaf and slice the loaf into six portions. Roll each portion into a flat circle, brush with melted butter, and cut into eight pie-shaped wedges. Combine the ham and sour cream and mix well. Place this stuffing in the center of each wedge. Shape the wedges into crescents by rolling toward the tips. Brush the crescents with the beaten egg and place on a well greased baking sheet. Allow to rise until doubled in size. Bake at 425° until golden.

Hladetina
Pork in Aspic

2 lbs. pork feet, ears and skin
1 c. vinegar
1 large carrot, sliced
1 parsley root
2 qts. cold water
1 large onion
4 cloves of garlic
1 bay leaf
1 tsp. whole black pepper
1 ½ tsp. salt
1-2 hard cooked eggs for garnish

Clean the meat well. Mix the vinegar and the water and pour it over the meat. Wash the meat again in this solution and cut it into small pieces. Place it along with the bones in a deep pot. Cover with water to which 4-5 tablespoons vinegar have been added. Cook over low heat for about an hour and a half. Add the remaining ingredients and simmer for another hour or two until the meat is tender. Bone the meat when it has cooled enough to handle. Set the liquid aside. Place the pork in a well greased mold. Garnish with the vegetables and sliced hard cooked eggs. Cover with the liquid in which the pork was cooked. Refrigerate overnight so the jelly has a chance to set. The following day, turn the jelly mold out onto a serving platter. Garnish with sliced fresh vegetables for color.

Ploškice od Jetre
Liver Slices

1 lb. chopped goose liver
3 eggs, well beaten
½ c. sour cream
¼ c. butter
1 tsp. flour
1 c. bread crumbs
¼ c. milk
1 tsp. chopped parsley
1 tsp. powdered garlic
paprika, salt and pepper to taste

Soak the bread crumbs in the milk for about ten minutes. Melt the butter in a saucepan and add the liver to it. Cover and simmer for about five minutes. Mash the livers in a deep bowl. Add the soaked bread crumbs, paprika, garlic and finely chopped parsley, the cream, the eggs and the salt and pepper. Grease and flour a jelly mold. Place the liver mixture into the mold and cover with greased foil. Tie the foil with string. Place the mold into a saucepan. Add enough water to come two thirds of the way up the mold. Steam over medium low heat for about 1½ hours. Turn the liver mold out onto a serving platter and slice it very thinly, but maintaining its shape of the mold. Serve with crackers and a bowl of sour cream.

Pašteta od Jastoga
Lobster Spread

10 slices bread
¼ c. butter
½ c. lobster meat
1 tsp. mayonnaise
12 large olives, halved
juice of one lemon
salt to taste

Finely chop the lobster meat. Cut the bread into various shapes with cookie cutters. Fry in hot butter until nicely browned. Drain on paper towels. Add the salt, mayonnaise and lemon juice to the lobster meat. Mix well. Spread this mixture on the bread. Garnish each canapé with a slice of olive. If desired, pipe finely mashed pickled beets around the edges for color. Crab meat or shrimp may be used in place of lobster.

Pašteta od Ovčeg Sira
Liptauer Spread

8 oz. Liptauer cheese
8 tbsp. butter
1 tsp. mustard
½ onion, chopped
1 anchovy
1 tsp. paprika
salt to taste

Pass the cheese through a sieve. Combine it with the butter, mustard, onion, salt and paprika. Mash the anchovy and blend it into the spread. Mix until smooth and creamy. Refrigerate, then serve on bits of bread or crackers.

Zakusci od Ikre
Caviar Eggs

6 hard cooked eggs
¼ c. sour cream
¼ c. caviar
salt and paprika to taste

Slice the eggs lengthwise and remove the yolks. Refill the eggs with caviar. Mash the egg yolks and mix in the sour cream. Pipe the egg yolk mixture around the edge of each egg. Sprinkle with salt and paprika. Refrigerate before serving.

Pohane Kamenice
Fried Oysters

30 fresh oysters
2 egg yolks
3 tbsp. grated Parmesan cheese
3 tbsp. fine bread crumbs
oil for deep frying

Check for freshness by making sure that the shell of each oyster is tightly closed. Remove the shells and drain the oysters. Beat the egg yolks well with one tablespoon of water. Roll the oysters in cheese, coat with the beaten eggs and then roll again in the bread crumbs. Heat the fat and deep fry each oyster for about one minute. Drain and serve hot.

Pečeni Sir
Fried Cheese

½ lb. Emmenthal cheese
1 egg
¼ c. flour
½ c. fine bread crumbs
oil for frying

Cut the cheese into wide strips or into large cubes. Season the flour with a little salt. Heat a generous amount of oil in a deep skillet to 350°. Dip the cheese strips in a little oil. Roll in the seasoned flour and dip the well beaten egg to which you have added a tablespoon of water. Coat with fine bread crumbs. Fry the cheese in the hot oil until golden on all sides. The oil must not be too hot or the cheese will melt. It must not be too cold or the batter will not stick. Drain the fried cheese on paper towels and serve hot.

Punjene Školjke
Anchovy-Stuffed Shells

1 ½ c. butter
7 egg yolks
7 egg whites, stiffly beaten
9 chopped anchovy fillets
¼ c. grated Parmesan cheese
15-20 scallop shells
2 tsp. paprika
2 tbsp. chopped parsley
salt to taste

Cream the butter. Add the egg yolks, one at a time, beating after each addition. Add the chopped anchovy fillets and mix well. Stir in the grated cheese and parsley. Fold in the stiffly beaten egg whites. Season with salt. Fill the scallop shells with this mixture. Sprinkle with paprika and bake at 450° for about twelve minutes.

Punjena Jaja
Stuffed Eggs

6 eggs
2 tbsp. fine bacon bits
¼ c. sour cream
salt and pepper to taste
paprika for garnish

Hard cook the eggs. Slice them in half lengthwise. You can make the eggs especially decorative by cutting V-shaped inserts into them, creating a zig-zag effect. Remove the yolks from the eggs. Mash them. Add the sour cream and the bacon. Season with salt and pepper. Mix well. Pipe the yolk mixture back into the egg whites. Garnish by sprinkling paprika over the eggs. Serve with small pieces of toast or with crackers.

Sjeckana Gusja Jetra
Chopped Goose Liver

3 goose livers, chopped
5 tbsp. butter
2 tbsp. chopped onion
3 tbsp. white wine
¼ c. sour cream
1 c. thinly sliced mushrooms
salt and pepper to taste
olives for garnish

Heat the butter. Saute the livers and the onion in the butter for 3-4 minutes, shaking the pan occasionally to prevent sticking. Add the mushrooms. Season with salt and pepper. Add the wine, a tablespoon at a time, stirring after each addition. Simmer until the goose livers are tender. Remove from heat. Stir in the sour cream. Serve on crackers or very thin slices of toast. Place half an olive on each canapé as a garnish.

Ploškice od Šunke
Ham Slices

½ lb. ground ham
½ c. butter
1 c. buttermilk
6 egg yolks, well beaten
6 egg whites, stiffly beaten
½ c. bread crumbs
½ c. grated cheese
1 tsp. chopped parsley
1 tsp. paprika
salt and pepper to taste

Cream the butter. Add the egg yolks to the butter and beat well. Add the ham, buttermilk, parsley and cheese. Beat well. Season with salt, pepper and paprika. Stir in the bread crumbs. Fold the egg whites into the mixture. Grease and flour an oven-proof mold. Place the mixture into the mold. Bake at 350° for 20-25 minutes. Turn out onto a serving platter. Slice thinly, being careful to maintain the shape of the mold. Serve hot with crackers.

Račići s Pohanim Lukom
Prawns and Onion Rings

2 c. prawns
1 medium onion, chopped
3 tbsp. olive oil
3 tbsp. šljivovica brandy
2 tbsp. water
¼ c. flour
1 egg, well beaten
½ c. bread crumbs
1 tomato, peeled and chopped

Heat the olive oil and brown the onion in it slightly. Add the tomato and prawns and cook for seven to eight minutes. Slowly pour the *šljivovica* over the prawns and light it with a match. Allow the liquor to burn out. Add the water. Stir. Cover and simmer slowly for a few minutes longer. Slice the onions and separate them into rings. Roll the onion rings in flour. Dip in the well beaten egg and roll in bread crumbs. Deep fry the rings in the hot oil until golden on both sides. Garnish the prawns with the onion rings, or if your prefer, serve the onion rings on the side.

Pašteta od Sira
Cheese Spread

½ c. soft cheese*
½ c. Roquefort cheese
½ c. grated Parmesan
½ c. butter
½ c. cottage cheese
2 tsp. paprika
salt to taste

*Zdenka Sir cheese is used in Croatia. However, any soft sweet cheese may be used in its place.

Cream the butter. Finely mince the Roquefort. Combine all the ingredients and mix well. Serve on small pieces of fried bread, pumpernickel bread or on small crackers.

Zakusci od Sardelica
Anchovy Canapés

¼ c. smoked anchovy paste
1 egg, hard cooked
10 stuffed olives, halved
¼ c. sour cream
¼ c. olive oil
5 slices of brown bread, quartered

Cut the crusts from the bread. Fry the bread in the olive oil. Mash the yolk of the egg and mix it with the anchovy paste. Spread this mixture over the quartered bread slices. Chop the egg white and add it to the sour cream. Mash well. Pipe a sour cream border around each of the slices. Garnish each slice with half an olive.

Zakusci od Jastoga
Lobster Canapés

6 tbsp. lobster meat, cooked
3 tbsp. sour cream
10 pitted olives, halved
1 tbsp. lemon juice
salt and pepper to taste

Combine lobster meat, sour cream, and lemon juice to make a smooth spread. Season with salt and pepper. Place on squares of toasted bread. Garnish with halved olives.

Zakusci od Gusje Jetre
Goose Liver Canapés

½ c. cooked goose liver
2 tbsp. butter
¼ c. sour cream
¼ lb. sliced cheese
2 tbsp. minced onion
salt and pepper to taste
parsley for garnish

Brown the onion slightly in the butter. Mash the goose liver and add it to the onion. Mix well. Add the sour cream. Season with salt and pepper. Place a slice of cheese on a cracker or bit of toast. Spread with goose liver spread. Garnish with parsley.

Pileća Juha s Okruglicama od Krupice
Chicken Soup with Semolina Dumplings

Soups

Although not all Croatian meals include a first course of appetizers, *ručak*, the noon-day meal, most frequently begins with a serving of soup. Croatian soups are many and diverse, ranging from the simple clear boths to the more elaborate combinations of meats and vegetables.

The two basic and most popular soups, *Goveđa Juha* (Beef Soup) and *Pileća Juha* (Chicken Soup), also serve as a base for many other soups. They are very appealing light soups which make an excellent first course for lunch or dinner. They continue to be prepared by boiling the meat with vegetables in water for several hours. They may be served with any garnishes or additives, but are most frequently served with simple home-made noodles.

Dalmatinska Juha is made from a beef stock base, thickened with a roux and served with macaroni and Parmesan cheese. Beef and chicken stock may be used to enhance the flavor of many vegetable soups. These are made in many combinations ranging from single vegetable soups to the thick and hearty *Juha od Povrća* made with a wide array of fresh garden vegetables. *Juha od Gljiva* can be made with fresh mushrooms, but if these are not available, dried mushrooms may be substituted. A very popular version of potato soup, *Juha od Krumpira,* is made with rich cream and a well beaten egg.

The more bland vegetables are given zest with seasonings and other vegetables. The popular Juha od *Kiselog Zelja* is a sauerkraut soup thickened with a brown roux made of lard and flour. Like many other vegetable soups, it is flavored with smoked meat. The popularity and abundance of dairy products is evidenced in many of the Croatian soups. *Juha sa Sirom*, an interesting cheese soup, and *Juha od Mlijeka*, a thick milk soup are both as nourishing as they are flavorful. In addition, sour cream is added to a large number of the thick vegetable and goulash soups.

Fish and other seafoods also form the base for many soups. Although carp and cod are most frequently used for Riblja Juha, almost any fresh or saltwater fish can be successfully substituted.

Pileća Juha
Chicken Soup

3-3 ½ lb. chicken
1 carrot
1 celery stalk
½ bay leaf
½ tsp. black peppercorns
1 medium onion
salt to taste

Cut the chicken into pieces. Wash and chop the vegetables. Place the vegetables and all the chicken pieces except the breast in a deep pot. Add enough water to fill the pot. When the water comes to a boil, add the seasonings and the breast meat. Reduce the heat to low and simmer until the meat is tender. Strain the cooked soup. Garnish, and if desired, bone the chicken pieces, dice, and add them to the strained soup.

Gulaš Juha
Goulash Soup

½ lb. stewing beef, cubed
2 oz. smoked bacon
¼ c. chopped onion
2 tsp. paprika
¼ tsp. marjoram
½ tsp. minced garlic
2 tbsp. flour
6 c. beef stock
1 potato, cubed [optional]
salt and pepper to taste

Chop the bacon and fry lightly in its own fat. Add the chopped onion and sauté until lightly browned. Add the garlic and the cubed beef and allow the beef to brown. Stir frequently to prevent sticking. Add a little cold water and simmer over low heat for approximately twenty minutes. Stir in the flour and season with paprika, marjoram, salt and pepper. Add the stock gradually, stirring constantly. Simmer gently for 25-30 minutes. Diced potatoes may be added with the stock. Serve with crisp, warm rolls.

Juha od Jastoga
Lobster Soup

1 medium lobster
4 c. milk
1 c. water
1 tbsp. flour
4 tbsp. butter
1 tsp. paprika
salt and pepper to taste

Melt the butter over low heat. Increase the heat until the butter begins to foam. Add the flour and cook for a minute or two, but do not allow it to brown. Add the milk gradually, stirring constantly. Set aside along with the green glands and the coral. Finely chop the tail meat. Place the meat, broken claws and shell into cold water over medium heat. Simmer just below the boiling point for approximately twenty-five minutes. Stir in the milk sauce. Dice the remaining lobster meat and add it to the soup. Season with salt, pepper and paprika. Mash the coral to a paste and mix it with the green glands just before serving. Add the paste to the soup, mix thoroughly, reheat and garnish.

Juha sa Prženim Lukom
Onion Ring Soup

¼ c. flour
6 c. beef stock
1 c. small onions
1 tsp. paprika
salt and pepper to taste
¼ c. grated Parmesan Cheese
fat for deep frying

Peel and slice the onions and separate them into rings. Season the flour with salt, pepper and paprika. Flour the onion rings. Deep fry the floured onion rings in hot fat until they are golden on both sides. Drain on paper towels. Bring the beef stock to a boil and add half the cheese. Serve immediately, while the onions are still crisp. Serve the remaining cheese on the side.

Goveđa Juha sa Rezancima/Clear Beef Soup with Egg Noodles {page 43}

Goveđa Juha
Clear Beef Soup

2 lbs. beef
1 beef bone
6 c. water
1 whole carrot
1 whole stalk of celery
½ onion
½ tsp. peppercorns
½ tsp. parsley
1 bay leaf
salt to taste

Place the beef, beef bone and vegetables in the water. Season with bay leaf, peppercorns, parsley, and salt. Cook for approximately 2 hours. Strain to remove the vegetables to get a clear beef stock. Garnish as desired or use as a base for other soups.

Dalmatinska Juha
Dalmatian Soup

6 c. beef stock
¼ lb. cooked macaroni
¼ c. butter
3 tbsp. flour
2 tbsp. chopped onion
¼ c. grated Parmesan cheese

Melt the butter over low heat. Increase the heat and brown the onion in the hot butter. Add the flour and make a golden roux. Add this roux to the beef stock and stir well. Allow the soup to cook for 20-25 minutes. Add the cooked macaroni and grated cheese. Bring to a boil just before serving.

Juha od Povrća
Vegetable Soup

½ lb. smoked pork
6 c. beef stock
¼ c. diced potatoes
¼ c. diced carrots
¼ c. rice
¼ c. sliced onion
¼ c. green peas
¼ c. sauerkraut
¼ c. chopped spinach
¼ c. diced celery
¼ c. diced eggplant
1 tbsp. tomato paste
2 firm, ripe tomatoes, diced
1 tbsp. chopped parsley
¼ c. grated Parmesan
salt and pepper to taste

Place the smoked pork in a deep pot. Add enough water to cover. Add the beef stock, potatoes, carrots and rice. Cover and bring to a boil. Cook for about twenty minutes. Add the remaining vegetables and seasonings. Bring to the boiling point. Reduce the heat and cook slowly until the vegetables are tender. Remove the meat and serve on the side. Pass the soup through a sieve or blend in a blender. Sprinkle with grated Parmesan cheese.

Juha od Šparge
Asparagus Soup

6 c. water
½ lb. asparagus
3 tbsp. butter
3 tbsp. flour
½ c. sour cream
salt and pepper to taste

Cook the asparagus stems in salted water until tender. Drain the stems, but save the water. Mash the asparagus stems. Melt the butter in a medium saucepan. Add the flour. When it begins to brown, stir in enough warm water to make a thick sauce. Combine this mixture with the water in which the stems were cooked. Add the mashed asparagus to the soup. Cook for about fifteen minutes. Add the sour cream and bring to a boil. Sprinkle with parsley and serve with bread sticks or toasted buns.

Juha od Luka i Rajčica
Onion and Tomato Soup

4 tbsp. tomato puree
2 tbsp. minced garlic
¼ c. butter
1 whole stalk of celery
1 whole carrot
2 large onions, chopped
6 c. beef stock
2 tbsp. chopped parsley
½ tsp. paprika
salt and pepper to taste

Melt the butter in a large saucepan. Sauté the onion and garlic in the butter until the onion is slightly browned. Add the tomato puree and the parsley and stir well. Add the celery, carrot and beef stock. Cook over moderate heat for about half an hour. Season with salt, pepper and paprika. Remove the celery and carrot before serving. Serve with a little sour cream on the side.

Juha od Špinata
Spinach Soup

½ lb. chopped spinach
1 small onion, chopped
4 tbsp. butter
3 tbsp. flour
6 c. warm milk
salt and pepper to taste
1 egg

Sauté the spinach and onion in one tablespoon of butter for about fifteen minutes. Melt 3 tablespoons of butter. Add the flour and make a light roux. Add the milk gradually, stirring constantly. Cook for about five minutes. Add the spinach and cook for another ten minutes. Mix the egg with about ¼ cup of water and slowly pour into the boiling soup. Cook for approximately 1 minute and serve immediately.

Juha od Teletine
Veal Soup

½ lb. veal, cubed
2 carrots, sliced
¼ c. peas
¼ c. cauliflower
6 c. water
3 tbsp. butter or shortening
¼ c. flour
1 tbsp. chopped parsley
¼ c. finely chopped onion
salt and pepper to taste

Bring the water to a boil. Melt the butter or shortening in a saucepan. Add the flour to make a white roux. Brown the onion in the roux. Add the veal to the mixture and allow it to brown slightly. Dilute with a little cold water. Add the mixture and vegetables to the boiling water. Season with salt and pepper. Cook the soup until the vegetables and the meat are tender. Add the chopped parsley a few minutes before the soup is fully cooked. Serve with hot buttered rolls.

Juha od Mrkve
Carrot Soup

6 c. beef stock
1 lb. carrots, sliced
2 tbsp. butter
2 tbsp. bread crumbs
¼ c. sour cream
1 tbsp. chopped parsley
salt and pepper to taste

Cook the sliced carrots in salted water until tender. Mash them. Melt the butter over low heat. Add bread crumbs and sauté to make a golden paste. Add the mashed carrots to this paste. Add enough water to make a thick sauce, stirring constantly to avoid lumps. Add the beef stock and season with salt and pepper. Cook for 20-25 minutes. Add the chopped parsley and the sour cream just before serving.

Juha od Crvenog Graha
Kidney Bean Soup

1 lb. kidney beans
1 tsp. ground paprika
½ lb. smoked ham
3 tbsp. butter or shortening
3 tbsp. flour
1 c. cold water
salt and pepper to taste

Place the beans and the ham in a deep pot. Cover with water. Season with salt and cook for about an hour and a half until the beans are tender. Melt the butter or shortening over medium heat. Stir in the flour to make a golden roux. Stir in enough water to make a thick sauce. Bring this sauce to a boil and add it to the bean soup after removing the ham and three quarters of the beans. Cook the soup for another ten minutes. This soup is especially convenient because it provides soup, the main course (ham) and a side dish (beans) for a simple lunch or supper.

Juha od Cvjetače
Cauliflower Soup

6 c. beef stock
1 lb. cauliflower
3 tbsp. butter
3 tbsp. flour
1 tbsp. chopped parsley
¼ c. sour cream
salt and pepper to taste

Clean the cauliflower. Place it in a bowl of cold, salted water and allow it to sit upside down for about half an hour. This will draw out the dust and other impurities. Cook the cauliflower in boiling salted water for 25-30 minutes until tender. Break it into flowerettes. Leave one third of the flowerettes to garnish the soup, mashing the remainder of the cauliflower. Melt the butter over medium heat. Add the flour to make a golden roux, stirring constantly. Stir in the mashed cauliflower, and add a little water. Add this sauce to the beef stock. Stir well, and cook for another five minutes over moderate heat. Add the sour cream. Season with pepper and garnish with the cauliflower flowerettes and parsley.

Juha od Mahuna
Green Bean Soup

6 c. water
1 lb. green beans
2 tbsp. butter
1 tbsp. flour
¼ tsp. minced garlic
½ c. sour cream
1 tbsp. chopped parsley
salt and pepper to taste

Melt the butter or shortening over low heat. Add the flour and garlic and sauté until golden. Chop the green beans and add them to the salted water. Allow to cook over moderate heat until the beans are tender. Season with salt and pepper. Add the chopped parsley and the sour cream just before serving. Serve with bread sticks.

Juha od Soma
Catfish Soup

6 c. cold water
1 ½ lb. catfish, cleaned
1 tsp. red paprika
1 tsp. sugar
½ c. sour cream
1 bread roll
2 carrots, chopped
1 onion, chopped
1 tbsp. vinegar
1 bay leaf
2 tbsp. lard
2 tbsp. flour
2 celery stalks, chopped
2 tbsp. parsley, finely chopped
2 tbsp. butter
salt and pepper to taste

Place the cleaned fish, vinegar, bay leaf, salt, pepper and onion in boiling water and cook until tender. Drain the liquid and save. Cook the vegetables in the strained liquid until tender. Melt the lard and add the flour to make a golden roux. Add the parsley and red paprika. Mix in the cold water, stirring constantly. Add this sauce to the soup. Cook for 10-15 more minutes. Remove and bone the fish. Add it to the soup with the sour cream. Garnish and serve.

Banatska Juha
Banat Soup

6 c. cold water
1 lamb, pork or veal liver
1 tbsp. vinegar
1 parsnip
1 carrot, cut into strips
2 tbsp. butter
2 tbsp. flour
½ onion, diced
1 tsp. sweet paprika
¼ c. rice
¾ c. sour cream
salt to taste

Set the water to boil. Cut the liver into small pieces and add it to the boiling water. Add the vegetables and vinegar. Season with salt. Cook until the liver is tender. Melt the butter over medium heat. Brown the onion in it. Add the flour and paprika and sauté until golden brown. Pour this roux into the soup and mix well. Add the rice and cook until it becomes tender. Add the sour cream just before serving.

Kisela Juha sa Jajima
Sour Soup with Eggs

3 tbsp. lard or butter
1 tsp. sugar
3 tbsp. flour
1 whole medium onion, chopped
1 c. sour cream
2 bay leaves
6 c. water
wine vinegar to taste (1-2 tbsp.)
3-4 eggs, well beaten
salt and pepper to taste

Melt the lard and add the sugar. Sauté until it turns a dark brown. Add the flour and onion. When the mixture darkens and onion is tender, add the vinegar, bay leaves and pepper and cook for a minute or two longer. Add boiling salted water, stirring to avoid lumps. Continue cooking for about half an hour, stirring occasionally. Add the sour cream and well beaten eggs. Cook for another minute or two before serving.

Slavonska Juha od Rajčica
Slavonian Tomato Soup

5-6 medium cooked tomatoes strained, or
6 oz. tomato paste
3 oz. sliced smoked bacon
1 stalk celery, finely chopped
1 small onion, finely chopped
6 c. water
salt and pepper to taste

Fry the bacon in a medium saucepan in its own fat. Stir in the flour and allow it to turn a golden color. Stir in one cup water gradually, stirring constantly. Bring the mixture to a boil. Add the salt, pepper and tomato paste and stir well. Cook for 5-6 minutes. Bring 6 cups of water to a boil. Add the tomato sauce to the water. Bring the soup to a boil. Add the celery and onion. Cook the soup for 25-30 minutes. Garnish with croutons, spooned dumplings, or noodles.

Juha od Gljiva
Mushroom Soup

½ lb. mushrooms
1 egg yolk
¼ c. sour cream
2 tbsp. flour
2 tbsp. butter
3 c. milk
3 c. water
1 tbsp. minced onion
salt and pepper to taste
2 rolls, diced and fried as croutons

Slice the mushrooms. Melt the butter over low heat. Add minced onion and sauté until golden brown. Add the mushrooms and allow to simmer until the mushrooms begin to brown. Set a few mushrooms aside to garnish the soup with. Sprinkle the remaining mushrooms with flour and simmer for a minute or two longer. Add the water gradually, stirring constantly. When the mixture thickens, blend it in a blender or food processor. Return to the saucepan and stir in the milk. When the soup begins to boil, add the well beaten egg yolk and the sour cream. Serve garnished with sliced mushrooms or croutons.

Srijemska Juha
Sriem Soup

1 stewing chicken
1 medium onion
2 tbsp. butter
2 tbsp. flour
1 tbsp. chopped parsley
3 egg yolks
3 tbsp. sour cream
2 tbsp. wine vinegar
1 tsp. sweet paprika
salt and pepper to taste

Wash the chicken. Cut it into pieces and place in enough boiling water to cover. Reduce the heat and allow to simmer slowly. Add onion, salt, pepper, paprika and more water as required. Melt the butter over low heat. Make a golden roux by slowly stirring in the flour. Place this roux in the soup when the meat is cooked and tender. Add the vinegar and allow to cook a little longer. Remove the chicken. When it is cool enough to handle, bone the cooked chicken. Beat the egg yolks and the sour cream together in the serving bowl. Pour the soup over the egg yolks. Add the parsley and chopped chicken pieces before serving.

Juha sa Sirom
Cheese Soup

½ c. hard cheese, diced
3 tbsp. shortening
3 tomatoes, sliced
1 medium onion, sliced
6 c. beef stock
1 tbsp. chopped parsley
½ c. smoked ham, diced
salt and pepper to taste

Fry the onion in the shortening until it becomes clear. Add the tomatoes and fry a little longer. Add the beef stock and the cheese and simmer slowly until the cheese melts. Add the ham and parsley and cook for ten minutes longer. Season with salt and pepper.

Riblja Juha
Fish Soup

1 ½ lb. fish
2 carrots
1 tbsp. ground parsley
2 stalks celery
1 potato
1 medium onion
6 c. water
1 tbsp. butter
¼ tsp. black pepper, whole
salt to taste

Clean and wash the fish. Wash and chop the vegetables. Place the fish in salted boiling water and allow to cook gently until tender. Melt the butter over low heat. Brown the onion in the butter and add it to the soup along with the other vegetables. While the fish is cooking, add the whole black pepper. Remove the fish and the remaining black pepper before serving. This soup can be made from all larger types of fish. It is especially practical when the fish is used as an entrée or main course.

Zagorska Juha
Zagorje Soup

½ lb. chopped chicken
½ lb. chopped veal
6 c. water
½ tsp. sweet paprika
1 tsp. chopped parsley
1 medium carrot
1 medium onion
1 stalk celery
salt and pepper to taste

Bring the water to a boil and add the meat. Cook for a few minutes. Skim the water as froth forms. Add the vegetables and simmer gently for about two and a half hours over low heat. Remove the vegetables and season with salt and pepper. Sprinkle with paprika and chopped parsley.

Juha od Bijelog Graha
White Bean Soup

2 c. navy beans
2 lbs. smoked ham
1 tbsp. lard or shortening
1 tbsp. flour
1 medium onion, chopped
6 c. water
salt and pepper to taste
grated cheese or sour cream

Soak the beans overnight in cold water. The following day, place the ham in the water in a deep pot. Cook for about half an hour. Add the soaked beans and cook until they become tender. Remove the ham, slice it and set it aside. Brown the onions in the shortening. Add the flour and allow it to become a deep brown color. Add this roux to the beans and cook for another ten minutes. Serve with grated cheese, or add a little sour cream. Serve the ham with the bean soup on the side.

Juha od Poriluka
Leek Soup

1 ½ lb. leeks
2 large onions, sliced
3 tbsp. butter or shortening
6 c. beef stock
½ lb. potatoes, cubed
½ c. sour cream
salt and pepper to taste

Wash and cut the leeks into small pieces. Melt the butter over low heat. Add the leeks and sauté slowly. Add the onions and allow them to brown lightly. Add the beef stock and cook until the vegetables are tender. Pass everything through a sieve, or blend in a blender and return it to the saucepan. Bring the soup to a boil again. Add the potatoes and cook until they become tender. Add the sour cream just before serving, or serve it on the side.

Juha od Mlijeka
Milk Soup

3 tbsp. butter
3 tbsp. flour
1 ½ tbsp. ground parsley
3 c. milk
3 c. water
salt to taste

Melt the butter over low heat in a deep pot. When it becomes very hot, gradually stir in the flour and sauté to make a white roux. Do not allow the flour to brown. Add the water and the milk gradually, stirring to avoid lumps. Bring to a boil. Add the parsley and cook for about fifteen minutes. Add noodles and cook until tender.

Krumpir Juha
Cream of Potato Soup

3-4 large potatoes
2 large carrots, whole
2 parsnips
¼ c. flour
¼ c. butter
6 c. beef stock
1 egg yolk
¼ c. lard
1 tbsp. chopped parsley
½ c. sour cream
salt to taste

Peel the potatoes, slice them and fry in half the butter. Add the flour, brown lightly, then add the beef stock. Add the carrots and parsnips. Cook for half an hour, then run everything through a sieve. Beat the egg yolk until light and fluffy. Add the cream and beat again. Pour the egg and cream mixture into the soup just before serving. Serve with croutons. Add the croutons to the soup immediately before serving.

Turopoljska Juha
Turopolje Soup

½ c. sour cream
3 tbsp. flour
3 eggs
6 c. chicken stock
salt to taste
1 tbsp. wine vinegar (optional)

Salt the chicken stock as required and bring it to a boil. Beat the eggs. Add the sour cream and flour. Mix well. Pour this mixture into the boiling stock, stirring constantly. Reduce the heat and simmer for ten minutes. For a slightly tart flavor, add vinegar with the egg mixture.

Juha od Kiselog Zelja
Sauerkraut Soup

1 ½ lb. sauerkraut
1 ½ lb. smoked pork ribs
¼ c. smoked bacon, diced
1 tbsp. flour
2 onions, chopped
½ lb. smoked sausage, sliced
1 tbsp. finely chopped garlic
½ c. sour cream
1 tsp. sweet paprika
6 c. water
salt and pepper to taste

Place the smoked pork, sauerkraut, onions and garlic in a large pot. Add enough water to cover. Cook until the meat becomes tender, then remove the meat. Fry the bacon well in its own fat. Add the paprika and sausage. Mix well and add this mixture to the cooked sauerkraut. Add the water. Mix one tablespoon of flour with the sour cream. Add this mixture to the soup. Simmer slowly. When the soup comes to a boil, garnish and serve immediately.

Juha od Leće
Lima Bean Soup

½ lb. lima beans
3 tbsp. butter or margarine
3 tbsp. flour
6 c. beef stock
1 tbsp. finely chopped onion
salt and pepper to taste

Clean the lima beans and place them in a large pot. Cover with water. Melt one tablespoon butter or margarine over medium heat. Sauté the onion in it until it becomes lightly browned. Add the onion to the lima beans and cook the beans until tender. Mash the cooked lima beans. Melt the remaining butter. When the foam subsides, add the flour and make a golden roux. Add the mashed lima beans to this paste. Thicken the beef stock with the mixture. Cook for another five minutes, then garnish.

SOUP ADDITIVES

Rezanci za Juhu
Egg Noodles for Soup

1 egg
2 tbsp. milk
1 tsp. salt
1 tbsp. oil
3 c. flour

Combine all the ingredients but the flour in a mixing bowl. Stir in the flour. Knead on a board until you get a smooth, glossy dough. Divide the dough into two sections. Roll each section out as thinly as possible. Sprinkle the dough with a little flour and allow to dry for approximately ten minutes. Fold the dough over several times until you have a section three or four inches wide. Using a sharp knife slice each section approximately ¼" wide. Separate into noodles and allow to dry for at least two hours. The noodles can be used immediately or dried for several hours and stored in an airtight container for several weeks.

Okruglice od Sira
Cheese Dumplings

2 c. cottage cheese
2 egg yolks
2 egg whites, stiffly beaten
3 tbsp. wheat germ
2 tbsp. bread crumbs
2 tbsp. butter
¼ c. flour
½ tsp. salt

Cream the butter and egg yolks. Add the cheese which has been mashed with a fork, the wheat germ, the bread crumbs and salt. Fold in the stiffly beaten egg whites, and enough flour to make a smooth dough. Shape the dumplings with wet hands. Drop into boiling soup and cook for 10-12 minutes.

Okruglice sa Maslacem
Butter Dumplings

¾ c. flour
½ c. milk
2 eggs
1 tbsp. melted butter
salt to taste

Beat the eggs well. Add salt, pepper and melted butter to the eggs. Work all the ingredients together. Add the flour and milk alternately, beating after each addition, to make a soft dough. Drop the dumplings from a spoon into boiling soup. Dip the spoon in the boiling soup before taking a spoonful of dough so the dough will not stick. Cook for 10 minutes. Do not overcook. Serve with clear or cream soups.

Okruglice od Krupice
Semolina Dumplings

2 eggs, well beaten
2 tbsp. butter at room temperature
2/3 c. semolina flour
1 tsp. salt
1 tbsp. chopped parsley

Cream the butter, then add the eggs and mix well. Add the salt, semolina and chopped parsley. Flour your hands and shape the dough by teaspoonfuls into little dumplings or pinch the dough with a melon baller and place the dumplings into hot boiling soup. Cook for approximately 20 minutes. Use the dough immediately. If allowed to sit, the semolina will harden and the dumplings will be hard.

Illustrated on page 28.

Riža od Jetre
Liver Rice

6 c. beef stock
¼ c. lard or shortening
1 egg
1 tbsp. lard or shortening
2 ½ tbsp. onion, chopped
2 bread rolls
¼ c. bread crumbs
½ lb. calf's liver
parsley
salt and pepper to taste

Sauté the onion in one tablespoon of lard until golden brown. Soak the rolls in a little beef stock or water and mash them with a fork. Add the egg, onion, parsley and mashed rolls to the lard. Mix well. Chop the liver and add to the lard mixture. Season with salt and pepper. Add the bread crumbs to the liver mixture and mix well. Grind the mixture in a grinder and add to boiling soup. Allow to cook until tender before serving.

Rezanci od Krumpira
Potato Noodles

6 medium potatoes, cooked
2 tbsp. butter
1-1 ½ c. flour
1 or 2 eggs
½ c. lard or shortening
¼ c. bread crumbs

Mash the potatoes. Add the butter and eggs and mix well. Add one cup of flour and mix to make a medium soft dough. Sprinkle a board with the remaining flour and knead the mixture until the dough becomes smooth. Divide the dough into three or four sections. Roll each section out thinly and cut the dough into strips about three inches long and ¼" wide. Cook the noodles for a few minutes in salted boiling water. Drain. Fry the bread crumbs in the melted butter. Add the drained noodles, mix well and fry for a minute or two. These noodles make an excellent side dish. Any leftover potato noodles can be cut into smaller pieces and cooked in soup.

Savijače od Mesa
Meat Savijača as a Soup Additive

1 savijaca recipe
6 c. clear beef stock
½ lb. chopped ground beef
2 tbsp. lard or shortening
1 onion, finely chopped
1 tbsp. chopped parsley
1 tbsp. oil
1 egg
salt and pepper to taste

Brown the onion in the lard. Add the meat and allow it to brown. Season with salt, pepper and parsley. Allow the mixture to cool. Add the egg and mix well. Stretch the savijaca dough. Brush with oil and add the meat filling. Roll up the savijaca. Place in a well greased and floured pan. Brush the top with a little melted butter. Bake in a hot oven, 400° until the savijaca is golden brown. Cut into small sections. Serve separately with the soup. Do not put the savijaca sections in the soup before serving, or they will become soggy.

Tarana
Tarana

5 eggs
4 c. flour
1 tbsp. butter
1 tbsp. salt

Combine all the ingredients in a large bowl and mix until you get a firm dough. Turn the dough onto a floured board and knead until smooth. Separate the dough into three or four sections. Pass each piece of dough through a sieve or grinder. You will get little pieces of dough about the size of rice. Allow the dough pieces to dry overnight. The dried *tarana* may be stored for several weeks in airtight containers until ready to use. It may be cooked in water and served as a side dish like rice or added to soup.

Žličnjaci
Spooned Dumplings

2 tbsp. butter
1 egg
6 tbsp. flour
½ tsp. salt

Beat the butter well until it becomes light and frothy. Add the lightly beaten egg and flour and beat well with a spoon. Spoon the dough into boiling soup and cook until tender.

Ljevanci
Poured Soup Additive

1 egg
2 tbsp. milk
3 tbsp. flour
salt to taste

Beat the egg well. Stir in the milk, flour and salt and mix well. Pour into boiling soup. Cook for a minute or two before serving.

Žličnjaci od Kukuruzne Krupice
Cornmeal Dumplings

1 tbsp. butter, softened
6 tbsp. cornmeal
1 egg
½ tsp. salt

Beat the butter and the egg. Add the cornmeal and the salt. Spoon into hot soup and cook for approximately twenty minutes.

Žličnjaci od Špinata
Spinach Dumplings

1 tbsp. butter, softened
2 eggs
¼ c. finely chopped spinach
3 tbsp. milk
½ tsp. salt
½ c. flour

Cream the butter. Add the egg and beat well. Add the remaining ingredients and mix together well. Spoon into hot soup and cook for approximately twenty minutes.

45

Dalmatinski Jastog
Lobster à la Dalmatine

Fish and Seafood

Fishing is one of Croatia's major industries. Consequently, seafood plays a significant role in the Croatian diet. The Adriatic Sea is a veritable cornucopia of seafood abounding in a seemingly inexhaustable variety of saltwater fish and shellfish. It has been claimed that it contains at least 365 varieties. The most popular sea forms can all be found in the Croatian cook's repertoire.

Bakalar, unsalted dried cod, has developed as an important staple along the entire Croatian coast where it was an important food for fishermen and mariners because it could easily be stored. Bakalar is especially important for Christmas Eve, Ash Wednesday and Good Friday. We have included a recipe for Cod and Potatoes, but every Dalmatian housewife prides herself with her special method of preparing bakalar. For those same meatless holidays, inland Croatia prepares *Fiš Paprikaš*, a delicious paprikash usually made with carp or catfish. It is traditionally cooked outdoors and every man prides himself with his special method of preparation!

The countless flowing rivers and icy mountain streams found throughout the inland regions of Croatia supply a delicious assortment of freshwater fish. Salmon, trout, eel, perch, carp, catfish and pike are all found in great abundance. Trout has been a long-time favorite with Croatians. This freshwater fish is a specialty when prepared stuffed with prunes, and baked in a warm oven with frequent basting.

The popularity of sturgeon helps to account for the relatively frequent use of caviar and its popularity as an appetizer. A variety of fresh and saltwater fish is available in the well stocked open air markets of the big cities and of the larger towns.

Dalmatia has developed an excellent seafood cuisine and is the country's undisputed leader in seafood cooking. Among the numerous soups, gumbos and stews, *brodet* is one of many examples of excellent Dalmatian fish dishes enriched with just the right vegetables and seasonings.

Smoked, grilled, and broiled fish and seafood are also very popular. Grilling is perhaps the most popular method of preparing fish. We have included a recipe for grilling salmon, but most large fish can be prepared in the same manner.

Although it would be impossible to present all of the seafood specialties which the Croatian cooks have developed over the centuries, we have included those which we find to be representative of Croatian seafood cuisine.

Barbun na Jadranski Način
Red Mullet Adriatic Style

2 ¾ lbs. red mullet
3 sardines, chopped
¾ c. olive oil
1 tsp. minced garlic
1 tsp. chopped capers
1 tbsp. chopped parsley
1 lemon, sliced

Clean the fish. Fry the sardines lightly in the olive oil. Add the mullets and brown slightly on each side. Season with garlic and parsley. Allow the fish to simmer slowly until tender. Arrange the mullets on a heated platter. Season the pan juices with the chopped capers and continue to simmer for a few minutes. Pour this over the fish before serving. Garnish with lemon slices.

Pirjana Štuka
Stewed Pike

2 lbs. pike
1 tbsp. minced garlic
1 tbsp. chopped parsley
2 tbsp. shortening
¾ c. sour cream
¼ c. sliced onion
1 tsp. paprika
2 tbsp. tomato paste
1 c. red wine
salt to taste

Clean the pike and season it with salt. Heat the shortening in a large saucepan and sauté the onion in it until it turns golden brown. Place the fish in the saucepan with the onions. Remove the pan from heat and add garlic and paprika. Add the wine and tomato paste. Simmer gently until the fish is tender. Add the sour cream just before serving and garnish with chopped parsley. The fish may be cooked a little longer after the sour cream is added, but do not allow the cream to come to a boil.

Sabljan na Žaru
Skewered Swordfish

1 ½ lbs. swordfish steaks
3 tbsp. olive oil
2 tbsp. chopped onion
juice of one lemon
10 bay leaves
1 tbsp. chopped parsley
½ tsp. paprika
1 ½ tsp. salt
dash of pepper

Cube the fish into bite-sized chunks. Combine the olive oil, onion, paprika, salt, pepper, bay leaves and lemon juice. Place the fish cubes in this marinade and refrigerate overnight. The following day remove the fish from the marinade, drain, and place on skewers. Grill over hot coals for about ten minutes, turning occasionally. Garnish with chopped parsley and serve with Olive Sauce or Lemon Butter Sauce.

Ragu od Kamenice
Oyster Stew

30 oysters
2 tbsp. olive oil
½ onion, chopped
½ c. sliced mushrooms
1 ½ c. tomato paste
1 ½ c. water
2 tbsp. melted butter
1 clove garlic, chopped
salt and pepper to taste

Shuck and drain the oysters. Heat the olive oil and brown the onion in it. Add the mushrooms and sauté lightly. Add the tomato paste. Simmer for another 15 minutes. Add the water, oysters and garlic. Bring the oyster stew to a boil. Season with salt and pepper. Stir in the melted butter before serving.

Dalmatinski Brodet
Dalmatian Brodet

2 lbs. assorted salt water fish
¼ c. olive oil
3 tbsp. flour
3 tbsp. butter
½ c. sliced onion
1 c. wine
1 clove garlic, chopped
1 tbsp. parsley, chopped
½ lb. tomatoes or
1 c. tomato sauce
salt and pepper to taste

Clean the fish and cut it into fairly large steaks. Season with salt and pepper. Roll the steaks in the flour and fry them in the hot olive oil. Melt the butter over low heat. Increase the heat and brown the onions in the butter. Add the parsley, garlic, wine and the sliced tomatoes or tomato sauce. Simmer slowly for about half an hour. Add the fish and enough water to cover. Continue to simmer but do not stir. Instead, shake the pan occasionally. Carefully arrange the fish on a serving platter. Cover with the tomato and onion sauce. Serves 4-5.

Pastrva sa Gljivama
Croatian Trout

3 large trout
1 lb. pitted prunes
3 eggs
1 c. olive oil
1 tbsp. minced garlic
½ c. dry white wine
1 c. water
juice of half lemon
lemon slices
1 tbsp. chopped parsley
salt and pepper to taste

Soak the prunes in cold water for about an hour. Wash the fish and season it with salt and pepper. Drain the prunes well. Make incisions along the sides of the fish about one inch deep and one inch long. Stuff a prune into each cut. Grease a deep baking dish with part of the olive oil. Place the trout in the dish. Season with parsley and garlic. Combine the oil, water, lemon juice, and wine. Pour this mixture over the trout. Bake at 450° for half an hour to 45 minutes. Carefully place the fish on a warm serving platter. Scramble the eggs in the juices in which the trout was baked. Place the scrambled eggs on top of the trout and garnish with lemon slices.

Smuđ sa Kiselim Vrhnjem
Perch with Sour Cream

2 lbs. pike perch
1/3 c. oil
1 c. sliced mushrooms
¼ c. butter
½ c. sour cream
salt to taste

Fillet the fish and season with salt. Roll the fillets in oil. Pour the remaining oil into a deep baking dish. Place the fish in the oil and bake at 425° for approximately 10 minutes. Reduce the heat to 350° for another 15 minutes until the fish is tender. Sauté the mushrooms in the butter. Place the mushrooms over the fish. Pour the sour cream over the mushrooms. Place the pike back in the oven for another 10-15 minutes. Serve immediately.

Pečeni Smuđ
Baked Perch

2 large perch fillets
4 anchovy fillets
1 tsp. capers
1 tbsp. chopped parsley
rind of ½ lemon, grated
2 tbsp. melted butter
salt and pepper to taste
lemon slices

Wash and dry the fillets. Cut them into large chunks. Grease a covered baking dish generously. Arrange the chunks of fish closely in the dish and dot with capers. Season with salt and pepper. Sprinkle with grated lemon. Cut the anchovy fillets into thin strips and arrange them across the fish. Pour the melted butter over the fish. Cover the baking dish and bake at 425° for about ten minutes. Reduce the heat to 350° and bake for another twenty minutes until the fish is tender. Garnish with finely chopped fresh parsley and lemon slices. Serve with hot lemon sauce.

Marinirana Tunina
Marinated Tuna

2 lbs. tuna
½ c. olive oil
¼ c. flour
2 c. water
2 medium onions
1 clove garlic, chopped
1 bay leaf
1 tsp. salt
1 tbsp. parsley, finely chopped
1 tsp. whole black pepper
1 c. wine vinegar
2 tbsp. sugar
rind of one lemon

Clean the fish and cut it into thick slices. Roll it in flour. Heat the oil. Brown the fish well on both sides in the hot oil. Arrange the fried fish in a shallow serving dish. Thinly slice the onions. Brown the onion, garlic and parsley lightly in the oil in which the fish was fried. Add the salt, pepper, bay leaf, wine vinegar, lemon rind, sugar and water. Bring the mixture to a boil. Reduce the heat and simmer for about 10-15 minutes. Allow to cool slightly. Pour this marinade over the fish and refrigerate overnight. Marinated tuna should be served cold. Mackerel can be prepared in the same manner.

Loptice od Bakalara
Codfish Balls

2 c. cooked cod
1 c. mashed potatoes
3 tbsp. milk
3 tbsp. olive oil
2 eggs, well beaten
1 tbsp. lemon juice
oil for deep frying
salt and pepper to taste

Combine the cod and potatoes with the milk, lemon juice and olive oil. Mash well. Stir in the eggs. Season with salt and pepper. When the mixture is well combined, shape into balls. Deep fry in hot oil until the balls are a golden color. Serve hot.

Jesetra sa Lukom
Sturgeon with Onions

2 lbs. sturgeon
1/3 c. flour
¼ c. vegetable oil
2 tbsp. flour
3 c. Croatian Tomato Sauce
1 c. sliced onion
salt, pepper and paprika to taste

Slice the sturgeon into large chunks. Season with salt, pepper and paprika. Roll the fish in the seasoned flour. Heat the oil and brown the sturgeon in it. Place the fish in a well-greased baking dish. Brown the onion in the oil in which the fish was fried. Season with salt and pepper and sprinkle with 2 tablespoons of flour. Add the Croatian Tomato Sauce to the onions. If necessary, add a little water. Pour this mixture over the fish. Bake at 400° for approximately half an hour.

Bakalar s Krumpirom
Codfish Casserole

2 lbs. dried codfish
2 lbs. potatoes
½ c. oil
1 c. bread crumbs
1 tbsp. ground parsley
2 cloves garlic, chopped
salt and pepper to taste

Pound the codfish well with a meat tenderizer. Soak it in cold water for 24 hours. Clean the fish and cook it in boiling water until it becomes tender. Drain and allow the fish to cool. When it has cooled sufficiently to handle, remove the bones. Peel and slice the potatoes. Peel and cut the fish into fairly large chunks. Place the fish and potatoes in a deep baking dish in alternate layers. Sprinkle each layer with bread crumbs, garlic and parsley. Season each layer with salt and pepper and add a few tablespoons of hot water. Heat the oil and pour it over the casserole. Bake at 400° until the potatoes are tender. Serve with fresh or cooked sauerkraut.

Pirjana Pastrva sa Gljivama
Trout Sautéed with Mushrooms

2 ¾-3 lbs. trout
1 c. sliced mushrooms
2 tbsp. lemon juice
¾ c. butter
¾ c. sour cream
salt and pepper to taste

Clean the fish and remove the bones and heads. Sauté the mushrooms in butter until soft. Remove the mushrooms and add the fish. Season with salt and pepper. Sauté for 3-4 minutes. When nicely browned, place the fish and the mushrooms on a serving dish. While the butter is still warm, add the lemon juice and sour cream without allowing the sauce to come to a boil. Pour this sauce over the fish and mushrooms just before serving.

Pečena Kečiga
Baked Sterlet

1 medium sterlet or other sturgeon
½ c. butter
½ tsp. parsley, finely chopped
1 tsp. paprika
juice of two lemons
salt to taste
1 lemon, sliced

Skin and clean the fish. Season it with salt, parsley and paprika. Place the fish in a greased baking dish. Melt the butter and pour it over the sterlet. Bake at 350° for half an hour until the fish is tender, but does not fall apart. When baked, transfer the fish to a hot buttered serving dish. Beat the lemon juice into the butter that the fish was cooked in to make a rich, creamy sauce. Pour this sauce over the sterlet and garnish with the lemon slices.

List sa Bijelim Vinom
Sole Fillets in White Wine

1 ½ lbs. sole fillets
1/3 c. butter
1 c. sliced mushrooms
1 c. bread crumbs
1 tbsp. flour
1 ½ c. white wine
salt and pepper to taste

Wrap the fillets in a clean kitchen towel to remove the moisture. Melt the butter. When hot, place the fillets in the butter to coat them completely. Remove from the butter and season both sides with salt and pepper. Roll the fish in bread crumbs. Fry the fillets in the hot butter until they turn a golden brown. Remove and place them in a warm, greased serving dish. Sauté the mushrooms in the butter in which the fish was cooked. Sprinkle with flour. Simmer for 10-15 minutes. Add the wine and continue to simmer a little longer. Remove from heat and pour over the sole. Serve immediately.

Rak u Umaku
Creamed Crayfish

2 c. crayfish meat
1 c. chopped mushrooms
1/3 c. butter
½ tsp. paprika
2 tbsp. onion, finely chopped
1 tsp. chopped parsley
1 c. sour cream
¼ c. wine
salt and pepper to taste

Melt the butter over low heat in a large saucepan. Turn up the heat and add the onion, mushrooms, crayfish meat and parsley. Season with salt, pepper, and paprika. Reduce the heat and simmer slowly for about 20 minutes, stirring occasionally. Place the crayfish in a buttered oven dish. Add the wine to the sour cream and beat well. Pour this mixture over the fish. Bake at 375° for about 20 minutes or until the top becomes golden brown.

Losos na Žaru
Grilled Salmon

6 skinless salmon fillets or steaks
4 tbsp. olive oil
¼ c. chopped onion
4 cloves garlic, minced
1 tsp. minced rosemary

Combine the oil, onion, garlic and rosemary. Rinse the fish and pat it dry. Season with salt and pepper. Soak the salmon in this marinade while you prepare the grill. Grease the grill and lay the fish steaks directly on it approximately six inches from the coals. Cover the grill with the hood or with foil. Cook the salmon for approximately eight to ten minutes if the steaks are less than one inch thick or twelve to fifteen minutes for fish up to an inch and a half thick. Turn the steaks once, but baste often with the reserved marinade. Transfer to a warm platter.

Pečeni Losos
Broiled Salmon

2 large salmon steaks
½ c. clarified butter
1 lemon, sliced
salt and pepper to taste

Grease a broiling pan well with part of the butter and preheat it under the broiler. Arrange the steaks on the pan. Pour the melted butter over the steaks. Broil for approximately half an hour at 6 inches from the heat. Turn the steaks occasionally and baste frequently while broiling. Place on a serving platter. Season with salt and pepper and garnish with lemon slices. Serve a Lemon Butter Sauce or Sour Cream Sauce on the side. Serves 4.

Jegulje u Vinu
Eels in Wine

1 ½ lbs. eel
½ c. melted butter
2 tbsp. tomato paste
1 tsp. lemon juice
2 tbsp. water
½ c. white wine
3 bay leaves
1 clove of garlic, chopped
salt and pepper to taste

Slice the eels into bite-size cubes and brown them in the butter. Combine the wine, water, tomato paste, lemon juice, bay leaves and garlic. Add these to the eels. Season with salt and pepper and simmer until the eels become tender. Serves 4.

Jadranski Jastog
Adriatic Lobster

4 (1 lb.) lobsters
½ c. olive oil
2 c. tomato sauce
2 tbsp. melted butter
2 cloves garlic, chopped
½ c. water
3 tbsp. chopped parsley
½ tsp. oregano
salt and pepper to taste

Tie the lobster with string and cook in a boiling salted water for about ten minutes. Split and clean the lobsters. Place the lobsters in hot olive oil with the split side down in a large skillet. Sauté for five minutes. Combine the tomato sauce, butter, garlic, parsley and oregano. Season with salt and pepper. Pour this sauce and the water along the sides of the lobsters to cover the bottom. Cover and simmer for about half an hour to 45 minutes. Serves 4.

Dalmatinski Jastog na Žaru
Lobster à la Dalmatine

5 lobsters
¼ c. melted butter
½ tsp. powdered garlic
salt and pepper to taste

Split and clean the lobsters. Combine the garlic and butter. Liberally brush the meat of each lobster with the garlic butter. Season with salt and pepper. Place in the oven and broil for 15 or 20 minutes if the lobsters are small, 25-30 minutes if they are large. Baste frequently with the remaining butter. Serve hot or cold with Lemon Butter Sauce. Serves 5.

Illustrated on page 46.

Pečene Girice
Fried Smelts

1 lb. smelts or other small fish
½ c. flour
½ tsp. salt
¼ tsp. pepper
3 tbsp. vegetable oil
3 tbsp. butter
lemon slices
dill sprigs

Clean the fish. Combine the flour with the salt and pepper and roll the fish in it. In a large skillet, heat the oil. Add the butter and when the butter has melted, add the fish a few at a time. Cook until crisp on both sides, approximately five minutes. Serve on a bed of rice. Garnish with lemon slices and fresh dill.

Jadranske Školjke
Adriatic Mussels

4 lbs. mussels
¼ c. tomato paste
2 tbsp. white wine vinegar
½ c. olive oil
3 cloves, crushed
1 clove garlic, minced
salt and pepper to taste

Steam the mussels for about ten minutes. When they open, remove them from the shells. Combine the tomato paste, white wine vinegar, olive oil, garlic, cloves, salt and pepper. Marinade the mussels in this mixture, refrigerated, for two to three hours before serving. Serves 4.

Lubin sa Koprom
Dill-Stuffed Sea Bass

1 2½ lb. sea bass
1 medium onion, finely chopped
1 large tomato, chopped
½ c. chopped green pepper
6. tbsp. butter
½ c. white wine
1 tbsp. chopped parsley
1 tsp. chopped dill
salt and pepper to taste

Remove the scales from the bass. Cut an opening, clean the fish and rinse well. Wipe the fish dry. Melt three tablespoons of butter and fry the onion, pepper and tomato in it until the onion begins to brown lightly. Add the dill and parsley. Season with salt and pepper. Stuff the fish with this mixture and sew up the opening on the fish with kitchen thread. Place the fish in a greased baking dish. Melt the remaining three tablespoons of butter. Combine it with the wine and pour over the fish. Bake at 425° for approximately twenty minutes, basting frequently with its own juices. Garnish with fresh dill before serving.

Som sa Kiselim Vrhnjem
Catfish With Sour Cream

one 4 lb. catfish
½ c. flour
½ lb. sliced mushrooms
½ c. melted butter
¾ c. bread crumbs
1 tsp. paprika
1 ½ c. sour cream
dash of nutmeg
salt and pepper to taste

Wash and clean the catfish. Slice into half inch thick steaks. Roll the steaks in flour. Lightly sauté the mushrooms in hot butter. Add the fish and fry for 5 minutes until lightly browned. Lower the heat and add the sour cream, salt, pepper, nutmeg and paprika. Place this fish casserole in a deep baking dish and sprinkle with bread crumbs. Bake at 350° for approximately half an hour. Increase the heat to 425° for an additional five minutes to brown the bread crumbs.

Iverak sa Gljivama
Flounder With Mushrooms

2 lbs. flounder
1 c. chopped mushrooms
1 c. olive oil
1 tsp. chopped parsley
¼ c. bread crumbs
juice of one lemon
salt and pepper to taste

Wash the flounder and dry with a clean kitchen towel. Make several deep slashes in the sides of the fish. Place the fish in a well greased baking dish. Combine the mushrooms with the parsley, lemon juice, bread crumbs and olive oil. Stir well. Pour this mixture over the fish. Season with salt and pepper. Grease the cover of the baking dish. Cover the flounder casserole and bake at 350° for approximately an hour. Serve with a hot or cold sauce. Serves 4.

Peceni Iverak i Rizi Bizi/Fried Flounder and Rice and Peas [page 122]

Pečeni Iverak
Fried Flounder

2 lbs. fresh flounder fillets
2 tbsp. vegetable oil
2 tbsp. butter
½ c. flour
1 egg, beaten
½ c. bread crumbs
½ tsp. salt
¼ tsp. pepper
2 tbsp. lemon juice
1 tbsp. chopped parsley

Rinse the fillets and pat them dry. Season the flour with salt and pepper. Dredge them in the flour and shake off the excess. Coat the pieces in the egg. Heat the oil. Add the butter and heat until just melted. Arrange the fish in the skillet without crowding. Cook on each side for four or five minutes until they are nicely browned. Tranfer to a warm serving platter. Repeat with any remaining pieces. Add the lemon juice and the chopped parsley to the butter. Pour over the fried fish. Garnish with lemon slices and fresh parsley. Any flatfish fillet (sole, turbot, halibut, etc.) can be prepared in this manner.

Bijelica u Vinu
Whitefish in Wine

2 lbs. whitefish fillets
½ lb. sliced potatoes
1 ½ c. mushrooms, thinly sliced
3 tbsp. butter
¾ c. white wine
1 c. sour cream
salt to taste

Butter a deep baking dish and place a layer of potatoes in it. Place chunks of butter over the potatoes. Cover them with half of the sour cream. Heat the wine and cook the mushrooms in it for five to ten minutes. Pour this mixture over the sour cream. Add the fillets and season with salt. Cover with the remaining cream. Bake at 375° for about half an hour until the potatoes are tender.

Smuđ sa Gljivama
Croatian Baked Perch

2 lbs. fresh perch
1 lb. mushrooms, sliced
¼ c. butter or margarine
1 tbsp. lemon juice
½ c. olive oil
1 c. sour cream
salt and pepper to taste

Clean and fillet the fish and season with salt and pepper. Heat the olive oil and fry the fish until lightly browned. Grease a baking dish well. Arrange the fillets in the baking dish. Sauté the mushrooms in the butter. Add the lemon juice to the mushrooms and stir well. Place the mushrooms over the fish. Pour the sour cream over the casserole and bake at 350° for about 15-20 minutes.

Jastog u Umaku od Mlijeka
Lobster in White Sauce

1 boiled lobster
1 tsp. chopped parsley
1 egg yolk, well beaten
1 tsp. lemon juice
Milk Sauce [page 129]

Remove the meat from the lobster and dice finely. Add to the milk sauce along with the chopped parsley and lemon juice. Heat the mixture so that the lobster is heated thoroughly, but do not allow the sauce to boil. Stir in the egg yolk and cook for another minute or two, stirring constantly.

Pijani Šaran
Drunken Carp

3 lbs. carp
2 tbsp. chopped garlic
¼ c. oil
2 c. white wine
¼ c. onion, finely chopped
salt and pepper to taste
paprika for garnish

Wash and clean the carp, leaving it whole. Season with salt. Refrigerate for 2-3 hours. Stuff the fish with the onion and garlic. Dip it in oil and sprinkle with pepper. Place the fish in a deep baking dish and bake at 350° for 45 minutes to an hour. While the fish is baking, baste frequently with the wine. Garnish with paprika before serving.

Rižoto sa Lignjama
Squid Risotto

2 lbs. squid
4 tbsp. olive oil
3 cloves garlic, minced
½ c. white wine
1 c. uncooked rice
2 c. fish stock
1 tbsp. chopped parsley

Clean the squid as described for preparing Grilled Stuffed Squid on page 21. Cut the body of the squid into rings. Heat the oil and sauté the onion and garlic in it until tender. Add the squid rings and tentacles and sauté for another minute. Season with salt and pepper. Add the wine and the parsley. Cover and cook for approximately 20 minutes. Add the rice and fish stock. Bring the mixture to a boil again. Reduce the heat. Cover and cook over low heat for another 20 minutes.

Fiš Paprikaš
Fish Paprikash

2 lbs. catfish or carp
2 tbsp. butter or oil
1 medium onion
1 tsp. paprika
salt to taste
1 c. sour cream

Cut the fish into chunks. Season it with salt. Heat the oil and sauté the onion in it until it begins to brown. Add the fish and sauté for another minute or two. Add the paprika and about half a cup of water and simmer over low heat, adding more water as required, for approximately twenty minutes until the fish becomes tender. Shake the saucepan from time to time to keep the fish from sticking. Add the sour cream and bring to just below the boiling point. Serve immediately with more sour cream on the side, if desired.

Šaran sa Češnjakom
Baked Carp with Garlic

one 3 lb. carp
5 cloves garlic, minced
1 tbsp. flour
1 tbsp. chopped parsley
4 tbsp. oil
2 tbsp. vinegar
salt, pepper and paprika to taste

Clean the fish and make a large slit on the side. Season inside and out with salt and pepper. Rub it with a halved clove of garlic. Combine the minced garlic with the oil, parsley, vinegar, flour, paprika, salt and pepper. Place the carp in a greased baking dish. Pour the garlic mixture over the fish and bake for approximately half an hour at 425°.

Jastog na Kotorski Način
Lobster, Kotor Style

4 small lobsters
3 onions, chopped
3 cloves garlic
1 c. white wine
2 tbsp. tomato purée
2 tbsp. bread crumbs
1 tbsp. chopped parsley
¼ c. olive oil
salt and pepper to taste

Cook the lobsters in salted boiling water for fifteen minutes. Allow to cool slightly, then remove the meat. Cut it into chunks. Heat the oil and saute the onions in it until they begin to brown slightly. Add the tomato purée and season with salt and pepper. Add the wine. Bring to a boil and simmer for two minutes. Add the lobster pieces and the bread crumbs and allow to cook for another two to three minutes. Serve on a bed of rice or with freshly baked bread for dunking.

Podvarka
Croatian Roast Turkey

Poultry and Game

Croatia raises a plentiful assortment of poultry and fowl. The home bred birds are of the best quality because they are allowed to roam freely in the farmyards and are fed only the finest grain, resulting in very flavorful birds.

Chicken is the most abundant and most easily obtainable bird. The methods of preparing poultry range from roast and fried fowl to paprika-seasoned stews and goulashes which are simmered over low heat, blending the flavors of the seasonings with the meat and stock.

Duck is popular in Croatia, but the more flavorful wild duck is not as readily available as the domestic fowl. It is most commonly roasted, but because it tends to be quite fat, it is often cooked in soups or stews. The boiled duck can then be served cold with a white sauce or with a rich wine gravy.

The turkey was introduced to Europe in the sixteenth century from North America and gained immediate acceptance in Croatia. The distinctive *Podvarka* is a popular national turkey preparation. The bird is stuffed with a mixture of liver and bread crumbs and roasted slowly on a bed of sauerkraut. The popular *Pura s Mlincima* is a preparation of roast turkey served on a bed of homemade pasta called *mlinci*.

Traditionally, the most highly appreciated fowl has been the goose. The goose provides such delicacies as chopped goose liver, goose liver slices and the world renowned *paté de foie gras*. Geese are force-fed so that the livers will grow plump. This pattern of feeding gives the liver extra succulence. Goose is frequently roasted for festive occasions and served surrounded by a bed of colorful vegetables. Roast goose is generally stuffed with apples, its own liver, chestnuts or sauerkraut. We have included a recipe for *Međimurska Pečena Guska* which is stuffed with apples.

Hunting has always been a favorite pastime of Croatian sportsmen. Hunters from around the world come to her rich forests which abound in a variety of wild game and fowl. They often bag wild duck, partridge, grouse and pheasant along with wild hare, wild boar and deer in the woods of central and Northern Croatia. For those who have a taste for these exquisite game animals, several methods of preparation are included with our less dramatic and more traditional poultry recipes.

Pohani Kunići
Breaded Rabbit

1 young rabbit
½ c. oil or shortening
½ c. butter
¼ c. flour
½ c. bread crumbs
2 eggs, beaten
salt and pepper to taste

Wash the rabbit and cut it into pieces. Season each piece with salt and pepper. Roll in flour, dip in egg and then roll in bread crumbs. Heat the butter and oil or shortening together in a large saucepan. Reduce the heat to moderate and fry the breaded rabbit pieces until golden on all sides. Serves 4.

Bosanska Piletina
Bosnian Chicken

2 medium fryers, cut into pieces
¼ c. butter or margarine
1 large onion
1 c. chicken stock
2 c. sliced okra
2 tbsp. chopped parsley
2 c. Croatian Tomato Sauce
salt, pepper, and paprika to taste

Wash the chicken pieces and dry with a kitchen towel. Season well with salt and pepper. Melt the butter over low heat. Increase the heat and fry the pieces in the butter until they become golden brown on all sides. Place the pieces in a deep pot. Slice the onion and fry it in the butter. Place the onion over the chicken pieces. Season with paprika. Add a layer of okra over the onions. Combine the chicken stock and Croatian Tomato Sauce and bring to a boil. Pour this mixture over the chicken and okra. Cover and simmer slowly for approximately 45 minutes. Sprinkle with parsley before serving. This is an excellent dish to make in a crock pot, adjusting the cooking time for your particular appliance.

Riža S Gusjom Jetrom
Rice With Goose Liver

½ lb. goose liver, chopped
1 ½ c. rice
½ lb. chopped mushrooms
1 c. green peas
¼ c. butter
6 tbsp. shortening
1 c. grated Parmesan cheese
1 tbsp. chopped parsley
¼ c. tomato sauce
¼ c. onion, chopped
½ c. chicken stock
pinch marjoram
salt and pepper to taste

Sauté the mushrooms, chopped liver and onion in the butter and shortening. Add tomato sauce and chicken stock. Stir and cook for 3-5 minutes. Add the rice, green peas, salt, pepper and marjoram and stir in half the grated cheese. Place in a well greased baking dish. Sprinkle the remaining grated cheese over the casserole. Bake in a hot oven (450°) for 5-6 minutes until the cheese is lightly browned. Garnish with chopped parsley. Serve immediately. Chicken liver may be substituted if goose liver is not available. Serves 3-4.

Slavonska Pržena Gusja Jetra
Slavonian Fried Goose Liver

2 lbs. goose liver
1 tsp. paprika
½ c. chopped onion
¼ c. oil or shortening
salt and pepper to taste

Cut the liver into strips or cubes. Heat the oil or shortening and fry the onion in it. When the onion clarifies, add the goose liver. Season with salt and pepper. Fry for 2-3 minutes, shaking the pan so that the livers do not stick. Do not stir. This will avoid breaking the livers. Add the paprika and stir carefully just before serving.

Pečena Pura s Mlincima
Roast Turkey With Mlinces

4 c. flour	1 medium turkey
2 eggs	½ c. oil
½ c. water	salt and pepper to taste
1 tsp. salt	

Season the turkey inside and out with salt and pepper. Place in a large roaster and pour melted butter over the bird. Place one cup water in the bottom of the roaster. Roast the turkey, covered, for twenty minutes per pound of weight. Remove the cover and bake for another hour, basting frequently with the turkey's own juices. When the turkey is roasted, allow to cool enough to handle. Strain the pan drippings and set aside.

While the turkey is roasting, make the mlinces. Combine the eggs, water, salt and flour and work into a medium dough. Turn onto a well-floured board and knead until the dough is smooth and firm, adding more flour as required. Cut the dough into four or five pieces and roll each piece out separately on a floured board. The thinner the dough is rolled, the better. Place each sheet of dough on a warming plate and heat on the lowest setting for approximately half an hour on each side. When the mlinces begin to turn golden brown, remove and allow to cool. Make the remaining mlinces in the same manner. Allow the mlinces to dry while the turkey roasts. Break each of the mlinces into small pieces and place in a large bowl. Pour boiling water over the mlinces and cover the bowl. Allow to stand for five minutes. Drain. Pour strained pan drippings from the turkey over the mlinces and serve with the turkey.

65

Pečeni Puran
Roast Turkey With Chestnut Stuffing

1 roasting turkey
½ c. oil or shortening
½ lb. bacon, sliced
½ lb. ground pork
½ c. milk
1 tbsp. flour
1 lb. cooked chestnuts
¼ c. melted butter
2 eggs
4 slices bread
1 tbsp. tomato paste
1 tsp. salt
¼ tsp. pepper

Soak the chestnuts and bread in milk for approximately 15 minutes. Clean the turkey well. Season the turkey inside and out with salt and pepper.

Combine the eggs, salt, pepper, butter, chestnuts, bread mixture and ground pork. Stuff the turkey with the chestnut mixture. Sew up the opening. Wrap the turkey in bacon slices. Place in a deep roasting pan. Pour the oil or melted shortening over the bird. Pour ½ cup water in the bottom of the pan. Cover and roast at 350° for about 20 minutes for each pound of weight.

When the turkey is nearly tender, remove the bacon and continue to roast until the turkey becomes crisp and golden. Baste frequently in its own juices. Turn the turkey over occasionally. Remove the thread before serving.

Strain the pan drippings from the roasted turkey. Fry the tomato paste in the pan drippings. Add the flour and allow it to brown. Add enough water to make a creamy gravy. Serve this gravy on the side.

Pashalna Piletina
Passover Chicken

1 large chicken
2 c. sliced mushrooms
3 pieces matzo
1 ½ c. chopped chicken liver
1 onion, finely chopped
¼ c. chicken fat
2 eggs
1 green pepper
1 medium tomato
1 medium onion
2 cloves garlic
¼ c. bread crumbs
1 tbsp. chopped parsley
salt and pepper to taste

Soak the matzo in warm water until soft, then squeeze dry. Melt the chicken fat. Add the chopped onion and cook until it clarifies, but do not allow it to brown. Add the chicken livers, parsley and mushrooms. Allow to simmer for about five minutes. Remove from heat and allow to cool. Add the matzo and grind the mixture. Season with salt and pepper. Beat the eggs. Add the eggs and the bread crumbs to the chicken liver mixture. Mix well, then refrigerate for an hour.

Soak the chicken in salted ice water for about an hour. After removing the chicken from the ice water, dry with a kitchen towel. Season well inside and out with salt and pepper. Stuff with liver stuffing and sew up the opening.

Slice the vegetables. Grease a baking dish with chicken fat. Line the bottom with the sliced vegetables. Season with garlic, salt and pepper. Add one quarter cup of water. Place the chicken over the vegetables and bake at 350° until the chicken is well roasted. Keep the chicken warm while preparing the sauce.

Put the vegetables through a sieve. Add the sieved vegetables to the pan drippings and serve on the side with the chicken. Place the chicken back in the pan and allow to crisp for another five minutes at 400° just before serving.

Pečene Jarebice
Roast Partridge

3 partridges
3 tbsp. butter
6 slices bacon
1 tbsp. flour
1 c. sour cream
salt and pepper to taste
bread stuffing or apples

Wash and dry the partridges. Season with salt and pepper inside and out. Roll them in flour. Stuff with bread stuffing or apples, if preferred. Lard the breasts of the birds by sewing in strips of bacon slices or lay the bacon slices over the birds to baste them while they are roasting. Melt the butter in a baking dish. Arrange the birds in this dish and roast at 350° until the meat is tender, approximately one hour. Increase the heat to 400° and leave the birds in the oven another ten minutes to crisp the skin. Pour sour cream over the roasted birds. Return to the oven for another 5-6 minutes. Transfer to a serving platter and garnish with parsley.

Želuci u Umaku od Paprike
Chicken Giblets in Paprika Sauce

½ lb. chicken livers
½ lb. chicken hearts
1 lb. chicken giblets
¼ c. diced bacon
½ c. onion
1 tsp. paprika
1 c. chopped tomatoes or
3 tbsp. tomato paste
1 c. diced green peppers
2 tsp. minced garlic
salt and pepper to taste

Wash the giblets well. Cut them into bite-sized pieces. Fry the bacon in its own fat. Drain all but one tablespoon of the fat. Add the onion and allow it to brown slightly. Remove from heat. Add the paprika and a tablespoon or two of water. Place the giblets in the onion and bacon mixture. Season with salt and pepper. Add the garlic and return to heat. Simmer slowly, covered for about half an hour. Add water as required. Add the tomatoes and green peppers and continue to simmer until the vegetables are tender. Serve hot with dumplings.

Pileći Perket
Chicken Perket

2 lbs. chicken, chopped
3 tbsp. butter or margarine
2 onions, thinly sliced
1 clove garlic, minced
2 tbsp. paprika
1 c. chicken stock
salt and pepper to taste
½ c. sour cream

Melt the butter over low heat. Increase the heat and brown the chicken in the butter. When the meat has browned, remove from the pan and add the onions to the butter. Sauté the onions until tender. Add the garlic and paprika and cook for another minute or two. Place the chicken pieces over the onions. Add chicken stock to cover and simmer slowly, covered, for about an hour. Add a little water while cooking, if required. Do not stir the chicken while cooking. Instead, shake the saucepan occasionally so that the chicken does not stick. Add the sour cream. Bring to just below the boiling point. Remove from heat and serve immediately with more sour cream on the side.

Purji Kotleti
Breaded Turkey Cutlets

1 ½ lbs. turkey breast, sliced
½ c. flour
2 eggs
1 tbsp. water
¾ c. bread crumbs
¾ c. butter
¼ c. oil
1 tsp. salt
¼ tsp. pepper

Pound the turkey slices with a meat tenderizer until they are no more than ¼" thick. Stir the salt and pepper into the flour. Beat the eggs slightly with the water. Roll the cutlets in flour, dip in the egg and coat with bread crumbs. Heat the oil and add the butter. When the butter has melted, increase the heat to moderate and fry the cutlets in the hot fat on both sides until the cutlets are a light golden color.

Pečena Patka
Roast Duck

1 medium duck (approximately 4 lbs.)
2 tbsp. butter
1 c. bread crumbs
2 eggs, well beaten
1 c. mushrooms, sliced
½ c. sour cream
2 tbsp. chopped green onion
1 tsp. chopped parsley
salt and pepper to taste

Melt the butter over low heat. Increase the heat and sauté the mushrooms in the butter. Mix together the mushrooms, bread crumbs, parsley, green onion and sour cream. Add the well beaten eggs and season with salt and pepper. Stuff the bird with this mixture. Place dabs of butter on the duckling. Season the outside with salt and pepper. Place the duck in the oven and roast at 350° until the duck is golden and the skin is nicely crisped.

Bunjevačka Piletina
Chicken à la Backa

1 large fryer, cut up
2 tbsp. oil
½ tsp. paprika
3 tbsp. tomato paste
3 medium tomatoes, diced
1 small onion
2 green peppers, cut into strips
½ c. water
1 c. chicken stock
1 small bunch parsley
salt and pepper to taste

Sauté the onion in the oil until it begins to brown slightly. Remove from heat. Season with paprika. Stir. Add the water. Place the chicken pieces in this mixture. Season with salt and pepper. Return to heat and simmer for about 45 minutes, stirring occasionally. If necessary, add a little water each time. Add the vegetables to the chicken and stir well. Add the chicken stock. Bring to a boil. Reduce the heat and simmer another half hour until the vegetables are tender, but not overcooked. Be careful that the chicken does not break away from the bones when it is placed in a serving dish over rice or noodles. Cover with the sauce that the chicken was cooked in. Sprinkle with parsley and garnish with fresh tomato slices and pepper rings, if desired.

Pržena Gusja Jetra
Fried Goose Liver

2 lbs. goose liver
1 tsp. powdered onion
2 c. milk
½ c. butter
¼ c. oil or shortening
salt and pepper to taste

Soak the liver in the milk for approximately an hour until all the color is drained from it. When it becomes white, drain. Slice the liver and season it with salt, pepper and onion. Sauté the slices in a mixture of half the butter and the oil or shortening. The shortening will keep the butter from burning at high heat. Heat the remaining butter and pour it over the fried goose liver just before serving. Season again with salt and pepper.

Istarska Piletina u Umaku
Istrian Creamed Chicken

1 medium chicken, cooked
¼ c. bread crumbs
2 tbsp. olive oil
1 small onion
1 clove garlic, chopped
2 tbsp. flour
6 anchovy fillets, chopped
1 tsp. chopped parsley
1 tsp. paprika
juice of half lemon
1 c. chicken stock
1 tsp. salt
¼ tsp. pepper

Bone the chicken and chop the meat into bite-sized pieces. Heat the olive oil and fry the onion in it until it becomes clear, browning slightly. Add the bread crumbs, garlic, parsley, paprika, lemon juice and anchovies. Simmer for a few minutes. Add the chopped chicken and the flour. Season with salt and pepper. Stir well. Add the chicken stock and simmer until the sauce begins to thicken. Pour into a well greased baking dish. Bake at 350° for about an hour. Serves 4-5.

Pirjana Piletina
Stewed Chicken

1 frying chicken
1 large onion, chopped
3 tbsp. butter
1 tbsp. chopped parsley
1 tsp. paprika
2 c. chicken stock
2 tbsp. tomato paste
½ c. mushrooms, sliced
salt and pepper to taste

Wash and cut the chicken into pieces. Sauté the onion and the sliced mushrooms in the butter until the onion turns golden brown. Add the parsley and the chicken pieces, including the chicken liver and chicken giblets. Season with salt and pepper. Stir in the paprika. Add the tomato paste and the chicken stock and simmer over low heat until tender. Shake the pan occasionally to prevent the chicken from sticking. Remove the chicken to a serving platter, being careful to maintain its shape. Pour the sauce over the chicken. Serve with rice or dumplings.

Pečena Divlja Patka
Roast Wild Duck

3 lb. wild duck
juice of one lemon
2 c. cubed smoked bacon
1 c. water
¼ c. oil
½ c. butter, melted
salt and pepper to taste

Wash the duck and pat dry. Coat the cavity and the outside with oil and the juice of one lemon. Place one cup of cubed bacon in the cavity and sprinkle the remaining bacon over the bird. Pour the melted butter over the duck. Season well with salt and pepper. Add the water to the bottom of the pan. Place the bird in the oven. Bake at 350° for approximately an hour and a half. Baste frequently. Increase the heat to 425° and bake another ten minutes until the duck is well done and the skin has crisped.

Pohana Piletina
Fried Chicken

2 medium fryers
3 eggs
2 tbsp. water
½ tsp. salt
¼ tsp. pepper
½ c. flour
1 c. bread crumbs
¾ c. oil or shortening
¾ c. butter

Wash the chickens and cut them into pieces. Beat the eggs well with the water and add the salt and pepper. Dredge the chicken pieces with flour and shake off the excess. Dip them in the well beaten eggs, then roll in the bread crumbs. Heat the oil, then allow the butter to melt in the hot oil. Fry the chicken in the hot fat (375°) until golden. Be careful not to allow the oil to get too hot or too cold. In the first case the coating will burn while the inside will remain raw. In the second case, the coating will not adhere to the chicken and it will fall off. Fry the larger pieces together so that they will become well done. Serve hot.

Zec na Seljački Način
Country Style Rabbit

1 medium rabbit
2 medium onions, chopped
3 tbsp. oil
2 carrots
2 tbsp. flour
2 tbsp. butter
¼ c. sour cream
2 bay leaves
1 c. red table wine
salt and pepper to taste

Heat the oil and sauté the onion in it until it clarifies. Cut the rabbit into serving size pieces and add the pieces to the onion. Allow the rabbit pieces to brown on both sides. Add the carrot and bay leaves. Season with salt and pepper. Add the wine and bring to a boil. Reduce the heat and simmer until the pieces become tender. Stir the rabbit pieces occasionally and add water as required. Mix the flour with the butter and add this mixture to the rabbit. Add enough water to make a smooth gravy. Stir in the sour cream. Bring to just below the boiling point. Remove from heat and serve immediately.

Zečji Paprikaš
Rabbit Paprikash

1½ lb. rabbit, cut into pieces
1 green pepper, diced
1 tbsp. paprika
½ c. water
1 tbsp. flour
2 tbsp. tomato paste
3 tbsp. butter or margarine
½ c. sour cream
½ c. chopped onion
1 hard roll, diced
salt to taste

Wash the rabbit and cut it into pieces. Melt the butter over low heat and sauté the onion and green pepper in it. Place the rabbit pieces in the butter and season with paprika. Allow the rabbit to brown, then add the water. Simmer for about an hour, or until the meat is tender. Add the tomato paste and stir well. Slowly add the cream to make a thick soup. Fry the diced roll in two tablespoons of butter to make croutons.

Međimurska Pečena Guska
Medjimurian Roast Goose

1 medium goose
½ tsp. ground marjoram
5-6 cooking apples
1 tbsp. flour
1 c. poultry stock
salt and pepper to taste

Season the goose very well with salt and pepper, inside and out. Season the cavity with the marjoram. Pare, core and slice the apples. Stuff the goose with the apple slices. Cover the bottom of a roasting pan with warm water. Place the goose in the pan and roast for approximately two and a half hours at 350°. Turn the goose over when half roasted to brown and crisp both sides. Make little perforations in the skin to allow the fat to flow out. When tender, increase the heat to 400° and roast for another 5-10 minutes until the skin of the goose is crisp. Pour the strained pan juices into a small saucepan. Stir in the flour. Add the chicken stock and bring to a boil. Cook until the sauce thickens. Serve this gravy separately with the roast goose.

Pečeni Fazan
Roast Pheasant

2-2 ½ lb. pheasant
1 c. cubed bacon
2 tbsp. butter
1 c. diced bread
1 c. chestnuts
1 tsp. paprika
strips of bacon fat
salt and pepper to taste

Boil and chop the chestnuts. Lard the pheasant with strips of bacon fat. Combine the cubed bacon, chestnuts and diced bread. Season with salt and pepper. Stuff the bird with this mixture. Dab the pheasant with butter and grease the roasting pan well. Season the inside and the outside of the bird with salt and pepper. Sprinkle with paprika. Place the bird in a 425° oven and roast for approximately 15 minutes. Reduce the heat to 350° and roast for approximately 45 more minutes, basting frequently.

Piletina u Umaku od Kopra
Chicken in Dill Sauce

1 medium fryer, cut into pieces
¼ c. butter
2 tbsp. flour
¼ c. chopped onion
¼ c. sour cream
2 tbsp. chopped dill
1 tsp. grated lemon rind
salt and pepper to taste

Season the chicken pieces with salt and pepper. Melt half the butter over medium heat. When the butter begins to foam, increase the heat and fry the chicken in the hot butter until nicely browned on both sides. Remove from heat. Heat the remaining butter in the same manner and fry the onion in the hot butter until it becomes clear. Stir in the flour and cook for one minute. Add ½ c. water and cook the mixture for about five minutes, stirring constantly. Place the chicken pieces in this sauce and allow to simmer over medium low heat for about 45 minutes until tender. Remove the chicken pieces from the sauce and place in a serving bowl. Add the sour cream, dill and lemon rind to the sauce. Stir and cook over low heat until the sauce reaches the boiling point, but do not allow the mixture to boil. Pour the sauce over the chicken pieces and garnish with fresh dill and lemon slices.

Pečeni Golub s Gljivama
Roast Pigeon with Mushrooms

6 small pigeons
2 lbs. sliced mushrooms
1 c. butter
2 tbsp. flour
1 tbsp. chopped parsley
salt and pepper to taste

Clean the birds. Split them down the center. Melt half the butter in the bottom of a deep baking dish. Place a layer of sliced mushrooms in the butter. Place two pigeon halves over the mushrooms. Alternate layers of mushrooms and pigeon until all are used up. Melt the remaining butter and season it with salt and pepper. Pour the seasoned butter over the pigeon casserole. Cover tightly and bake at 350° until the pigeons are tender. Make a smooth roux from the flour and some of the juice that the pigeons were cooked in. Add enough water to make a smooth sauce. Pour this sauce over the pigeon casserole. Stir and bake for another twenty minutes. Garnish with chopped parsley.

Pečena Guska
Roast Goose

1 medium goose
1 goose liver, chopped
½ c. cubed bacon
½ c. chopped mushrooms
2 tbsp. white wine
1 egg, well beaten
1 tbsp. butter
1 c. bread crumbs
salt and pepper to taste

Fry the liver and bacon in the butter. Add the mushrooms and simmer until they become soft. Remove from heat. Add the bread crumbs, wine and egg. Mix well and season the mixture with salt and pepper. Clean the goose. Season with salt and pepper, making sure to season the cavity well. Stuff the goose with the liver stuffing. Sew up the cavity. Roast at 350° for approximately three hours until the goose is an even golden brown color on the outside and tender on the inside. Increase the heat to 425° and roast the goose for another 5-10 minutes to crisp the skin.

Podvarka
Croatian Roast Turkey

1 medium turkey
1 turkey liver
1 tsp. paprika
2 c. coarse bread crumbs
1 c. sour cream
2 lbs. sauerkraut
2 potatoes, grated
2 onions, grated
salt and pepper to taste

Season the turkey very well inside and out with salt, pepper and paprika. Finely chop the turkey liver. Combine it with the bread crumbs and sour cream and mix well. Stuff the turkey with this mixture. Close the opening with thread or metal skewers. Mix the sauerkraut, grated potatoes and grated onion and season with pepper. Place this mixture in the bottom of a well-greased roasting pan. Place the turkey on top of the sauerkraut mixture and bake in a 350° oven. Allow the turkey to roast for 20 minutes per pound of weight. Baste frequently with melted butter. Turn the turkey when half roasted. Serve hot on a bed of the baked sauerkraut.

Illustrated on page 62.

Pileći Rižot
Chicken With Rice

1 lb. chicken pieces
1 c. rice
2 tbsp. tomato purée
1 tbsp. oil
1 c. white wine
1 large onion
1 tbsp. parsley
salt and pepper to taste
¼ c. Parmesan cheese

Heat the oil and sauté the onion until it becomes clarified. Add the chicken pieces and sauté until they are nicely browned on all sides. Add the tomato purée and chopped parsley. Stir in the wine. Season with salt and pepper. Simmer over medium heat for approximately half an hour. Add the washed rice and one cup water. Continue to simmer for another twenty minutes until the rice is tender. Sprinkle with Parmesan cheese. Serve additional cheese on the side.

Pileći Paprikaš
Chicken Paprikash

1 medium frying chicken
3 tbsp. butter
2 tsp. paprika
2 tbsp. flour
1 large onion, chopped
1 c. chicken stock
1 c. sour cream
salt and pepper to taste

Clean the chicken and cut it into pieces. Melt the butter over medium heat. When it begins to foam, increase the heat and sauté the chopped onion in it. When the onion begins to brown, add the chicken pieces and sauté until they are browned on both sides. Remove from heat. Season with salt, paprika and pepper. Sprinkle with flour. Add the chicken stock. Stir well and cover the saucepan. Bring the stock to a boil. Reduce the heat and simmer until the chicken is tender. From time to time, add a little water if required. When the chicken is tender, add the sour cream and bring to just below the boiling point. Serve with dumplings or noodles.

Piletina s Ružmarinom
Rosemary Chicken

1 medium frying chicken
3 tbsp. white wine vinegar
1 tbsp. crushed rosemary
3 tbsp. olive oil
salt and pepper to taste

Wash the chicken and pat dry. Cut into pieces. Combine the vinegar, oil and rosemary. Season the chicken with salt and pepper. Heat ¼ c. olive oil and fry the chicken pieces in the hot oil until lightly browned on all sides. Reduce the heat and cook for another half hour. Turn the chicken several times while cooking. It will be done when the juices run clear if the chicken is pierced with a knife. Remove from heat. Transfer the chicken to a serving platter. Heat the oil again and add the vinegar mixture. Bring to a boil. Simmer for five minutes. Pour over the chicken and serve immediately.

Pečen Srneći But
Roast Leg of Venison

1 leg of venison
2 c. vinegar
1 c. water
1 tsp. peppercorns
1 onion, halved
1 stalk celery, chopped
1 bunch parsley
2 bay leaves
1 tbsp. lemon rind
6 oz. smoked bacon
3 tbsp. oil
2 tbsp. flour
¼ c. sour cream
salt to taste

Make a marinade from the vinegar, oil, peppercorns, onion, carrots, celery, bay leaves, lemon rind and parsley. Allow this marinade to cook for half an hour.

Pour the hot marinade over the leg of venison and allow the meat to marinade for 24 hours. The following day, remove the meat from the marinade and pat dry. Season with salt and lard with the smoked bacon. Generously grease the leg of venison with oil and place in a roaster.

Pour the water into the bottom of the pan. Roast at 350° until tender. Baste frequently with the pan juices and occasionally with the remaining marinade.

When the meat is well baked, allow it to cool enough to handle. Slice the meat and arrange it on a warmed serving platter. Mix the sour cream with the flour.

Strain the pan drippings into a saucepan. Add 2 tablespoons of marinade and the flour mixture. Cook until you obtain a smooth gravy. Pour some of the gravy over the meat and serve the rest in a gravy boat.

Dalmatinska Pašticada
Dalmatian Pot Roast

Meats

Perhaps it is the home-grown quality of the pork produced in Croatia that accounts for its widespread popularity throughout the country. The preparation of pork dishes is expressed in a variety of ways. It may be simmered in delicately seasoned sauces, braised in its own juices with vegetables, mushrooms or sauerkraut, or it may be used in stews and casseroles. Pork chops may be stuffed, braised in a tomato sauce or fried.

In addition to these methods of preparation, succulent pork roasted over a glowing bed of live coals has evolved into a national tradition for all festive occasions. Pork also finds its way into the Croatian diet in the form of richly smoked hams and bacon, along with a vast array of tempting *kobasice* (pork sausages), *krvavice* (blood sausages), *kulen*, a Croatian smoked salami made with choice cuts of pork chopped into chunks) and other *charcuterie*.

The fondness for pork exhibited by Christian Croatians is equalled only by the love that Moslem Croatians have for lamb. A whole young lamb roasted over an open fire is specialty that is enjoyed throughout the country, but is especially popular in Bosnia and Herzegovina. For smaller gatherings roast leg of lamb is especially suitable. The versatility of lamb is expressed in countless ways. Bosnian Lamb Pilav is created by combining cubed young lamb with rice and seasonings.

Beef is most popular braised, although it may be used to make a beef goulash, or *Dalmatinske Polpete* with tomato sauce. Veal is more popular than beef in Croatia and is considered a festive meat. *Zagrebački Odresci* are a delightful specialty of golden breaded veal cutlets stuffed with a paper thin slice of prsut ham and Trappist cheese. Adriatic veal cutlets are given their distinctive flavor by coating them with bread crumbs and grated Parmesan cheese before frying. Breast of veal stuffed is often roasted with a sour cream stuffing .

Čevapčići and *ražnjići*, skewered and grilled meats, are a national specialty. They are often served on a mixed grill plate, *mješano meso sa ražnja*, along with grilled sausage, pork chops and lamb chops. *Čevapčići* are prepared by combining finely ground lamb, pork and veal, then shaping miniature sausages which are grilled over an open barbecue grill. To prepare *ražnjići*, veal, pork and lamb are cubed into bite-sized morsels, alternated on a skewer and grilled until the meat becomes an enticing dark brown on the outside and the morsels are very well done on the inside.

Jadranski Teleći Odresci
Adriatic Veal Cutlets

6 veal cutlets
1 egg, well beaten
3 tbsp. flour
1 lb. cooked potatoes
1 c. fine breadcrumbs
½ c. grated Parmesan cheese
¼ c. olive oil
¼ c. butter
1 tbsp. chopped parsley
salt, pepper and paprika to taste

Season the flour with salt and pepper. Roll the cutlets in the seasoned flour, then dip them in the egg. Roll in breadcrumbs which have been combined with the grated cheese. Fry over medium heat in the olive oil and butter. If necessary, add more oil and butter. Remove the cutlets when they are an even golden color and thoroughly cooked. Slice the potatoes. Season with salt, pepper and paprika. Fry lightly in the fat in which the cutlets were fried. Drain on paper towels. Arrange the potatoes around the cutlets and garnish with fresh or chopped parsley.

Svinjski Odresci sa Zeljem
Braised Pork Chops

2 ½ lbs. pork chops
¼ c. oil
2 medium onions, chopped
1 small cabbage, shredded
1 green pepper, sliced
3-4 firm ripe tomatoes, sliced
1 c. red wine
1 tsp. paprika
salt and pepper to taste

Heat half the oil over medium heat. Sauté the onion in the hot oil until golden. Brown the pork chops in the remaining oil in a large saucepan. Add the onion and vegetables. Season with salt, pepper and paprika. Cover and simmer for 45 minutes to an hour. Add the wine and simmer for another 15 minutes.

Bunjevačko Meso s Rižom
Pork with Rice

2 lbs. pork shoulder, cubed
6 tbsp. lard or oil
3 large green peppers
3 firm ripe tomatoes, peeled
¼ c. chopped onion
1 c. beef stock
1½ c. rice
1 tsp. paprika
salt and pepper to taste

Heat half the lard or oil. Sauté the onion in the hot lard or oil until it becomes golden. Remove from heat. Stir in the paprika and 4 tablespoons water. Cook for a few minutes. Add the meat and sauté until the meat has browned. Add the beef stock and simmer over medium low heat for about an hour. Stir occasionally, adding water as required. Fry the rice in the remaining lard or oil until it becomes transparent. Add it to the meat together with the vegetables. Cover and simmer slowly, stirring occasionally until both the meat and the vegetables are tender. Add more water if necessary. Transfer to a heated platter and garnish with slices of fresh tomato and green pepper.

Seljački Pirjani Popečci
Country-Style Braised Beef

1½ lbs. beef steak
2 large onions, thinly sliced
¼ c. lard or oil
2 tbsp. flour
1 tsp. paprika
Salt and pepper to taste

Wash the beef. Slice it into small cutlets. Pound the cutlets with a meat tenderizer and season with salt, pepper and paprika. Dredge the cutlets in the flour and shake off the excess. Heat the oil or lard. Brown the onions in the hot fat. Add the cutlets. Sauté until golden on both sides. Add a little water, cover and simmer the meat slowly in its own juices until tender. Do not overcook or the meat will toughen.

Pečeni Odojak
Roast Suckling Pig

1 suckling pig
½ c. lard or oil
2 oz. smoked bacon, sliced
1 c. beer
salt to taste

Clean and wash the suckling pig well. Dry it inside and out with a kitchen towel. Season the piglet very well with salt. Refrigerate for several hours or overnight. The following day, wipe the piglet with a kitchen towel to remove any excess salt. This will prevent the skin from blistering while roasting. Place an empty bottle in the stomach cavity to keep the piglet from collapsing while roasting and sew up the edges. Place the piglet on a metal rack in a large roasting pan. Pour hot oil over the roast. Place it in a warm oven and roast at 325° for about 20 minutes for every pound of weight. Baste frequently with the smoked bacon slices which have been dipped in beer. If the ears and tail begin to brown too soon, cover them in aluminum foil so that they will not become overly crisp. When the roast is an even golden brown, remove from the oven. Allow to cool for about five minutes. Remove the bottle from the cavity. Place an apple in the pig's mouth and serve whole.

Bunjevački Juneći Odresci
Sirloin Steak à la Backa

6 sirloin steaks
¼ c. flour
2 tbsp. oil
1 c. onions, sliced
1 c. beef stock
½ c. smoked bacon, sliced
into 1 inch strips
2 tsp. minced garlic
2 green peppers
2 firm ripe tomatoes, peeled
1 tbsp. tomato paste
½ c. mushrooms, sliced
1 tsp. paprika
pinch marjoram
salt and pepper to taste

Dredge the steaks in flour seasoned with salt and pepper and shake off any excess. Heat the oil in a large saucepan and brown the steaks in hot oil.

Remove the steaks to a plate and sauté the onions in the oil until they become golden brown. Add the paprika, tomato paste, garlic, marjoram and two tablespoons water. Stir well. Cook this sauce for a few minutes.

When nicely thickened, return the steaks to the saucepan. Add the beef stock and enough water to cover. Cover the saucepan and simmer over low heat until the meat is nearly tender. Turn the steaks occasionally, adding water from time to time as required.

Fry the bacon in its own fat, but do not crisp. Add the mushrooms, sliced tomatoes and green peppers. Season with salt and pepper and simmer, covered, for about 10-15 minutes. Add this vegetable sauce to the steaks and continue cooking slowly until both the vegetables and the steaks are tender.

Podravski Odresci
Veal Cutlets à la Podravina

2 lbs. veal scallops
½ c. lard or butter
2 onions, finely chopped
1 tsp. paprika
2 cloves garlic, minced
tomato paste
1 c. red wine
1 tbsp. parsley
3 tbsp. sweet cream
2 hard rolls, diced
salt and pepper to taste

Heat the lard or butter over medium heat. When the foam subsides, brown the onion in it. Stir in the rolls. When the rolls have browned, add a little water and simmer until they become soft. Add the veal scallops and garlic. Season with salt and pepper. Add a little water and simmer slowly until the meat becomes tender. Mix the tomato paste with the wine. Pour this mixture over the scallops. Cook for approximately 15-20 minutes. Add the cream and sprinkle with parsley before serving.

Suho Meso sa Kiselim Zeljem
Smoked Pork With Sauerkraut

1½ lb. smoked pork
(or Canadian bacon)
½ lb. sauerkraut
1 lb. potatoes
½ large onion, chopped
salt, pepper and paprika to taste

Clean the meat. Peel and cube the potatoes. Place the meat in the bottom of a large pot. Cover the meat with the sauerkraut. Place the potatoes over this layer. Sprinkle with the finely chopped onion. Season with salt, pepper and paprika. Add just enough water to cover. Cover and simmer slowly for an hour to an hour and a half.

Zagrebački Odrezak
Zagreb Veal Cutlet

6 large veal cutlets
6 thin slices smoked ham
6 thin slices Trappist cheese*
¼ c. flour
2 tbsp. milk
2 eggs, well beaten
½ c. fine breadcrumbs
¼ c. butter
¼ c. oil
salt and pepper to taste

*Trappist cheese is not readily available everywhere. Port du Salut, a French version of this famous Croatian cheese makes a good substitute.

Pound the veal cutlets with a meat tenderizer very well. Place a slice of cheese and a slice of ham on half of each cutlet. Fold the cutlet over and squeeze the edges firmly so that the filling does not show. Heat the oil and the butter together. Beat the eggs with the milk. Roll the cutlets in the flour. Dip them in the eggs. Roll each cutlet in breadcrumbs until it is well coated. Fry the cutlets on both sides over moderately high heat until they become an even golden color. Garnish with parsley and slices of lemon.

Čevapčići
Chevapchichi

1 lb. ground beef
1 lb. ground pork
¼ lb. smoked bacon
2 tbsp. lard or oil
½ c. onion, finely chopped
2 cloves garlic, chopped
2 tbsp. flour
1 tbsp. parsley
1 egg, lightly beaten
1 tsp. paprika
salt and pepper to taste

Heat the lard or oil in a medium saucepan. Add the onions and garlic and cook them for a few minutes until the onions are slightly browned. Transfer the onions to a deep bowl. Add the meat, egg, flour, salt, pepper, parsley and paprika. Mix well. When all the ingredients are well combined, shape little sausages from the mixture about two inches long and arrange them on a plate. Cover the plate and refrigerate the *cevapcici* for at least an hour before cooking. *Cevapcici* are most frequently barbecued on an open charcoal grill. Grill them for about 15-20 minutes. They should be a dark brown on the outside and very well done on the inside. Turn them over frequently while grilling. If preferred, they can be cooked in a saucepan in a little hot oil. They must be turned often so that they do not stick. Serve sprinkled with chopped onions or with an onion salad. *Cevapcici* can be served as an appetizer.

Sarajevske Pljeskavice
Sarajevo Patties

1½ lb. ground lamb
½ onion, chopped
1 garlic clove, chopped
salt and pepper to taste

Combine the onion and the lamb. Season with garlic, salt and pepper. Shape the meat into patties about one inch thick. Place the lamb patties on an outdoor grill over hot coals. Brown both sides evenly. Serve with an onion salad or a green salad.

Pljeskavica
Croatian Hamburger

1 lb. ground veal
1 lb. ground pork
1 c. chopped onion
1 tsp. paprika
2 cloves garlic, chopped
1 egg
salt and pepper to taste

Combine the veal, pork, egg, onion, paprika and garlic. Season with salt and pepper. Knead the mixture until all the ingredients are mixed. Roll the meat mixture into a loaf and slice the loaf into patties or shape patties with floured hands. Place the patties on an outdoor grill over hot coals. Grill until the outside is a dark brown and the inside is well done. Serve with an onion salad or simply with chopped onions.

Dalmatinske Polpete
Dalmatian Meatballs

¾ lb. ground steak
¾ lb. ground pork
1 egg, slightly beaten
2 cloves garlic
1 egg
1 onion, finely chopped
¼ c. oil
salt, pepper and paprika
2 c. Croatian Tomato Sauce

Combine the meat, egg, onion, and garlic. Season to taste with salt, pepper and paprika. Shape into small balls and fry in the hot oil. Arrange the polpete in a serving dish. Pour Croatian Tomato Sauce over the polpete and serve with pasta or rice.

Bosanski Janjeći Pilav
Bosnian Lamb Pilav

2 lbs. shoulder of lamb, cubed
2 tbsp. vegetable oil
2 tbsp. butter
1½ c. rice
¼ c. tomato paste
1 c. beef stock
1 onion, finely chopped
1 clove garlic, chopped
2 c. water
salt and pepper to taste

Sauté the lamb in the oil for approximately fifteen minutes until browned on all sides. Add the crushed garlic and season with salt and pepper. Add the tomato paste and the water. Cover and simmer slowly for approximately an hour, stirring occasionally. If necessary, add a little more water. Sauté the onion in the butter until it clarifies. Add the green and red peppers and continue to sauté for another three minutes. Add the rice and allow the rice to clarify. Add the beef stock, cover, and simmer slowly until tender, approximately twenty minutes. Place the rice on a large serving platter. Place the lamb in the center and serve immediately.

Punjena Teleća Jetra
Stuffed Veal Liver

1 ½ lb. veal liver
¼ c. lard or oil
½ c. diced smoked bacon
1 onion, finely chopped
1 tsp. chopped parsley
1 egg
½ c. sour cream
¼ c. breadcrumbs
salt and pepper to taste

Wash the liver well in warm water and wipe with a kitchen towel. Cut an opening into the liver horizontally. Melt half the lard or oil over medium heat. Increase the heat and add the bacon and onion. Fry for a minue or two, then add the bread crumbs and parsley. Continue cooking until the ingredients are soft. Remove from heat. Whip the cream, then beat the egg into it. Season with salt and pepper. Add to the breadcrumb mixture. Mix well. Fill the opening of the liver with this mixture and sew up the edges. Grease a baking sheet with the remaining lard or oil. Place the liver in a hot oven and bake at 425° for ten minutes. Reduce the heat to 325° and bake for another hour, basting frequently.

Odrezak Tomislav
Tomislav Veal Cutlet

6 veal cutlets
6 slices sheep's cheese
6 thin slices Prsut ham
4 oz. cooked spinach
2 oz. morel mushrooms
½ c. white wine
½ c. heavy cream
1 medium onion, finely chopped
1 tsp. chopped parsley
¼ c. oil
salt and pepper to taste
¼ c. flour
1 c. beef stock

Pound the meat with a meat tenderizer so that the cutlets are ¼" thick. Season with salt and pepper. Place a slice of cheese and a slice of Prsut ham on each cutlet. Divide the spinach and mushrooms in 6 equal portions. Place one portion of each on each cutlet. Fold the cutlet over and fasten with a toothpick. Dredge the cutlets in flour and shake off the excess. Fry them in the hot oil until browned on both sides. Remove the cutlets from the oil. Sauté the onion in the oil that the cutlets were fried in until it clarifies. Add 2 tablespoons flour, the beef stock and the wine and stir well. Return the cutlets to the saucepan and season with salt and pepper. Simmer for approximately ten minutes. Add the cream. Bring to just below the boiling point. Arrange on a warmed serving platter and sprinkle with parsley.

Goveđi Gulaš
Beef Goulash

2 lbs. lean beef, cubed
3 large onions, sliced
2 tbsp. butter
1 tsp. minced garlic
2 ½ c. beef stock
1 tbsp. paprika
salt and pepper to taste

Melt the butter in a large saucepan over low heat. Brown the onion slices in the butter. Add the beef, garlic and paprika. Sauté until the beef is lightly browned. Season with salt and pepper. Stir in the beef stock. Cover and simmer gently for about one and a half hours.

Slavonski Gulaš
Slavonian Goulash

1 lb. lean beef, cubed
1 lb. lean veal
2 large onions, chopped
2 tbsp. oil
1 tsp. paprika
2 medium tomatoes
1 tsp. chopped parsley
salt and pepper to taste

Heat the oil in a large saucepan. Brown the onions in hot oil. Add the meat and allow it to brown well. Season with salt, pepper and paprika. Peel and slice the tomatoes. Place them over the meat. Season again with salt, Cover the saucepan and simmer for about an hour until the meat is tender. Add water as required while the goulash is cooking. Sprinkle with parsley before serving.

Banatski Gulaš
Goulash à la Banat

2 lbs. beef, cubed
3 tbsp. oil
1 c. chopped onion
1 tsp. minced garlic
1 tsp. paprika
1 c. beef stock
pinch marjoram
1 lb. potatoes
3 green peppers
3 firm ripe tomatoes
1 head kale
salt and pepper to taste

Heat the oil in a large skillet. Brown the onion in the hot oil. Add the cubed beef. Season with salt and pepper. Add the garlic, paprika and marjoram. When the beef is well browned, add the beef stock to cover the bottom. Allow to simmer gently for about half an hour. Stir occasionally, adding water as required. Wash and chop the vegetables. When the meat is almost tender, add the chopped vegetables and a little more water. Continue to simmer until the meat and vegetables are tender.

Dalmatinska Pašticada
Dalmatian Pot Roast

2 lbs. beef
2-3 cloves
4 cloves garlic, slivered
2 oz. bacon slices
1 onion, finely chopped
8 oz. dried prunes (optional)
1 c. red table wine
1 tbsp. tomato paste
1¼ c. beef stock
¼ c. lard or oil
salt and pepper to taste

Wash the roast, wipe it with a kitchen towel and lard it with bacon. Make small slits in the side of the roast and insert the garlic and clove in each one. Season with salt and pepper and refrigerate overnight. The following day, heat the oil and brown the meat on all sides in the hot oil. Add the onion and simmer slowly until the meat soaks up all the juices. Add the wine and tomato paste. Simmer for approximately twenty minutes. Add the beef stock and simmer slowly for approximately two hours. If necessary, add a little water occasionally. Remove the roast, slice thinly and place on a serving platter. Strain the gravy and cook it for another half hour. If required, thicken the gravy with a little flour browned in hot fat. Pour this sauce over the sliced roast before serving.

Illustrated on page 76.

Kobasice sa Kiselim Zeljem
Sausage with Sauerkraut

2 lbs. smoked pork sausage
1 lb. sauerkraut
2 tbsp. lard or oil
1 small onion, chopped
2 cloves garlic, chopped
1 tsp. paprika
salt and pepper to taste

Heat half the lard in a large saucepan. Brown the onion in the hot fat. Add the sauerkraut and sauté for about half an hour. Fry the sausage in the remaining fat. When the sausage is well browned, add it to the sauerkraut and continue to simmer slowly until the sausage becomes tender.

Jezik u Umaku
Beef Tongue

1 beef tongue
1 carrot
2 parsley roots
1 bay leaf
¼ lb. bacon
1 medium onion
¼ c. lard or oil
2 tbsp. anchovy paste
2 tbsp. flour
½ lb. smoked sausage
1 c. sour cream
1 c. beef stock

Place the carrot, parsley roots, bay leaf and onion in salted water. Add the tongue and cook with the vegetables until tender. Remove the tongue, wash it and lard it with bacon. Spread the tongue with anchovy paste. Brown the onion in half the lard or oil. Add the cooked vegetables and paprika. Cook for about 15 minutes, then mash the vegetables. Make a roux of the remaining lard or oil and the flour. Add the beef stock. Cook well. Add the mashed vegetables. Slice the sausage and add it to this mixture. Place the tongue in this sauce and continue cooking for about 15-20 minutes. Remove the tongue. Slice it and arrange the slices on a serving platter. Add the sour cream to the sauce. Stir well and pour this over the beef tongue slices. Garnish with mashed potatoes, if desired.

Janjeći Odresci
Grilled Lamb Chops

2 lbs. lamb chops
1 tbsp. olive oil
1 tbsp. minced garlic
1 tbsp. wine vinegar
2 tbsp. minced onion
salt and pepper to taste

Wash the meat and dry with a kitchen towel. Pound the chops with a meat tenderizer until they are about ½ inch thick. Make a marinade from the remaining ingredients. Place the meat in the marinade and refrigerate overnight. Drain before broiling or barbecuing on an outdoor grill. Use the marinade to baste the chops while cooking.

Slavonski Svinjski Odresci
Slavonian Pork Chops

2 lbs. pork chops
6 tbsp. flour
3 tbsp. lard or oil
¼ c. diced bacon
1 c. sliced smoked sausage
3 tbsp. tomato purée
½ lb. green peppers, sliced
2 large tomatoes, sliced
1 clove garlic, minced
1 tsp. paprika

Season the pork chops with salt and pepper. Roll in flour and fry in hot lard or oil. Fry the bacon in its own fat. Add the sausage to the bacon and stir well. Drain any excess fat. Season with paprika. Allow the sausage to brown a little. Add the garlic, tomatoes, green peppers and tomato purée. Allow to simmer over low heat until the vegetables are half cooked. Add the pork chops and continue to simmer until everything is tender. Serve with mashed potatoes or on a bed of rice.

Pohani Teleći Odresci
Breaded Veal Cutlets

6 veal cutlets
3 tbsp. flour
2 eggs, well beaten
¼ c. breadcrumbs
1 tsp. paprika
salt and pepper to taste
oil and butter for deep frying

Season the flour with the salt, pepper and sweet paprika. Roll the cutlets in the seasoned flour. Coat with egg and roll in fine breadcrumbs. Heat the oil and allow the butter to melt in the hot oil. A combination of half butter and half oil is ideal for frying breaded cutlets because the oil keeps the butter from burning. Place the cutlets in the hot fat, reduce the heat to moderate and fry for about 8-10 minutes on each side. The cutlets are ready when they are an even golden brown color.

Teletina sa Graškom
Spring Veal With Baby Peas

2 lbs. young veal, cubed
6 tbsp. oil
1 ½ c. rice
¼ c. onion, finely chopped
3 c. chicken stock
1 tbsp. chopped parsley
2 c. cooked peas
½ c. grated hard cheese
1 tsp. paprika
salt and pepper to taste
¼ c. grated Parmesan cheese

Heat half the oil and brown the onion in it. Add the meat. Season with salt, pepper and paprika. When the meat has browned, add a little water. Cover and simmer slowly for about an hour. Stir occasionally and add more water as required. Heat the remaining oil and fry the rice in it. Add the parsley, meat and stock. Cover and simmer slowly until the rice is tender, stirring occasionally. Add the cooked peas and garnish with grated cheese.

Zenički Janjeći Odresci
Lamb Chops à la Zenica

6 lamb chops
¼ c. butter
1 tsp. chopped parsley
1 c. sliced mushrooms
¼ c. flour
salt and pepper to taste

Soak the lamb chops in hot water. Melt the butter over low heat. Increase the heat and sauté the mushrooms and parsley in the hot butter. Drain the lamb chops and blot them on a kitchen towel. Season them with salt and pepper. Roll them in flour. Add the lamb chops to the mushrooms. Simmer slowly over low heat until the chops are tender. Place them in a deep dish. Serve a brown sauce on the side.

Seljački Svinjski Odresci
Country Pork Chops

2 lbs. pork chops
3 tbsp. oil
1 c. beef stock
½ c. smoked bacon, chopped
½ c. small onions, sliced
2 lbs. potatoes, cubed
1 tsp. minced garlic
1 tsp. chopped parsley
1 tsp. flour
salt and pepper to taste

Melt the oil over low heat. Increase the heat and fry the cutlets in it. Remove the cutlets. Drain the fat into another saucepan. Add the cutlets and the beef stock. Bring to a boil. Reduce the heat and simmer, covered, until tender. Fry the bacon in its own fat. Add the onions and sauté until they become golden. Add the potatoes and stir well. Line a serving dish with the cutlets. Cover with potatoes and pour a hot gravy or sauce over the potatoes. Serve immediately.

Punjeni Svinjski Filet
Croatian Stuffed Pork Chops

2 lbs. pork chop fillets
½ lb. Trappist cheese*
½ c. flour
1 egg
1 tbsp. milk
½ c. bread crumbs
½ c. butter
½ c. oil
salt and pepper to taste

*Port du Salut cheese may be substituted.

Remove the bones from the pork chops if they have not already been filleted. Pound the meat with a meat tenderizer until very thin. Season with salt, pepper and garlic. Place a thick slice of Trappist cheese on half the cutlet and fold the other half over the first. If the pork chops are especially small, place a second cutlet over the cheese instead of folding the meat over. Dredge the stuffed cutlet with flour and shake off the excess. Beat the egg with the milk and season with salt and pepper. Dip the cutlets in the egg mixture, then roll in the bread crumbs. Heat the oil in a large skillet over medium heat. Melt the butter in the hot oil. Fry the cutlets in the hot (350°) oil and butter until golden on both sides.

Ražnjići
Raznjići

1 lb. veal
1 lb. pork or lamb
1 clove garlic, chopped
2 tbsp. chopped onion
3 tbsp. oil
small bay leaves
1 tbsp. ground parsley
salt to taste

Cut the meat into 1½ inch cubes. Dry the cubed meat between a few sheets of paper towel. Place the meat in a deep bowl. Season with salt and pepper. Add the oil, onion, garlic and parsley. Mix well. Cover and refrigerate for at least three hours. Place the meat cubes on skewers alternating the pork and veal with half a bay leaf between each cube. Broil the *ražnjići* in a preheated oven broiler or grill them over hot coals on an outdoor barbecue grill for about twenty minutes until well done. The pork must not be undercooked. Baste the *ražnjići* with the oil and seasoning marinade in which they were soaked earlier, while cooking. Serve the *ražnjići* on the skewers on which they were grilled. Sprinkle with chopped onion just before serving or serve with an onion salad. Like *čevapčići*, *ražnjići* make excellent appetizers.

Janjeći But
Roast Leg of Lamb

1 leg of lamb, 6-7 lbs.
1 c. melted butter
1 c. water
4 cloves garlic
1½ lbs. new potatoes
1 bunch of fresh parsley
salt and pepper to taste

Wash the lamb and pat dry. Peel and crush 5 cloves of garlic and rub into the surface of the lamb or insert into slits in the meat. Season well with salt and pepper. Place the lamb in a covered roasting pan and pour the melted butter over it. Add half the water. Roast the lamb at 350° covered, for approximately two hours, basting frequently. Half an hour before the lamb is fully roasted, pour the pan drippings into a bowl. Scrub off the skin of the new potatoes and toss them in the bowl with one tablespoon chopped parsley, the remaining clove of garlic, crushed, and a little salt. Place the potatoes in a baking pan and bake in the oven for half an hour, turning them at least once. Serve the leg of lamb on a very warm platter on a bed of the new potatoes. Garnish with the remaining parsley.

Goveđi Odresci S Lukom
Sirloin Steak With Onions

2 lbs. sirloin steak
½ c. lard or oil
3 tbsp. flour
1 c. small onions
salt and pepper to taste

Pound the steaks with a meat tenderizer. Season with salt and pepper. Roll in flour. Slice the onions and sprinkle with the remaining flour. Heat the lard or oil in a large skillet and fry the onions in it until browned. Remove the onion and drain on paper towels. Set the onion in a warm place. Fry the steaks in the remaining lard or oil on both sides. Place the steaks on a hot serving dish and arrange the fried onion over them. Serve with a hot sauce or meat gravy.

Svinjski Paprikaš
Pork Paprikash

2 lbs. fresh cubed pork
1 ½ lb. sauerkraut
½ c. lard or oil
2 medium onions, chopped
1 c. sour cream
1 tbsp. garlic powder
salt and pepper to taste

Wash the sauerkraut. Heat half the lard or oil. When it becomes frothy, add half the onion and sauté until it becomes golden. Add the sauerkraut and simmer slowly until it becomes tender. Heat the remaining lard or oil and brown the rest of the onion in it. When the onion is golden, add the meat. Sauté the meat over moderate heat until nicely browned. Reduce the heat, cover and simmer for a few minutes. Add the sauerkraut and stir together well. Season with salt, pepper, garlic and paprika. Simmer over moderately low heat for another half hour. Add the sour cream before serving and continue to cook gently long enough to heat the sour cream. If desired, this dish can be prepared in advance, adding the sour cream and reheating before serving.

Turopoljska Pirjana Govedina
Turopolje Braised Beef

2 lbs. beef steak
1 c. mushrooms
½ c. butter
½ c. onions
1 tbsp. chopped parsley
1 tsp. minced garlic
1 tbsp. tomato paste
1 green pepper, cored and sliced
½ c. red wine
salt and pepper to taste

Cut the meat into long strips. Heat half the butter and brown the onion in it. Add the garlic, wine, green pepper and tomato paste. Cook for 4-5 minutes, stirring constantly. Add the meat. Season with salt and pepper. Cover and simmer slowly, turning occasionally. Wash and slice the mushrooms. Sauté them in the remaining butter. When the meat is almost tender, add the mushrooms and parsley. Continue to simmer until the meat becomes tender.

Sinjski Teleći Kotleti
Veal Cutlets à la Sinj

6 veal cutlets
½ c. butter
2 tbsp. chopped onion
1 clove garlic, chopped
1 c. chopped green olives
½ c. finely diced ham
salt and pepper to taste

Season the cutlets with salt and pepper and allow them to sit for about ten minutes. Heat the butter in the saucepan. Add the cutlets and fry them on both sides until golden. Add the onion, garlic and ham. Allow to simmer slowly until the onion becomes clear. Cover and continue to cook for about twenty minutes. Remove the cutlets to a warmed serving dish. Add the olives to the sauce that the cutlets were cooked in. Continue to cook the sauce for another minute or two, then pour it over the cutlets. Serve immediately.

Punjena Teleća Prsa
Stuffed Breast of Veal

2 lbs. veal breast
2 rolls
2 eggs
1 onion
½ c. sour cream
2 tbsp. lard or oil
1 tsp. finely chopped parsley
salt and pepper to taste

Wash the meat and remove the ribs. Salt the meat inside and out. Cut the rolls into small cubes and cover the chopped onion which has been sautéd in the lard or oil. Beat the eggs in a deep bowl. Add the sour cream, chopped parsley and the salt and pepper. Add this mixture to the cubed rolls. Mix well. Stuff the breast with this mixture and sew up the opening. Place the ribs in a well-greased baking dish and add the stuffed breast over the ribs. Pour some hot oil or lard over the meat. Bake in a moderate oven at 350° until golden brown. Baste with the juices to which a few tablespoons of water have been added. Serve with a meat gravy or a sauce made from the pan drippings.

Paprika Popečci
Paprika Veal Chops

2 lbs. veal chops
¼ c. lard or oil
¼ c. smoked bacon, diced
3 tbsp. chopped onion
1 c. beef stock
2 tbsp. tomato paste
2 tbsp. flour
1 c. sour cream
salt, pepper and paprika to taste

Fry the bacon in its own fat. Add the onion and allow the flour to brown. Season with salt and paprika. Add the beef stock and tomato paste. Allow this sauce to simmer slowly. Pound the veal chops with a meat tenderizer. Season with salt and pepper. Heat the lard or oil. Brown the chops in the hot lard or oil quickly on both sides. Simmer them slowly for approximately half an hour in the tomato sauce. Add the sour cream to the sauce just before serving.

Pečena Jetra
Fried Liver

2 lbs. liver
2 onions, sliced
1 tsp. paprika
¼ c. lard or oil
flour
salt and pepper to taste

Cube the liver or slice it into thin slices. Season the flour with salt, pepper and paprika. Roll the liver in the seasoned flour. Heat the lard or oil in a skillet. Fry the liver in the hot lard or oil. Drain on paper towels. Sauté the onions in the skillet that the liver was fried in. Serve the liver on a bed of the sautéd onions. Calf, lamb or pork liver can be prepared in this manner.

Janjetina u Umaku
Lamb in Sour Cream Sauce

3 lbs. lamb roast
½ c. smoked bacon, diced
2 tbsp. lard or oil
2 tbsp. flour
1 c. sour cream
1 c. chicken stock
salt to taste

Wash and dry the lamb roast with a kitchen towel. Lard the roast and season with salt. Melt the lard and pour it over the roast. Place the meat in a warm oven and roast for approximately an hour and a half until the outside is crisp and golden. Baste frequently with the hot lard or oil. When the lamb is roasted, pour the lard or oil into a skillet. Fry the flour in the hot lard or oil. When it has browned, dilute with the stock. Add the sour cream and mix well. Pour this sauce over the lamb roast. Return to the oven and bake long enough for the sauce to come to a boil. The roast may be sliced before serving or at the table. Pour the sauce over the roast just before serving.

Teleći Popečci sa Gljivama
Paprika Veal With Mushrooms

2 lbs. veal cutlets
¾ c. sour cream
1 green pepper
1 medium onion
1 lb. mushrooms
2 tbsp. flour
2 tbsp. butter or margarine
1 tsp. paprika
1 tbsp. chopped parsley
salt and pepper to taste

Chop the onion and green pepper and slice the mushrooms. Heat the butter, add the onion and cook until clear. Dredge the veal in flour and shake off the excess. Add the veal to the onion and brown nicely on both sides. Add the green pepper and paprika and cook over low heat until the veal becomes tender, approximately 30 to 40 minutes. Add the mushrooms. Stir well and cook for another five minutes until they soften. Stir in the sour cream and heat to just below the boiling point. Arrange the veal cutlets in a serving platter. Place the mushrooms over the veal and garnish with parsley.

Svinjetina u Mirodijama
Herbed Roast Pork

one 4 lb. boneless pork roast
1 glove garlic, minced
2 tsp. dried rosemary, crushed
1 tsp. dried thyme leaves, crushed
1 tsp. dried basil leaves, crushed
2 tbsp. oil
salt and pepper to taste

Combine the garlic, rosemary, thyme, basil, salt and pepper with the oil. Coat the meat with this seasoning mixture. Place the meat, fat side up, on a rack in a baking pan. Roast for one hour and an half at 325° or until the roast is nicely browned. Remove to a serving platter and slice into serving portions. Serve the gravy on the side.

Gravy

¼ c. strained pan drippings
3 tbsp. flour
1 c. cold water
¼ tsp. salt
¼ tsp. pepper

Pour the drippings into a small saucepan. Stir in the flour. Cook over low heat, stirring constantly, until the mixture comes to a boil. Gradually stir in one cup water. Stir in the salt and pepper.

Rolada od Govedine
Croatian Beef Tenderloin

3 lb. beef tenderloin
2 cloves garlic, minced
4 oz. sliced bacon
3 tbsp. chopped parsley
salt and pepper to taste
4 hard cooked eggs, peeled
1 large onion, chopped
1 large carrot, cut into thin strips
2 c. tomato juice
1 c. sour cream

Split and flatten slightly the beef tenderloin. Pound it with a meat tenderizer on both sides. Season with salt and pepper. Sprinkle with garlic and parsley. Lay the bacon over the beef. Place the whole eggs in a row over the meat. Roll the meat into a large log and secure with skewers or tie with kitchen string. Heat the oil and sauté the onion in it until it clarifies. Add the carrot and sauté for another five or six minutes. Add the beef roll and cover with the tomato juice. Simmer over low heat until tender. Turn the roast occasionally and add water as required. When the pot roast is tender, remove to a serving platter. Allow to cool enough to handle. Remove the string and slice the roast. Add the sour cream to the sauce that the beef was cooked in. Bring to just below the boiling point. Pour this sauce over the sliced beef.

Pečena Rolada od Govedine
Stuffed Tenderloin

3 lb. beef tenderloin
6 tbsp. butter
8 oz. sliced mushrooms
½ c. chopped onion
3 c. bread crumbs
3 slices bacon
salt and pepper to taste

Split and flatten the tenderloin. Beat it slightly with a meat tenderizer. Sauté the onion and mushrooms in the butter. Stir in the bread crumbs. Spread this mixture over the tenderloin. Fasten the edges with skewers or tie with kitchen string. Season with salt and pepper. Place the bacon over the roast. Roast, uncovered at 325° for about one and a half hours.

Mesnate Kobasice
Meat Sausage

5 lbs. fresh pork
2 tbsp. salt for fresh sausage or
4 tbsp. salt for dry or smoked sausage
2 tsp. pepper
1 tbsp. paprika
6 cloves garlic, minced
¼ c. beef stock
natural pork casings

Allow the garlic to marinade in the beef stock for approximately half an hour. Cut the meat into ¼" pieces, or grind them in a meat grinder with holes approximately 3/8" in diameter. Mix the meat thoroughly with the salt, pepper and paprika. Add the beef stock one tablespoon at a time.

Pork casings come in bundles preserved in salt which can be kept for long periods of time in a cool place. Wash a length of pork casings under lukewarm water. Fit the end of the casing to the opening of a water faucet and allow warm water to run through the casing. Allow the casing to soak in warm water for fifteen minutes. Squeeze the water out and drain the casing.

Using the stuffer attachment of your meat grinder, gather the casings on the funnel. Leave a small piece of casing on the end so that trapped pockets of air can be pushed out when the sausage is made. Hold the tip of the casing so that it does not roll too fast. Fill the casing.

Using strong string, tie a knot at the end of the casing. Fold the casing over knot and tie again. You may tie the ends of the string to make a loop for hanging the sausage. Push the meat toward the tied end. Squeeze the sausage where you want it to end. Twist the sausage at the point where you squeezed it and tie the end with the string.

Continue squeezing and tying until you have made all the sausages from that piece of stuffed casing. Continue stuffing casing and making sausages until all the meat is used up. Refrigerate the sausage for two to three days to cure it if it is to be eaten fresh . The sausage can also be smoked or air dried during winter months. To air dry, hang them in a dry, cool place to avoid spoiling. The sausage can be eaten after it has dried for eight weeks and will keep for several months.

Teleći Perket i Žličnjaci s Jajima /Veal Perket an Egg Dumplings [page 122]

Teleći Perket
Veal Perket

2 lbs. veal, cubed
3 tbsp. butter
2 onions, thinly sliced
1 clove garlic, minced
2 tsp. paprika
3 tbsp. tomato paste
1 c. beef stock
salt and pepper to taste
½ c. sour cream

Melt the butter over low heat. Increase the heat and brown the onion in the butter slightly. When the onion is tender, add the meat and brown well. Remove from heat. Add the garlic and paprika. Return to heat and sauté for a minute or two. Add the beef stock and simmer slowly, covered for about an hour, adding more water as required. Add the tomato paste and continue to cook until the meat is tender. Remove from heat. Stir in the sour cream. Return to heat and heat until the sauce just reaches the boiling point. Serve immediately with more sour cream on the side.

Punjene Paprike
Croatian Stuffed Peppers

Entrées and Casseroles

Stews, ragouts and casseroles made of vegetables, meats and seasonings are favorites as entrées served between the soup and main course of formal dinners. They can also be served as one-dish meals for luncheon or supper.

Perhaps the best known Croatian entree is the famed meat-stuffed cabbage specialty known as sarma. This national dish is prepared by stuffing the leaves of pickled cabbage with a mixture of smoked pork, beef and rice. It is a delicious preparation that blends the delicate aromas of spices with the taste of fresh and smoked meat against the background of tart sauerkraut leaves. Equally popular are the various stuffed vegetables, including *Punjena Paprika*, stuffed green peppers which are slowly simmered in a rich tomato sauce.

Stews and casseroles are solid, hearty dishes prepared with meats, vegetables, parsley, onion, garlic and spices. They are very definite in flavor and soft in texture. The vegetables used in the stews and ragouts vary according to season and personal preference. Potatoes are frequently left out and the stew is served with a side dish of potatoes, noodles, rice or dumplings. The most typical Croatian casseroles are those baked in the oven for several hours. *Đuveč* and the various *složenci* are rich combinations of meats and vegetables which frequently include rice. Their versatility and ease of preparation make them very practical as supper or luncheon dishes.

Bosanski Lonac is a very substantial, flavorful meal made of pork and beef and cooked in white wine with a variety of vegetables and seasonings. It was traditionally cooked in a deep earthenware pot from which it derives its name. Because it must be simmered very gently over low heat for several hours, it is especially well suited for crock pot cookery.

These casseroles, stews, ragouts and other one dish meals reflect the rich and varied ingredients available to create such preparations. Originally, such meals were served after long hard hours of work outdoors. Although they are relatively simple to prepare, these dishes are wonderful in the way that they blend flavors and balance compositions and textures into subtle harmony.

From the earthy and simple to the most complicated and extraordinary, these combinations of meats, vegetables and spices make for interesting balances and contrasts of taste.

Punjena Paprika
Stuffed Peppers

1 lb. ground beef
1 lb. chopped smoked ham
12 large green peppers
2 large onions, chopped
¼ c. oil
1 c. sour cream
1 c. uncooked rice
1 tbsp. chopped parsley
2 tbsp. flour
2 c. beef stock
¾ c. tomato paste
salt and pepper to taste

Brown the onion in half the oil. Add the meat and cook it in its own juices until the water has evaporated. Allow to cool slightly. Add the rice, salt, pepper and parsley and mix well. Wash the peppers, core them and remove the seeds and ribs. Stuff the peppers with the meat mixture. Do not stuff the peppers too full because the rice will expand during cooking. Arrange the peppers in a deep pot. Brown the flour in the remaining oil. Add the tomato paste and the beef stock. Stir well. Pour this sauce over the peppers and simmer over low heat for approximately an hour and a half without mixing. Shake the pot occasionally so that the peppers do not stick. Carefully remove the peppers and arrange them in a warm serving dish. If desired, add sour cream to the tomato sauce. Cook for a few more minutes, then pour this sauce over the peppers.

Illustrated on page 98.

Lički Lonac
Lika Casserole

Follow the Bosanski Lonac recipe, substituting lamb for the beef and pork.

Hercegovački Đuveč
Herzegovinian Baked Casserole

1 lb. cubed beef
1 lb. cubed pork
1 c. sliced onion
½ c. olive oil
1 ½ c. rice
5-6 firm ripe tomatoes
8 green peppers
4 tbsp. sour cream or
¼ c. wine
salt and pepper to taste

Partially cook the rice in salted water. Drain. In a small saucepan heat the olive oil and brown the onions in it. Slice the tomatoes and cut the green peppers into strips. Place the onions in a deep baking dish. Place a layer of tomatoes over the onions, green peppers over the tomatoes and rice over the green peppers. Continue alternating the layers until all the tomatoes, green peppers and rice are used up. Season each layer with salt and pepper. Season the meat with salt and pepper and arrange it on top of the vegetables. Bake at 350° for about an hour. Remove from the oven and add the sour cream or wine. Return to the oven and continue baking until the meat is tender, approximately 45 minutes longer.

Govedina s Grahom
Beans and Beef Casserole

2 lbs. beef
½ lb. beans
½ lb. cabbage, shredded
½ lb. carrots, sliced
1 onion, finely chopped
2 c. beef stock
salt, pepper and paprika to taste

Wash the beans and soak them for several hours. Chop the meat into large cubes. Place the beans in the bottom of a large pot. Add the meat and then place the carrots and cabbage on top. Sprinkle with a layer of chopped onions. Season each layer with salt, pepper and paprika. Cover with beef stock and enough water to cover. Allow to cook over very low heat for about three hours.

Bosanski Lonac
Bosnian Casserole

1 lb. beef, cubed	2 sliced green peppers
1 lb. pork, cubed	2 carrots, sliced
1 clove garlic, chopped	1 tbsp. parsley
1 onion, sliced	¼ c. wine
½ cabbage, shredded	¼ c. chopped celery
5 potatoes	2 tsp. paprika
½ lb. green beans	water or beef stock
2 sliced tomatoes	salt and pepper to taste

Wash and cube the meat. Place it in the bottom of a large crock pot. Layer the vegetables over the meat. Season each layer with salt and pepper. Sprinkle the garlic over the vegetables. Leave the onion as the top layer. Add the wine and enough water or beef stock to cover. Cover the pot and allow to simmer for several hours until both the meat and the vegetables are tender.

Nadjevene Rajčice
Stuffed Tomatoes

6-8 large, firm, ripe tomatoes
½ lb. ground beef
¼ c. chopped onion
1 egg
1 tbsp. butter
3 tbsp. wine or beef stock
½ tbsp. chopped parsley
salt, pepper and paprika to taste

Wash the tomatoes, cut off the tops and remove the centers and seeds, which can be used later in the sauce. Sauté the onion in one tablespoon butter or margarine. When the onion has become a golden brown, add the ground beef and sauté until browned. Season with salt, pepper and paprika. Add the wine or beef stock and mix well. Cook for about five minutes. Remove from heat. When the mixture has cooled, stir in the whole egg and the chopped parsley. Stuff the tomatoes with this meat filling. Place the tomatoes in a large saucepan which has been well greased with oil. Cover the tomatoes with the sauce and sauté them in the covered saucepan for about half an hour. Stuffed tomatoes can be served as an appetizer or as a luncheon dish.

Sauce:

2 tbsp. butter
2 tbsp. flour
1 c. beef stock
2 tbsp. tomato paste
½ c. wine
1 tsp. sugar

Melt the butter over medium heat. Add the sugar. When the sugar has melted, add the flour and allow it to brown. Add the wine gradually, stirring constantly so that lumps do not form. Add the tomato paste and beef stock. Allow the sauce to cook for about ten minutes before pouring over the stuffed tomatoes.

Zemunske Paprike sa Sirom
Cheese-Stuffed Peppers

6 paprika peppers
1 lb. cottage cheese
½ c. sour cream
2 eggs, well beaten
salt and pepper to taste

Remove the tops from the peppers. Core them, removing the seeds and ribs. Beat the cottage cheese until smooth. Add the eggs. Season with salt and pepper. Stuff the peppers with this cheese filling. Arrange the peppers in a well greased baking dish. Place about a tablespoon of sour cream on each stuffed pepper. Bake at 450° for approximately 15-20 minutes.

Ričet
Beans and Barley

1 ½ lbs. smoked pork
½ lb. navy beans
½ lb. barley
½ onion, finely chopped
1 tbsp. oil or lard
2 tbsp. flour
¼ c. water
salt and pepper to taste

Soak the beans overnight. Place the beans, barley and meat in a large pot. Add enough cold water to cover. Cook over medium low heat until the beans and barley are tender. Brown the onions in the shortening. Stir in the flour and sauté until it begins to brown. Add the water and stir well. Gradually add some of the water in which the beans and barley were cooked. Add the beans and barley to the sauce. Season with salt and pepper. Allow to cook a little longer before serving. Slice the smoked pork and serve it on the side.

Punjeni Jastučići s Umakom od Rajčica/Stuffed Pillows with Croatian Tomato Sauce [page 134].

Punjeni Jastučići
Stuffed Pillows

1 ½ c. flour
2 tbsp. melted butter
¼ tsp. salt
3 tbsp. water
1 well beaten egg
3 c. Croatian Tomato Sauce
¼ c. grated Parmesan Cheese

Sift the flour with the salt into a deep bowl. Make a well in the center of the flour. Mix well. Add the egg and water alternately, mixing well after each addition. Knead the dough until smooth. Divide it into four portions. Roll each portion in a square approximately ¼ inch thick. Place the meatballs on one sheet approximately 2 inches apart. Place another dough sheet over the filled sheet. Lightly roll together, without stretching. Cut out two inch squares with a pastry cutter. Cook the stuffed pillows in salted water for approximately fifteen minutes. Drain on absorbent paper. Transfer to a heated serving dish. Add Croatian Tomato Sauce and sprinkle with grated Parmesan cheese.

Continued on next page.

Filling:

1 ½ lb. ground beef
1 tbsp. parsley
2 tbsp. butter
1 egg, beaten
2 tbsp. chopped onion
¼ c. bread crumbs
salt and pepper to taste

Melt the butter over low heat. Increase the heat and fry the onion and parsley in the butter until the onion is a golden color. Season with salt and pepper. When the meat has browned, remove from heat. Drain the excess fat. Add the bread crumbs and the egg and mix well. Divide the meat mixture into little balls about ½" in diameter. Roll in the remaining breadcrumbs. For variety, substitute veal, pork, chicken or rabbit meat.

Jastučići Punjeni Sirom
Cheese-Stuffed Pillows

1 ¼ c. flour
1 egg
½ tsp. salt
1 egg white
2 tbsp. butter
¼ c. water
2 tbsp. breadcrumbs

Sift the flour into a deep bowl. Make a well in the center. Place the egg, salt and water into the well. Knead the dough well. Add more water as required to make a smooth, silky dough. Separate the dough into two sections. Shape it into two loaves and allow it to sit for about half an hour. Roll the dough very thin and cut it into squares. Brush a little egg white around the edges of the squares. Place a tablespoon of filling on half the squares. Cover with the remaining squares and press the edges together with a fork. Drop into boiling salted water and cook for about fifteen minutes. Drain and place in a deep bowl. Fry the breadcrumbs in the butter. Pour this mixture over the stuffed pillows.

Filling:

4 tbsp. butter
1 egg
1 lb. cottage cheese
¼ c. sour cream
¼ tsp. salt

Cream the butter. Beat the egg. Combine the butter and the egg. Add the cheese, sour cream and salt and mix well.

Lizibaba
Grandmother's Potato Bake

3 lbs. potatoes
3 eggs
1 c. flour
1 c. milk
1 tsp. salt
¼ tsp. pepper

Filling:

1 lb. lean ground beef
4 oz. smoked bacon
1 small onion, finely chopped
1 clove garlic, crushed
1 tbsp. chopped parsley
1 c. sour cream [optional]

Peel and dice the potatoes. Place the diced potatoes in a large bowl and season with salt and pepper. Sprinkle with flour and stir in the milk. Fry the bacon in its own fat. Drain the excess fat, reserving one tablespoon. Fry the onion in the reserved bacon fat. Stir in the garlic. Add the onion to the beef and shape into ½" meat balls. Pour half the potato mixture in a greased baking dish. Place the meat balls over the potato mixture. Pour the remaining potato mixture over the meat balls. Bake at 350° until golden, approximately one hour. If desired, pour one cup sour cream over the potato bake and return to the oven for another ten minutes. Garnish with chopped parsley.

Sekeli Gulaš
Sekeli Goulash

1½ lbs. lean pork, chopped
4 tbsp. oil
3 medium onions, chopped
2 tsp. paprika
2 tbsp. tomato purée
1 tsp. caraway seed
1 lb. sauerkraut
salt and pepper to taste
¾ c. sour cream
1 tbsp. corn starch
2 tbsp. water

Rinse the sauerkraut. Heat the oil and sauté the onion in it. Remove from heat. Add the paprika, caraway seed and the pork. Return to the heat and sauté approximately ten minutes. Add the tomato purée, sauerkraut, salt and pepper. Stir, cover and simmer over low heat until the meat is tender. Stir the corn starch in the water and add to the goulash. Cook for another ten minutes. Add the sour cream and heat to just below the boiling point before serving.

Musaka
Moussaka

3 eggplants
2 medium onions, chopped
1 tomato, chopped
2 lbs. ground lamb or beef
1 ¼ c. hot milk
1 egg yolk
3 tbsp. chopped parsley
3 tbsp. flour
3 tbsp. butter
½ tsp. ground allspice
pinch nutmeg
tomato paste
oil for frying
salt and pepper to taste

Peel and slice the eggplants thinly, or slice them unpeeled. Sprinkle the slices generously with salt. Allow to drain in a strainer for about half an hour. Squeeze. Wash in cold water and dry with a towel. Fry lightly in a little oil on both sides. Remove and drain on absorbent paper.

Fry the onions in a little oil until they begin to brown. Brown the ground meat with the onions. Season with salt, pepper and allspice. Add the tomato and tomato paste. Stir in the parsley. Add a little water and simmer for about fifteen minutes.

When the meat is fully cooked and the water is absorbed, place alternate layers of eggplant, meat and onion in a deep baking dish. Begin and end with the eggplant.

Melt the butter in a saucepan. Add the flour and allow to brown only slightly, stirring constantly. Add the hot milk gradually, stirring constantly, until the mixture boils. Season with salt, pepper and nutmeg. Simmer until the sauce thickens.

Beat the egg yolk. Add to the sauce, but do not allow the sauce to come to a boil. Pour the sauce into the baking dish. Bake uncovered for about 45 minutes at 375°.

Musaka can be prepared in one large serving dish or in individual dishes.

Čolet
Cholet

1 lb. smoked pork
1 lb. kidney beans
3 tbsp. lard or shortening
2 tbsp. onion
1 tsp. paprika
flour
salt and pepper to taste

Soak the beans overnight in cold water. Place the beans and meat in a crock pot. Season with salt, pepper and paprika. Brown the onion in the hot fat. Add the flour and allow it to brown. When the flour has browned, add a little water. Add this roux to the beans and meat. Place the meat and beans in a crock pot. Season with salt, pepper and paprika. Cook overnight over very low heat. The following day, reheat for about half an hour before serving. Serves 4.

Bučnica sa Sirom
Squash Savijaca

1 recipe savijaca dough
2 lbs. grated squash
1 ½ lbs. cottage cheese
¾ c. sour cream
3 eggs, well beaten
½ tsp. salt

Salt the grated squash and drain in a colander for half an hour. Squeeze out any remaining water. Combine the squash with the cottage cheese, sour cream and the eggs. Mix well. Stretch the savijaca dough on a well-floured tablecloth on a large table. Allow to dry for about five minutes. Sprinkle or brush the dough with melted butter. Spread the filling over two thirds of the dough. Gently pull up on the tablecloth and allow the dough to roll to make a large log. Transfer the *savijaca* to a greased baking sheet, making a U-shape out of the *savijaca* to fit it onto the baking sheet. Brush the *savijaca* generously with butter. Bake at 425° for ten minutes. Reduce the heat to 350° and bake for another thirty minutes. (Makes two *bucnice*.)

Sarma
Croatian Stuffed Cabbage Leaves

2 heads pickled cabbage	2 tsp. paprika
1 lb. ground beef	1 onion, chopped
1 lb. smoked ham, chopped	1 egg
¼ c. smoked bacon, chopped	2 tbsp. oil
2 tbsp. flour	1 lb. smoked ham hocks or
1 c. uncooked rice	pork ribs

salt and pepper to taste

Fry the bacon in its own fat. Add the onion and sauté for about five minutes. Remove from heat and drain the excess fat. Allow to cool slightly. Combine with the ground beef, the chopped ham, rice, egg, 1 teaspoon paprika, salt and pepper. Mix well. Remove the large outer leaves of the cabbage. Cut off the outer ribs or the sarma will be difficult to roll. Place some filling in each cabbage leaf and roll it up from the center of the leaf to the outer edge. Tuck the sides into the center to hold the roll together.

Cut any remaining cabbage into strips. If desired, add another half pound of sauerkraut. Place half the sauerkraut in the bottom of a large pot. Arrange the cabbage rolls over the sauerkraut. Add the smoked ribs or ham hocks. Cover with the remaining sauerkraut.

Continued on next page.

Heat the oil. When it becomes very hot, brown the flour in it. Add one teaspoon paprika and enough water to make a thick roux. Cook for five minutes. Pour the roux over the cabbage rolls. Add enough water to cover the sarma and simmer over low heat for one and a half to two hours until the rice is fully cooked. Do not stir the sarma while it is cooking. Instead, shake the pot occasionally to prevent sticking. Transfer to a warm serving dish. Sarma can be reheated. In fact, it seems to get better each time that it is reheated.

Pickled Cabbage

Kiseli Kupus

3 large heads cabbage
2 gallons water
½ c. salt
½ c. vinegar

Choose a container with a well-fitting cover in which to pickle the cabbage. Sterilize this container by rinsing it with boiling water. Wash the cabbage and place it in the prepared container. Pour the water into a large pot. Add the salt and bring the water to a boil. Remove from heat and allow to cool. Add the vinegar to the water. Pour the water and vinegar mixture over the cabbage. Seal tightly. Allow the cabbage to pickle in this brine for ten to fourteen days before using.

Okruglice sa Šljivama

Plum Dumplings

2 lbs. potatoes
3 c. flour
1 tbsp. butter
1 egg
1 lb. plums
1 ½ c. bread crumbs
5 tbsp. butter, softened
powdered sugar or heavy cream,
or ground walnuts or ground poppy seeds

Cook the potatoes in boiling water for half an hour. Peel while the potatoes are still hot. Pass the potatoes through a sieve. Put the warm, grated potatoes in a large bowl. Add the flour, butter, salt and egg. Mix all the ingredients until you get a medium firm dough.

Turn the dough out onto a floured board and knead into a smooth, glossy dough. Divide the dough into four sections and roll each section into a log, approximately 3 inches in diameter. Cut the log into slices approximately ½" thick. Flatten each slice to ¼" in thickness. Place a pitted plum on each slice, wrap the edges of the dough around the plum to form a dumpling.

Drop the dumplings into briskly boiling water and cook for approximately ten minutes until the dumplings rise to the top of the water. Fry the bread crumbs in the remaining tablespoon of butter until they become golden. Roll the cooked dumplings in the fried bread crumbs. Arrange in a serving dish and sprinkle with powdered sugar, cream, ground walnuts or ground poppy seeds.

Burek
Burek

1 recipe savijaca pastry	¾ c. beef stock
1 medium onion, chopped	1 tbsp. chopped parsley
3 strips bacon, diced	1 tsp. paprika
1 lb. ground beef	1 egg, lightly beaten
½ lb. ground pork	¼ c. flour
¼ c. butter	½ tsp. salt
	¼ tsp. pepper

Fry the bacon in its own fat until crisp. Add the onion and sauté the onion until it becomes a golden brown. Add the ground meat and cook for about five minutes, stirring constantly. Drain any excess fat. Add the salt, pepper, paprika, parsley and egg to the mixture. Stir well over the heat for a minute or two. Melt the butter in another saucepan. Add flour to the butter, a little at a time, stirring after each addition. When browned, add the beef stock and simmer until thickened. Add the sauce to the meat mixture. Refrigerate while you prepare the *savijača* pastry.

Stretch the *savijača* dough on a well-floured tablecloth on a large table. Allow to dry for about five minutes. Sprinkle or brush the dough with melted butter. Spread the filling over two thirds of the dough. Gently pull up on the tablecloth and allow the dough to roll to make a large log. Transfer the *burek* to a greased baking sheet, making a U-shape out of the *burek* to fit it onto the baking sheet. Brush the *savijača* generously with butter. Bake at 425° for ten minutes. Reduce the heat to 350° and bake for another thirty minutes. Allow to cool enough to handle. Slice into small pieces and serve hot.

Burek sa Sirom
Cheese Burek

1 recipe savijaca pastry
½ c. melted butter
2 tbsp. milk
½ lb. cottage cheese
½ c. cream cheese
1 c. grated Parmesan
2 eggs
2 tbsp. butter
1 tsp. chopped parsley

Place the cottage cheese and cream cheese in a deep bowl. Mash them with a fork. Add the Parmesan cheese, eggs, butter, milk, and parsley and mix well. Stretch the savijaca pastry across a large table. Allow to dry for about five minutes. Brush the surface with melted butter. Sprinkle the filling over two thirds of the surface. Roll the pastry by lifting the ends of the tablecloth, beginning at the end which has the filling. Bake at 425° for ten minutes. Decrease the heat to 350°. Bake until the pastry is crisp and an even golden color. Allow to cool for about ten minutes. Slice and serve hot.

Okruglice od Mesa u Umaku od Rajčica
Meat Dumplings in Tomato Sauce

2 lbs. ground meat
2 rolls
1 egg
1 tsp. ground parsley
2 tbsp. shortening
1 medium onion
1 clove garlic, minced
salt and pepper to taste

Dice the rolls and soak them in a little milk or water. Squeeze the excess liquid out. Brown the meat in a small amount of hot oil. Combine the roll with the ground meat. Sauté the onion in the shortening until golden brown. Add the finely ground garlic, parsley and the slightly beaten egg to the meat mixture. Season with salt and pepper. Knead everything well and shape into small dumplings. Roll the dumplings in flour and fry in hot fat. Place the fried dumpling in a serving bowl and cover with tomato sauce. Serve with potatoes or over macaroni.

Tomato Sauce:

½ medium onion, sliced
1 carrot
1 parsley root
2 tbsp. oil
2 tbsp. flour
4 ripe tomatoes, sliced or
3 tbsp. tomato paste
¼ c. wine
¼ c. water
½ tsp. sugar
salt and pepper to taste

Heat the oil. Sauté the onion, carrot and parsley root in the hot oil. Sprinkle with flour and sauté over medium heat until the flour is slightly browned. Add the tomatoes or tomato paste, water, wine and sugar. Season with salt and pepper. Allow this sauce to simmer over medium heat for approximately half an hour. Pour over the cooked meat dumplings. *Croatian Tomato Sauce* may be substituted.

Osiječki Krumpir
Potatoes, Osijek Style

3 lbs. potatoes
6 hard-cooked eggs, sliced
½ lb. smoked ham, sliced
1 smoked sausage
1 tsp. salt
4 tbsp. butter
2 c. sour cream
1 tbsp. bread crumbs

Cook the potatoes in salted water until they are almost tender. Peel while they are still hot. Hard cook the eggs. Slice the cooked potatoes and the eggs. Grease a baking dish and sprinkle with bread crumbs. Arrange a layer of potatoes over the bread crumbs, a layer of ham and sausage, and a layer of eggs. Continue placing the ingredients in the baking dish, alternating layers until all are used up. Season each layer with salt and pepper. Place a layer of meat on top. Bake at 350° for approximately an hour. Pour the sour cream over the casserole and return to the oven for another half hour. Serve hot.

Zagorske Štrukle
Zagorje Cheese Štrukle

2 c. flour
2 tbsp. oil
4 tablespoons oil
1 egg
½ tsp. salt
½ c. warm water

Filling:

½ lb. cottage cheese
½ c. sour cream
3 eggs
½ tsp. salt

Combine all the ingredients for the filling. Make a dough following the instructions for *savijača.* Stretch the dough out on a floured tablecloth, but do not stretch it to transparency. Leave it approximately one eighth of an inch thick. Once the dough is stretched, brush with 4 tablespoons melted butter and spread the filling over the dough. Roll the dough into a sausage by lifting the tablecloth up and away from the table. Using a plate with a sharp edge, cut the sausage into pieces approximately 3 inches long. Strukle can be cooked in three ways:

1) Cook in salted boiling water for approximately ten minutes. Sprinkle with bread crumbs fried in hot butter.

2) Arrange the pieces in a well greased baking pan and bake at 425° for ten minutes. Decrease the heat to 350° and bake for another twenty-five minutes until golden. Serve immediately as an appetizer or as a soup additive, but do not serve it in the soup, or the strukle will become soggy.

3) Drop the strukle into boiling soup and cook for approximately fifteen minutes.

Pašta i Fažol
Beans and Pasta

8 oz. smoked ham, chopped
1 lb. beans, soaked overnight
½ lb. macaroni shells
1 medium onion, chopped
4 tbsp. oil
1 clove garlic, minced
1 tsp. paprika
salt and pepper to taste
1 tbsp. chopped parsley

Drain the beans. Place in a pot of boiling water and cook for approximately forty minutes. Heat the oil and sauté the onion in the hot oil. Remove from heat and stir in the paprika and garlic. Add the smoked meat and onion mixture. Season with salt and pepper. Continue to simmer until the beans are tender. Add the macaroni and chopped parsley and cook until the macaroni shells are tender. Strongly smoked meat makes this a delicious one-dish meal. Serve with bread fresh from the oven.

Slavonski Rezanci sa Sirom
Slavonian Noodles with Cheese

2 c. cooked noodles
½ lb. cottage cheese
¾ c. sour cream
½ lb. diced bacon
salt and pepper to taste

Fry the bacon in its own fat until crisp. Transfer the fried bacon to a small bowl. Drain all but two tablespoons of the fat. Place the cooked, drained noodles in a serving bowl. Add the cottage cheese and sour cream to the bacon fat and heat to just the boiling point. Season with salt and pepper and add half the fried bacon. Combine this cheese sauce with the noodles, sprinkle with the remaining fried bacon and serve immediately.

Nabujak od Jaja
Fluffy Eggs

Egg and Side Dishes

Eggs are a basic food which can be prepared in a variety of ways. In Croatia, fresh eggs are available in the early morning open-air markets. House-wives leave the home early to select fresh fruits, vegetables and eggs from among the many stands of produce. At the same time, they may purchase cheese to add to the eggs for a tasty breakfast or *marenda*.

In the rural areas, farms are considered incomplete without fowl. Therefore, it is not surprising that eggs are an addition to many Croatian foods, enhancing lunch and dinner dishes. Deviled eggs served with vegetables and breast of veal stuffed with egg are examples of interesting ways to enrich foods with eggs. A popular dish is Egg Satarash. It combines eggs, vegetables, bacon, and spicy seasonings. When the aroma of this specialty permeates the morning air, it is bound to awaken even the deepest sleeper.

We have included a collection of side dishes in this volume which complement main courses. Fried rice, served with a velvety smooth Butter Sauce, is a delightful addition to any meal. For those desiring a lighter specialty, there is the fluffy Potato Cheese Soufflé.

Rice and macaroni have long been prepared as favored side dishes in Croatia, and fresh ingredients such as Parmesan cheese, cottage cheese and butter are often incorporated into the recipes. These side and egg dishes can be served as an accompaniment to main dishes, but they also make nutritious and filling breakfast foods.

Nabujak od Jaja
Fluffy Eggs

2 eggs
1 tbsp. butter
salt to taste

Separate the eggs. Whip the egg whites until stiff. Season with salt. Melt the butter. Grease a baking dish with the melted butter. Place the egg whites in the baking dish like two nests. Carefully drop the egg yolks into the nests so as not to break them. Bake at 400° for approximately ten minutes.

Jaja s Vrhnjem
Sour Cream Eggs

2 eggs, well beaten
2 tbsp. sour cream
salt and pepper to taste

Add the sour cream to the eggs. Season with salt and pepper. Scramble in a little hot oil or butter. Makes one serving.

Pečena Jaja sa Kiselim Vrhnjem
Eggs in Sour Cream

8 eggs
¼ c. butter
2 c. sliced mushrooms
juice of half a lemon
1 pint sour cream
¼ c. breadcrumbs
1 tsp. chopped parsley
2 tbsp. chopped onion
salt, pepper and paprika to taste

Melt the butter over medium heat. Increase the heat and sauté the onions in the hot butter. Add the mushrooms and lemon juice and sauté for another 5 minutes. Add the sour cream. Season with salt, pepper and paprika and mix well. Pour this mixture into a greased baking dish. Break the eggs into the sour cream mixture. Sprinkle with bread crumbs and parsley. Pour the melted butter over the dish. Bake at 325° for approximately fifteen minutes.

Kajgana s Tuninom
Tuna Fish Omelette

6 eggs
½ c. canned tuna
4 tbsp. butter
3 anchovy fillets
salt and pepper to taste

Beat the eggs well. Season with salt and pepper. Flake the tuna with a fork and add it to the eggs. Melt half the butter in a medium skillet. Pour in the egg mixture. Cook over medium heat. When the omelette is half cooked, turn the edges toward the center. Cook until the bottom is golden brown and the top is set. Fold half the omelette over the other half. Mince the anchovy fillets and combine them with melted butter. Pour this mixture over the omelette. Serve immediately. Serves 3-4.

Krumpir sa Sirom
Cheese Potatoes

2 lbs. cooked potatoes
6 tbsp. butter
2 tbsp. bread crumbs
½ lb. cottage cheese
1 tsp. paprika
½ c. smoked bacon, diced
salt and pepper to taste

Thinly slice the potatoes. Grease a baking dish well. Sprinkle with half the bread crumbs. Combine the cottage cheese with the butter. Cook over medium heat until foamy. Remove from heat. Fry the bacon in its own fat until brown and crisp. Combine the remaining bread crumbs, salt, pepper and paprika with the potato slices. Stir in the cheese mixture. Arrange in the baking dish and bake at 350° for approximately half an hour. Turn out like a cake and serve hot.

Krumpirača
Potato Bake

10 medium potatoes
3 eggs, slightly beaten
1 c. flour
1 tsp. salt
1 tsp. lemon juice or vinegar
3 tbsp. oil

Grate the potatoes into the lemon juice or   vinegar to keep the potatoes from turning dark. Add the eggs, oil, flour and salt. Grease a shallow baking dish and pour the potato mixture into the baking dish. Bake at 350° for approximately an hour. The top and bottom should be golden. Serve immediately.

Kroketi od Krumpira
Potato Croquettes

1 ½ lb. potatoes
2 eggs
¼ c. grated Parmesan
¾ c. flour
3 tbsp. butter
¼ c. fine breadcrumbs
1 c. oil
salt and pepper to taste

Peel and cook the potatoes. Mash them and season with salt and pepper. Combine with one egg, the butter, grated Parmesan and flour. Shape the potato mixture into little croquettes, approximately 2 ½" long. Roll in a little flour, dip in the remaining slightly beaten egg and roll in bread crumbs. Fry in hot oil until the croquettes are an even golden brown on all sides.

Pita Zelenita
Spinach Pita

savijaca dough
1 lb. cottage cheese
1 c. sour cream
10 oz. cooked spinach
1 tsp. salt
¼ c. melted butter
4 eggs

Preheat the oven to 425°. Drain and chop the spinach. Beat the eggs well with a wire whisk. Add the cottage cheese, sour cream, salt, and spinach. Stretch the dough, following the directions for Basic Savijaca Dough. Brush well melted butter. Fill with the spinach mixture, but cover only two thirds of the dough. Roll the *savijaca* into a log and place in a well-greased baking pan. Brush the top with butter. Bake at 425° for ten minutes. Reduce the heat to 350° and continue baking until the top of the *savijaca* is golden brown, approximately 25 minutes. Cut into serving-size pieces and serve hot.

Gljive s Rižom
Mushrooms and Rice

1 c. rice
1 lb. sliced mushrooms
2 c. water
2 tbsp. chopped parsley
2 tbsp. chopped onion
4 tbsp. butter
salt and pepper to taste

Melt half the butter in a large skillet. Sauté the onion and rice in the butter until the rice becomes transparent. Stir in the water and simmer over low heat until the water is completely absorbed. In another skillet fry the mushrooms in the remaining butter for 10-15 minutes. Sprinkle with parsley. Combine the rice and mushrooms. Season with salt and pepper before serving.

Okruglice od Riže
Rice Dumplings

½ lb. rice
½ c. cooked beef, finely ground
2 tbsp. oil
2 egg yolks
2 egg whites, stiffly beaten
2 tbsp. flour
2 tbsp. smoked bacon, diced

Fry the rice in the oil. When it has clarified, cover with water. When the rice is half cooked, remove from heat and drain. Add the finely ground meat and the egg yolks. Fold in the egg white. Stir in the flour. Shape the dough into small dumplings and cook them in salted, boiling water for 10-15 minutes. Fry the bacon in its own fat. Drain the dumplings, place in a serving bowl and sprinkle with the fried bacon.

Palenta - Žganci - Pura
Palenta

1 ½ c. corn meal
4 c. water
1 tbsp. salt

Add the salt to the water and bring to a boil. Place the corn meal in a large dry skillet. Heat the corn meal over medium heat, stirring constantly until it barely begins to brown. Pour the boiling water over the hot corn meal and mix quickly. Reduce the heat and continue to cook until the water is fully absorbed. Serve hot with butter, grated cheese or sour cream.

Pržena Palenta
Fried Palenta

4 c. cooked palenta
3 tbsp. butter
1 c. grated Parmesan cheese

Stir the cheese into the hot palenta. Pack the mixture into a well greased baking pan. Allow to cool. When the palenta is cold, turn it out on a board and cut into squares or diamonds. Melt the butter over low heat. Increase the heat to medium and fry the palenta in the hot butter. Serve with a rich meat sauce or with stewed meats.

Prepržena Riža
Fried Rice

1 c. rice
4 tbsp. butter
2 tbsp. chopped onion
2 c. clear stock
salt and pepper to taste

Melt one tablespoon butter in a saucepan and sauté the onion in it. Add the rice and fry until lightly browned. Season with salt and pepper. Add the stock and stir well. Cook it on the stove until tender, or bake at 400° for approximately half an hour. Pour the remaining butter, melted, over the rice and serve hot.

Kajgana s Patlidanima
Eggplant Omelette

8 eggs
1 c. cooked eggplant, diced
¼ c. butter
1 clove garlic, chopped
pinch oregano
salt and pepper to taste

Season the eggplant with garlic, oregano, salt and pepper. Beat the eggs and stir into the eggplant. Cook until the eggs are firm, but not overcooked.

Kroketi od Riže
Rice Croquettes

1 c. cooked rice
2 tbsp. butter
2 tbsp. flour
2 tbsp. minced onion
½ c. flour
½ c. bread crumbs
2 eggs
oil for frying

Sauté the onion in the butter and combine with the cooked rice. Add one egg and 2 tablespoons flour. Mix well. On a floured pastry board, shape little croquettes from the rice mixture. Beat the egg slightly with one tablespoon water. Roll the croquettes in flour, dip them in the egg, then roll in bread crumbs. Fry in hot oil until golden on all sides. Season with salt.

Rezanci od Sira
Cheese Noodles

2 c. flour
1 lb. cottage cheese
1 tbsp. butter
1 egg
1 tbsp. wheat germ
½ tsp. salt

Combine the butter and the cottage cheese. Mash with a fork until very smooth. Add the egg, flour, wheat germ and salt. Make a smooth, thick dough. Allow the dough to sit for about half an hour. Roll it very flat and cut into small squares or strips. Cook for 5-10 minutes in boiling salted water. Drain the cooked noodles and roll them in breadcrumbs that have been fried in oil or butter.

Rolada od Špinata
Spinach Roll

½ c. butter	5 egg whites
5 egg yolks	¼ tsp. cream of tartar
½ c. yogurt	10 oz. cooked spinach
1 tsp. salt	3 hard cooked eggs
1 tsp. baking powder	4 oz. smoked bacon
1 c. flour	½ tsp. salt
	6 oz. cream cheese

Preheat the over to 350°. Combine the cream cheese and the well-drained spinach and set aside. Fry the bacon in its own fat. Drain on paper towels. Hard cook the eggs and mash them with a fork. Line a 10"x15" baking sheet with wax paper. Grease and flour the wax paper. Cream the butter and add the egg yolks, one at a time, beating well after each addition. Add the yogurt and continue beating until the mixture is light and fluffy. Sift together the flour, salt and baking powder and add to the yolk mixture. Beat the egg whites until frothy. Add the cream of tartar and continue beating until stiff peaks form. Gently fold the egg whites into the egg yolk mixture. Pour the batter onto the baking sheet and smoothen with a spatula. Bake at 350° for twelve to thirteen minutes until the top is golden and the cake springs back to the touch.

Continued on next page.

Invert the pan onto a lightly floured kitchen towel. Remove the wax paper. Cut away the edges of the cake. Roll the cake up with the towel and allow to cool for approximately five minutes. Spread a thin layer of the spinach mixture over the cake. Sprinkle with the fried bacon bits and mashed egg. Roll tightly with the help of the kitchen towel. Cut the ends of the roll and serve immediately.

Žličnjaci s Jajima
Egg Dumplings

2 eggs
6 tbsp. butter
1/2 c. water
1 tsp. salt
3 c. flour

Cream two tablespoons butter. Add the egg, water and salt. Add the flour and mix the ingredients just enough to give the dough an even texture. Bring a large pot of water to boil with 2 teaspoons salt. Drop the dumplings by spoonful into the boiling water. Cook for approximately ten minutes. When all the dumplings have come to the surface of the water, remove them with a slotted spoon and drain. Heat the remaining butter and fry the drained dumplings in the butter for just a minute or two. Serve with paprikrash, perket, or goulash.

Illustrated on page 97.

Rizi Bizi
Rice and Peas

1 ½ c. rice
1 tbsp. chopped onion
3 tbsp. butter
1 ½ c. cooked peas
¼ c. grated Parmesan cheese
3 c. chicken stock
salt to taste

Wash the rice and drain well. Melt the butter and brown the onion in it. Add the rice and fry it until it becomes clear and lightly browned. Season with salt. Add the stock. Cover and simmer for about half an hour without stirring. Remove from heat when the water has evaporated and the rice is tender. Mix in the cooked peas. Garnish with Parmesan cheese and serve immediately.

Illustrated on page 59

Sataraš od Jaja
Egg Satarash

8 eggs
½ lb. smoked bacon, diced
1 whole onion
1 zucchini
½ lb. mushrooms
2 firm ripe tomatoes
1 red bell pepper
1 greeen pepper
1 tsp. paprika
salt and pepper to taste

Slice the onion. Sprinkle with one teaspoon of salt and allow to sit for ten minutes. Slice the tomatoes, mushrooms and zucchini. Cut the peppers into strips. Fry the bacon in its own fat. When the bacon clarifies, add the onion. When the onion has clarified, add the remaining vegetables. Season with salt, pepper and paprika. Sauté until the vegetables are tender and the bacon is well crisped. Drain the bacon fat. Add the eggs and scramble.

Rezanci od Špinata
Spinach Noodles

2 eggs
1 tbsp. oil
1 tsp. salt
1 c. cooked spinach
2 ½ c. flour
3 tbsp. butter

Drain the spinach very well and dry between two paper towels. Pass the spinach through a sieve or blend it in a blender. Combine the eggs, oil, salt and spinach. Mix well. Add the flour and mix into a firm dough. Turn the dough onto a floured board and knead until smooth. Roll the dough to ¼" thickness and allow to dry for approximately 15 minutes. Fold the dough over several times and cut these folds into noodles, approximately 3/8" wide. Cook in boiling salted water for 5 minutes. Drain. Quickly fry the noodles in butter just before serving.

Riža s Umakom od Maslaca
Rice with Butter Sauce

1 ½ c. rice
3 tbsp. butter
3 tbsp. chopped onion
3 c. white stock
salt to taste
Butter Sauce
¼ c. Parmesan cheese, grated

Brown the onion in hot butter. Add the rice and fry it until it becomes transparent. Add the stock, season with salt and mix well. Allow to simmer for approximately half an hour over low heat. Do not stir. Grease a bundt cake pan well. Firmly pack the rice into the cake pan. Turn it over onto a large flat serving platter. Pour the butter sauce into the cavity. Place stuffed tomatoes or stuffed peppers around the rice. Sprinkle with grated Parmesan cheese and serve immediately.

Jaja s Gljivama
Eggs with Mushrooms

½ lb. mushrooms
2 tbsp. butter
1 tbsp. onion
½ tsp. chopped parsley
8 eggs, well beaten
salt and pepper to taste

Wash and thinly slice the mushrooms. Heat the butter in a large skillet. Sauté the onion in the butter until lightly browned. Add the mushrooms and sauté lightly. Season with salt and pepper. Sprinkle with chopped parsley. Pour the eggs over the mushrooms and scramble. Serves 4.

Kajgana sa Gljivama
Mushroom Omelette

1 c. sliced mushrooms
1 tbsp. butter
½ c. sour cream
6 egg yolks, well beaten
6 egg whites, stiffly beaten
1 tbsp. flour
salt and pepper to taste

Combine the sliced mushrooms, butter, sour cream, salt and pepper. Add the well beaten egg yolks and flour. Fold in the stiffly beaten egg whites. Melt enough lard or shortening to cover the bottom and sides of a large skillet. Pour the batter into the pan and cook over moderate heat until fluffy and golden on the underside. Loosen the edges. Slip a spatula underneath the omelette and fold one half over the other. Serve on a warmed serving platter. Serves 3 or 4.

Riža sa Sirom
Rice and Cheese

1 ½ c. rice
4 tbsp. butter
¼ c. grated Parmesan cheese

Cook the rice in salted boiling water until soft. Melt the butter in a large saucepan. Add the cooked rice. Fry the rice for a few minutes. The rice must be soft, but whole. When it has become crisped on the outside, but remains tender on the inside, place it in a serving bowl. Sprinkle with grated Parmesan cheese and serve.

Kajgana sa Kamenicama
Oyster Omelette

1 c. oysters
1 tbsp. flour
2 tbsp. butter
1 tbsp. lemon juice
1 c. sour cream
6 eggs, well beaten
salt and pepper to taste

Chop the oysters finely. Melt the butter over low heat. Increase the heat and brown the flour lightly in the butter. Add the lemon juice and sour cream to make a thick sauce. Season with salt and pepper. Fold in the eggs and add the oysters. Melt enough oil or shortening to cover the bottom and sides of a large skillet. Pour the batter into the skillet and fry the omelette until the underside is golden and the top is well done. Do not overcook. Slip the spatula underneath the omelette and fold one half over the other. Serve on a heated platter. Serves 3 or 4.

Sataraš od Jaja sa Suhom Kobasicom
Egg and Sausage Satarash

2 small onions
3 tbsp. butter
2 green peppers
1 smoked sausage
3 ripe tomatoes
8 eggs
1 tsp. paprika
salt and pepper to taste

Finely chop the vegetables and slice the smoked sausage. Sauté the onion in the hot butter until golden brown. Add the vegetables and smoked sausage. Simmer over medium heat for about fifteen minutes. Add the eggs to the mixture. Season with salt, pepper and paprika and scramble. Serves 4-5.

Hladni Umak od Sira
Cheese Sauce

Sauces

Sauces can play an important role in the composition of a meal. They serve as an accompaniment to various dishes, enhancing even the most humble preparations, or they may prove to be an excellent way to decorate less dramatic foods.

Sauces are appropriate for enhancing the flavor and texture of egg, meat, poultry, game, fish or vegetable dishes. Although they can vary from mild to very spicy according to the dish's main ingredients, they must never overpower or disguise the basic essence of the dishes that they are served with.

We present some basic sauces which may suit various types of dishes. These can be adapted by the use of the imagination and are intended to serve only as a sampling of the variety of sauces that can accompany Croatian foods.

The basic white sauces *Umak od Mlijeka* and *Bijeli Umak* go very well with chicken, egg, fish, veal or vegetable dishes. They may be flavored with grated cheese, eggs, mushrooms, wine, butter or a variety of herbs and spices.

Croatian Tomato Sauce, a delicious blend of green peppers, tomatoes and flavorings can accompany meats and poultry. It can also be used as a shortcut in preparing stews, ragouts and with numerous stuffed vegetable dishes.

Although at first glance our garlic sauce may appear to contain an excessive amount of flavoring, it need not intimidate anyone. Garlic loses its ferocity during the cooking process. The result is a wonderful sauce that is not at all out of place with lamb, pork or vegetable dishes.

The Lemon Butter Sauce is an excellent sauce for seafoods. Its tart flavor will enhance the flavor of any baked, broiled or grilled fish. The Rich Meat Gravy is as fine as its name implies. Its flavor can turn even the most humble cut of meat into a dining experience. It is certain to bring the chef compliments from his or her family and guests. Its richness can only be equalled by a fine mushroom sauce. The great abundance of mushrooms in Croatian forests helps to account for its popularity in cooking.

The sauces which are included in this collection demonstrate how simple, natural ingredients can be utilized to create fine sauces.

Umak od Kopra
Dill Sauce

3 tbsp. butter
2 tbsp. flour
½ c. sour cream
1½ tbsp. chopped dill
½ c. onion, finely chopped
1 c. beef stock
salt and pepper to taste

Melt the butter over low heat. Sauté the onion in the butter until it becomes golden brown. Make a golden roux by stirring the flour in gradually. Thin the roux by adding beef stock a little at a time. Stir constantly to avoid lumps. Add the sour cream. Continue stirring until smooth. Add the dill and season with salt. Bring the sauce to a quick boil and remove from heat. Continue to stir until it becomes very smooth and creamy. Serve with boiled or roasted meat.

Umak od Jaja
Egg Sauce

2 eggs, hard cooked
3 tbsp. butter
3 tbsp. flour
1 c. milk
¼ tsp. nutmeg
salt and pepper to taste

Melt the butter. Add the flour and cook for two or three minutes, stirring constantly. Do not allow the flour to brown. Gradually add the milk, stirring well so that lumps do not form. Simmer slowly until the sauce thickens. Add salt, pepper, nutmeg and finely chopped eggs. When the sauce begins to boil, remove from heat and serve immediately.

Umak od Maslaca
Butter Sauce

2 tbsp. butter
1½ c. chicken stock
2 tbsp. flour
salt and pepper to taste

Melt the butter over low heat. Raise the heat a little and add the flour gradually, stirring constantly so that lumps do not form. Add the chicken stock. Continue stirring. Season with salt and pepper and cook until the sauce thickens. Serve hot with vegetables, rice or boiled fish.

Umak od Paprike i Krastavaca
Pepper and Cucumber Sauce

1 medium cucumber
2 c. yoghurt
2 tbsp. oil
2 tbsp. vinegar
1 small red pepper, finely chopped
3 cloves garlic
salt and pepper to taste

Peel the cucumber and cut it into very thin slices. Season with salt and allow to sit, covered, for 20-30 minutes. This will allow the cucumbers to release some water. Drain the water from the cucumbers and season them with pepper. Add the finely chopped red pepper and garlic. Mix the oil and vinegar well. Pour this over the cucumbers. Add the yoghurt and mix well. This is an excellent sauce to serve with cold fish dishes. It can also be used in potato salads.

Riblji Umak
Fish Sauce

¼ c. fish stock
½ c. cream
4 egg yolks, well beaten
juice of 1 lemon
¼ tsp. sugar
salt and pepper to taste

Mix the cream into the well beaten egg yolks. Heat the fish stock and add slowly to the cream mixture. Beat well. Stir in the lemon juice. Season with salt and pepper. Beat the sauce for a few more minutes until it thickens. Add the sugar and refrigerate. Serve cold.

Umak od Mlijeka
Milk Sauce

3 tbsp. butter
1 c. warm milk
½ tbsp. flour
salt and pepper to taste

Melt the butter over low heat. Increase the heat and stir in the flour to make a white roux. Do not allow the flour to brown. Add the hot milk a tablespoon at a time, stirring constantly. Season with salt and pepper. Simmer the sauce gently until it thickens. Serve hot with vegetable, egg, fish or poultry dishes.

Umak od Hrena
Horseradish Sauce

½ tbsp. horseradish,
finely grated
2 tbsp. butter
2 tbsp. flour
1 c. milk
salt and pepper to taste

Melt the butter over low heat. Add the flour, a little at a time, stirring constantly so that lumps do not form. Allow this roux to brown, then stir in the milk gradually. Add the horseradish and season with salt and pepper. Continue cooking until the sauce thickens. Serve this sauce with pork.

Umak od Kiselih Krastavaca
Pickle Sauce

2 diced pickles
2 tbsp. oil
2 tbsp. flour
½ tbsp. finely chopped onion
½ c. sour cream
1 c. beef stock
salt and pepper to taste

Heat the oil over low heat and brown the onion in it. Stir in the flour to make a golden brown roux. Add the diced pickles to the roux. Slowly add the beef stock and sour cream, stirring constantly. Season with salt and pepper. Allow to thicken over medium heat. Garnish with a little chopped parsley before serving with boiled or baked fish.

Umak od Gljiva sa Vinom
Mushroom Wine Sauce

½ lb. mushrooms, chopped
2 tbsp. butter
2 tbsp. flour
1 tbsp. lemon juice
½ c. white wine
2 ½ c. hot beef stock
salt and pepper to taste

Melt half the butter over low heat. Stir in the flour. Cook for a minute or two, stirring constantly. Pour two cups of hot beef stock into the roux, a little at at time, stirring constantly so that lumps do not form. Melt the remaining butter in another saucepan and add the finely chopped mushrooms. Season with salt and pepper and allow to cook for 10-15 minutes. Add the remaining beef stock, the lemon juice and the wine to the mushrooms. Bring the mushroom sauce to a boil. Add the mushroom mixture to the roux and continue cooking for a few more minutes. This sauce makes an excellent accompaniment to boiled meat.

Umak od Kiselog Vrhnja
Sour Cream Sauce

2 c. sour cream
3 tbsp. butter
3 tbsp. flour
3 tbsp. lemon juice
½ tsp. minced parsley
salt and pepper to taste

Melt the butter over low heat. Increase the heat. Add the flour, stirring constantly. Season with salt and pepper. Cook for a few minutes. Do not stop stirring. When the roux has thickened, add the sour cream, a spoonful at a time. Remove from heat. When the sauce has cooled, add the parsley and lemon juice and beat well. Serve warm or cold. However, do not reheat this sauce or it may curdle.

Umak od Limuna
Lemon Sauce

3 tbsp. butter
3 tbsp. lemon juice
1 tsp. grated lemon rind
1 tsp. sugar
1 tbsp. chopped parsley
salt and pepper to taste

Melt the butter over low heat. Mix the lemon rind, sugar and parsley with the lemon juice. Stir this mixture into the melted butter. When all the ingredients are well mixed, remove from heat. Season with salt and pepper. Serve hot with cooked vegetables or with baked fish.

Umak od Vina
Wine Gravy

½ c. beef roast pan drippings
¼ c. flour
1½ c. beef stock
½ c. red table wine
salt and pepper to taste

Heat the pan drippings. Stir in the flour and cook over medium heat for a few minutes. Add the beef stock, stirring constantly so that lumps do not form. Stir in the wine. Season with salt and pepper. Cook until the sauce thickens. Serve with roast beef or lamb.

Umak za Ražanj
Gilled Meat Sauce

1 c. currant jelly
2 medium onions
½ c. Dijon-type mustard

Finely chop the onion. Mix all ingredients and heat to just below the boiling point. Serve with grilled meats or with *ražnjići* and *čevapčići*.

Umak od Gljiva
Mushroom Sauce

½ med. onion, sliced
½ lb. mushrooms, sliced
1 tbsp. butter
1 tbsp. chopped parsley
1½ tbsp. flour
1 tbsp. lemon juice
½ c. sour cream
salt and pepper to taste

Melt the butter over low heat. Brown the mushrooms and onion in the butter. Slowly stir in the flour and parsley. Add the lemon juice and sour cream, stirring constantly. Season with salt and pepper. Remove from heat when the sauce has thickened and serve hot.

Umak od Peršina
Parsley Sauce

1 tbsp. minced parsley
2 tbsp. butter
3 tbsp. flour
2 c. chicken stock
salt and pepper to taste

Melt the butter over very low heat. Add the flour, slowly, stirring constantly to avoid lumps. Add the stock, a little at a time. Season with salt and pepper. Continue stirring. Stir in the parsley. Mix well and serve immediately. This sauce can be served with cooked vegetables, but it is especially suitable for fish.

Bijeli Umak
White Sauce

3 tbsp. butter
2 tbsp. flour
½ tsp. vinegar
1 egg yolk
1 c. milk
salt and pepper to taste

Melt the butter in a medium saucepan over low heat. Add the flour slowly. Stir to make a smooth white roux. Do not allow the flour to brown. Add the milk gradually so that lumps do not form. Cook for two or three minutes. Beat the egg yolk well and add it slowly to the sauce. Allow the sauce to simmer a minute or two and season with salt and pepper. Stir in the vinegar. Serve with cooked vegetables.

Zeleni Umak
Green Sauce

½ tbsp. fresh chervil
2 tbsp. fresh parsley
2 tbsp. fresh sorrel
½ c. cream
2 c. clear stock
¼ c. butter
4 tbsp. flour
salt and pepper to taste

Chop all the herbs very finely. Melt the butter over low heat. Stir in the flour to make a smooth white roux. Thin the roux by adding the stock and cream slowly, stirring constantly. Add the herbs. Cook until the sauce thickens. Season with salt and pepper. Serve with grilled or baked fish.

Zelena
Green Sauce

5 canned anchovies
1 tsp. powdered onion
3 tbsp. oil
3 small pickles, chopped
3 tbsp. lemon juice
3 tbsp. mustard
1 tsp. chopped parsley
salt and pepper to taste

Mash the anchovies. Add the mustard and oil. When well blended, add onion, parsley, pickles and lemon juice. Season with salt and pepper. Continue stirring until well blended. Beat until the sauce becomes smooth and creamy. This sauce can be served with baked or broiled fish.

Bijeli Umak od Luka
White Onion Sauce

¼ c. onion, chopped
3 tbsp. butter
2 c. milk
3 tbsp. flour
salt and pepper to taste

Sauté the onion in the butter in a medium saucepan. Add the flour and sauté for about a minute, stirring constantly. Do not allow the flour to brown. Remove from heat. Stir in the milk, a little at a time. Return the sauce to the stove and cook until it thickens. Season with salt and pepper. Pass through a sieve before serving, if necessary. Serve hot.

Umak od Crnog Vina
Red Wine Sauce

½ c. red wine
3 tbsp. lemon juice
1 tsp. brown sugar
3 tbsp. flour
1 c. hot beef stock
3 tbsp. butter
salt and pepper to taste

Melt the butter over low heat. Stir in the flour. Add the hot stock, gradually, stirring constantly. When the sauce has thickened, stir in the brown sugar. Add the wine and mix well. Season with salt and pepper. Remove from heat. Stir in the lemon juice. Serve hot with grilled or baked fish.

Umak od Sira
Parmesan Sauce

3 egg yolks
2 tbsp. flour
2 tbsp. butter
3 tbsp. sour cream
1 c. beef stock
½ c. grated Parmesan cheese

Add the flour and beef stock alternately to the well beaten egg yolks, beating after each addition. Place in the top of a double boiler and heat well, stirring constantly. Do not allow to boil. Add half the butter and the sour cream. Mix well. Add the remaining butter and the Parmesan cheese. Continue stirring until the sauce thickens. Remove from heat when the sauce reaches the boiling point. Serve hot.

Umak od Česnjaka
Garlic Sauce

3 tbsp. butter or oil
3 tbsp. flour
½ c. sour cream
5-6 cloves garlic, minced
1 c. beef stock
salt and pepper to taste

Mix the salt and pepper with the garlic. Heat the oil over medium heat and stir in the flour. When the flour begins to brown, stir in the garlic slowly, mixing well so that lumps do not form. Dilute the roux with the beef stock. Allow to cook for about three minutes. Add the sour cream and bring the sauce to a boil, stirring constantly until creamy. Remove from heat and serve immediately. This sauce can be served with pork, lamb or fish, but may also be served with cooked vegetables.

Umak od Hrena sa Vrhnjem
Cream Horseradish Sauce

2 tbsp. grated horseradish
1 tsp. sugar
1½ tsp. wine vinegar
½ c. heavy cream

Mix together the wine vinegar, horseradish and sugar. Add the cream and stir well. Serve this sauce with cold meat cuts or with pork.

Umak od Sardela
Sardine Sauce

2 salted sardines
2 tbsp. oil
2 tbsp. flour
½ tbsp. minced onion
juice of half a lemon
1 tsp. chopped parsley
1 c. water

Cook the sardines and mash them, or mash two canned sardines. Fry the onion in the oil. When it begins to brown, stir in the flour to make a thick roux. Add the water gradually, stirring constantly. Allow to simmer slowly for a few minutes. Add the sardines, lemon juice and parsley. ½ c. sour cream may be added just before serving the sauce.

Umak od Jabuka
Apple Sauce

2 sour apples
2 tbsp. butter
2 tbsp. flour
¼ c. beef stock
1 tsp. lemon juice
1 tsp. lemon rind
2 tbsp. sugar
2 tbsp. sour cream

Peel and grate the apples and sauté them in butter for approximately five minutes. Stir the flour into the beef stock and add to the apples. When the sauce begins to thicken, stir in the lemon juice, lemon rind and sugar. Allow to simmer for another ten minutes. Remove from heat. Stir in the sour cream, return to heat and allow to reach just below the boiling point.

Hladni Umak od Sira
Cheese Sauce

½ c. blue cheese
½ c. soft cheese [Zdenka Sir]
½ c. cottage cheese
½ c. sour cream
1 tbsp. minced onion
1 tbsp. mustard
salt, pepper and paprika to taste

Allow the cheeses to come to room temperature. Blend in a blender or food processor until smooth and creamy. Add the remaining ingredients. Beat until fluffy. Chill. Makes an excellent dip to serve with crackers or chips or for dipping fresh vegetables.

Illustrated on page 125.

Umak od Poriluka
Leek Sauce

3 leeks
2 tbsp . butter
1 tbsp. flour
½ c. beef stock
3 tbsp. sour cream
½ tbsp. wine vinegar
salt and pepper to taste

Wash the leeks and cut them into small rings. Sauté in the butter for five minutes. Add the flour and cook for another minute. Stir in the beef stock and the vinegar and simmer until the leeks become tender. Pass the sauce through a sieve or blend in a blender. Add the sour cream. Place back on the heat and allow to reach just below the boiling point.

Umak od Sardelica
Anchovy Sauce

6-8 canned anchovies
3 eggs, hard cooked
¼ c. olive oil
¼ c. vinegar
1 tsp. chopped parsley
2 tbsp. butter
½ c. bread crumbs
2 tbsp. flour
1 c. boiling water
salt and pepper to taste

Combine and sieve the anchovies and eggs. Melt the butter over medium heat. Stir in the flour to make a white roux. Add the water slowly, stirring constantly. When the sauce is smooth and creamy, add the egg and anchovy mixture. Season with salt, pepper and parsley. Mix the breadcrumbs, vinegar and oil together well. Add this mixture to the sauce. Allow the sauce to cook for a minute or two longer before serving. Anchovy sauce is an excellent accompaniment to fried or baked fish.

Umak od Krastavaca
Cucumber Sauce

½ lb. cucumbers
2 tbsp. oil
2 tbsp. flour
1 tbsp. minced onion
1 c. water
1 tsp. vinegar
½ c. sour cream
1 tsp. chopped parsley
salt and pepper to taste

Peel and slice the cucumbers. Season with salt and pepper. Make a white roux of the flour and oil. Sauté the onion in a little fat. Add the onion and the water to the roux and allow it to cook for a few minutes. Drain the cucumbers and add them to the roux. Add the vinegar. Allow the sauce to cook for another ten or fifteen minutes. Stir in the sour cream and parsley just before serving. Serve with boiled or grilled fish.

Umak od Rajčica
Croatian Tomato Sauce

2 lb. green peppers
2 lb. potatoes
6 tbsp. oil
1 c. onion, chopped
¼ c. diced smoked bacon
salt and paprika to taste

Wash and core the green peppers and cut them into strips. Peel and quarter the tomatoes. Heat the oil over medium heat. Brown the bacon and onion in the hot oil. Season with paprika and salt. Mix the tomatoes and green peppers. Allow this mixture to simmer over low heat until a rich sauce is formed. Stir frequently, adding water as required. Croatian Tomato Sauce may be served with almost any type of meat, with many stuffed vegetables, and it may be substituted for fresh green peppers and tomatoes in many recipes.

Illustrated on page 101.

Umak od Maslina
Olive Sauce

12 pitted green olives
1 ½ tbsp. olive oil
5 anchovy fillets
3 c. clear stock
2 tbsp. flour
salt and pepper to taste

Heat the olive oil over medium heat. Add the flour, stirring constantly. Allow the roux to turn an even brown color. Slowly add the stock and bring the mixture to a boil. Continue stirring. Lower the heat and allow the sauce to cook for a few minutes. Finely chop the olives and the anchovy fillets. Add them to the sauce. Season the sauce with salt and pepper. This tangy sauce is excellent with lamb. It can also be served with grilled or baked fish dishes.

Fini Umak od Mesa
Rich Meat Gravy

½ c. cooked beef, minced
½ c. cooked pork, minced
1 onion, chopped
2 c. beef stock
½ c. red wine
2 bay leaves
2 tsp. minced garlic
1 clove
marrow from 3 large cooked beef bones
salt and pepper to taste

Remove the marrow from the beef bones. Add the meat, beef marrow, onion, clove, garlic and bay leaves to the beef stock in a medium saucepan. Season with salt and pepper. Simmer gently, covered, for approximately half an hour. Add the wine and simmer for another 15 minutes until the gravy is rich and creamy. If necessary, this sauce may be reheated, but do not allow it to come to a boil. Serve with any roasted meat.

Zagrebačka Salata
Zagreb Salad

Salads

Croatia is a climatic haven for the cultivation of vegetables. Mushrooms, tomatoes, cucumbers, red and green peppers and cabbage make favorite side dishes. These vegetables are as important to the meal as is the selection of the meat to be served.

Green salads of various types usually accompany the main course of a Croatian meal. They may be served raw in combinations of fresh, crisp radishes, green, red and yellow peppers, onions, mushrooms, tomatoes and cucumbers.

Lettuce and cabbage are favorite salad vegetables, frequently served alone or as the base for tossed salads. To add zest and flavor, salads are dressed simply with olive oil, vinegar, lemon juice or sour cream and various seasonings.

A dressing which is in almost every cook's repertoire is the popular Sour Cream Dressing. A variation of the standard oil and vinegar dressing is Olive Oil and Lemon Dressing. It will add a tartness to any fresh salad. A refined dressing that is certain to add flavor to a salad is the delectable White Wine Dressing.

The simple *Salata od Krastavaca*, Croatian Cucumber Salad, consists of thinly sliced cucumbers which are seasoned with salt, pepper and garlic and smothered in sour cream. Other salads are prepared with green and red peppers, raw or baked, cut into strips or rings and served alone or with tomatoes and onions. Eggs, cooked meats and fish are frequently added to salads as garnishes.

Istarska Salata combines head lettuce with a variety of vegetables, hard cooked eggs, cooked shrimp, and lobster meat. The Dalmatian Seafood Salad makes an excellent first course on a warm summer day. *Zagrebačka Salata* is a mélange of fresh garden vegetables dressed with vinegar and bits of smoked bacon.

Srijemska Salata
Srijem Salad

½ lb. tomatoes
2 green peppers
2 tbsp. oil
2 tbsp. vinegar
1 cucumber
1 large onion
1 tsp. chopped parsley
salt and pepper to taste

Wash and slice the vegetables. Mix them together. Combine the oil, vinegar, parsley, salt and pepper in a small bottle and shake well. Pour this dressing over the salad.

Salata od Špinata
Spinach Salad

12 oz. fresh spinach
6 slices bacon
3 small onions, sliced
1 c. sliced mushrooms
3 tbsp. lemon juice
6 tablespoons oil
1 clove garlic, crushed
salt and pepper to taste

Wash and drain the spinach well. Fry the bacon until crisp. Drain the fat and dice into small pieces. Sprinkle the fried bacon over the spinach leaves. Add the onion and mushrooms. Combine the lemon juice, oil, garlic, salt and pepper in a small bottle. Shake well. Pour over the salad and toss. Serve immediately.

Salata od Pečenih Paprika
Baked Green Pepper Salad

6 firm green peppers
1 tsp. minced garlic
2 tbsp. vinegar
2 tbsp. oil
salt and pepper to taste

Wash and wipe the green peppers. Place in a well greased pan and bake at 450° for about ten minutes. Allow to cool slightly. Peel the baked peppers. Remove the seeds and cut into strips or cubes. Add the garlic, salt, pepper, vinegar, and oil. Mix well.

Endivija Salata
Endive Salad

1 head endive lettuce
3 tbsp. oil
3 tbsp. vinegar
2 hard cooked eggs
1 clove garlic, minced
salt, pepper, and paprika to taste
1 tbsp. chopped parsley

Wash the endive and tear the leaves into pieces. Season with salt and pepper. Finely mash the eggs and add them to the oil and vinegar. Season the dressing with garlic, paprika and parsley. Mix or shake well. Pour over the salad and toss well.

Salata od Krastavaca
Croatian Cucumber Salad

4 large cucumbers
2 tbsp. oil
1 tsp. minced garlic
¾ c. sour cream
salt and pepper to taste

Wash the cucumbers and peel them. Slice the whole cucumber down the center. Keeping the two halves together, slice as thinly as desired. Season with salt, and pepper and refrigerate for at least half an hour. Drain. Pour the sour cream over the drained cucumbers. Add the garlic, salt, pepper, and oil. Mix well.

Zelena Salata sa Kiselim Mlijekom
Lettuce with Buttermilk Dressing

1 head lettuce
1 c. buttermilk
4 cloves garlic, minced
1 hard cooked egg
2 tbsp. oil
salt and pepper to taste

Wash the lettuce and tear the leaves into pieces. Season lightly with salt. Mash the egg yolks and combine with the oil, garlic, and pepper. Add the buttermilk and chopped egg whites. Mix well. Pour over the lettuce and toss well.

Slavonska Seljačka Salata
Slavonian Onion Salad

2 large onions
2 green onions
½ c. smoked bacon, diced
salt and pepper to taste

Slice the onions and green onions into rings. Place the rings into a deep bowl. Season with salt and pepper. Allow the onions to sit for a least an hour. This will soften the onions. Place the diced bacon in a small skillet and fry in its own fat. When the bacon is well crisped, remove from heat. Without draining the fat, scald the onion with the hot bacon. Serve immediately. This salad goes very well with cold meat, especially roast pork. It can also be served with fresh sausage.

Zelena Salata sa Jogurtom
Lettuce Salad With Yogurt Dressing

1 large head lettuce
½ c. yogurt or buttermilk
2 tbsp. olive oil
salt and pepper to taste

Wash and tear the lettuce into bite-sized chunks. Place in a serving bowl. Season with salt and pepper. Combine the yogurt and olive oil. Pour this dressing over the lettuce. Mix gently until the lettuce is well coated.

Salata od Krastavaca i Luka
Cucumber and Onion Salad

2 large cucumbers
2 medium onions
3 tbsp. oil
3 tbsp. vinegar
salt and pepper to taste

Peel the cucumbers and onions. Slice them thinly. Season with salt and pepper. Combine the oil and vinegar and shake well. Pour this mixture over the salad. Sour cream may be substituted for the oil and vinegar. If desired, the salad may be garnished with a little ground paprika just before serving.

Salata od Poriluka
Leek Salad

½ lb. leeks
3 tbsp. olive oil
1 tbsp. wine vinegar
10 black olives, pitted
salt and pepper to taste

Wash the leeks and slice them lengthwise. Cook them in boiling salted water until tender. Drain. Place in a long serving dish. Mix the olive oil, vinegar and salt and pepper to make a smooth dressing. Pour the dressing over the leeks and garnish with black olives. Serve immediately. This salad goes especially well with baked and broiled fish.

Zagrebačka Salata
Zagreb Salad

2 small tomatoes, sliced
1 medium head of lettuce
1 tsp. chopped fresh parsley
½ c. sliced fresh mushrooms
1 small cucumber, sliced
1 green pepper, chopped
1 stalk green onion, chopped
¼ c. sliced radishes
2 tbsp. vinegar
¼ c. smoked bacon, diced
salt and pepper to taste

Clean and wash the vegetables. Place them in a bowl and season with salt. Fry the bacon in its own fat. Add the vinegar to the bacon, but do not remove from heat. Pour over the salad, toss well and serve immediately. Season with salt, pepper and parsley just before serving.

Salata od Mahuna i Artičoke
Green Bean and Artichoke Salad

3 artichokes
1 lb. green beans
4 tbsp. butter
½ tsp. garlic powder
salt to taste

Wash the artichokes and remove the stems and leaf ends. Place in a deep pot with enough water to cover. Add one tablespoon of salt and cook for 35-45 minutes until tender. Drain. Cube the artichokes and cook for another five minutes in a little water. Clean the beans and cook for twenty minutes to half an hour until tender. Drain the beans and place them in a large serving bowl. Melt the butter over low heat. Pour the butter over the beans. Garnish by arranging the artichokes around the beans. Season with garlic powder and more salt, if desired.

Istarska Salata
Istrian Salad

1 head of lettuce
2-3 tomatoes
1 cucumber
1 medium onion
1 small bunch radishes
2 hard cooked eggs
6 olives
1 green pepper
¼ c. cooked lobster meat
¼ c. cooked shrimp
3 tbsp. lemon juice
3 tbsp. olive oil
1 tsp. powdered garlic
salt to taste

Wash the vegetables. Slice the tomatoes, cucumber, onion, green pepper, radishes and eggs. Halve the olives. Chop the lobster meat. Add the shrimp and lobster meat to the vegetables. Combine the lemon juice, olive oil, salt and powdered garlic. Mix well. Arrange the ingredients on a few lettuce leaves in a deep bowl. Pour the lemon juice and olive oil dressing over the salad. Do not toss.

Salata od Graha
Bean Salad

½ lb. cooked beans
4 tbsp. oil
3 small onions, sliced
1 tbsp. parsley, finely chopped
1 tbsp. celery leaves, chopped
3 tbsp. wine vinegar
salt, pepper and paprika to taste

Rinse the onion in several waters so it will not be too strong. Place the onions and beans in a large bowl and add the oil, stirring constantly. Add the parsley, celery, salt, pepper and paprika. Gently mix everything. Finally, while still stirring, add the wine vinegar. Chill for at least an hour before serving.

Krumpir Salata
Potato Salad I

½ lb. cooked potatoes
½ c. sliced pickles
3 hard cooked eggs
1 large green pepper
1 tsp. chopped parsley
¼ lb. tomatoes
1 onion
½ c. sour cream
¼ c. smoked bacon, diced
salt, pepper and paprika to taste
lettuce leaves and chopped parsley for garnish

Wash the vegetables. Slice the potatoes, onion and green pepper. Peel and dice the tomatoes. Peel and slice the eggs. Place the vegetables and egg in a serving dish. Add the salt, pepper, paprika and parsley to the sour cream. Fry the bacon in its own fat. Drain and add to the sour cream mixture. Pour this mixture over the vegetables and eggs. Stir gently, but coat everything well with the sour cream dressing. Serve on lettuce leaves. Garnish with chopped parsley.

Salata od Krumpira
Potato Salad II

½ lb. cooked potatoes
2 small sour apples, diced
2 pickles, chopped
2 carrots
2 stalks celery
1 tbsp. parsley
½ small head lettuce
1 c. cooked meat
¾ c. mayonnaise
2 tbsp. wine
salt, pepper and paprika to taste

Dice the potatoes and apples. Grate the carrots. Chop the meat, pickles and celery. Cut the lettuce into strips. Mix all the ingredients together and refrigerate for at least two hours. Garnish with lettuce, red beets or sliced hard cooked eggs.

Punjene Rajčice na Salati
Suffed Tomato Salad

6 large ripe tomatoes
2 hard cooked eggs
1 tbsp. vinegar
1 onion
1 tbsp. olive oil
¼ c.   tuna or sardines
salt and pepper to taste

Coarsely chop the eggs. Finely chop the fish and onion. Combine with the eggs in a large bowl. Add the olive oil and vinegar and season with salt and pepper. Core the tomatoes. Fill each with the fish mixture. Serve each tomato on a lettuce leaf.

Salad Dressings

Začin od Limuna i Maslinovog Ulja
Olive Oil and Lemon Dressing

5 tbsp. olive oil
3 tbsp. lemon juice
1 tsp. paprika
salt and pepper to taste

Add the seasonings to the olive oil. Slowly add the lemon juice a drop at a time, stirring well after each addition.

Začin od Česnjaka
Garlic Dressing

1 tsp. minced garlic
3 tbsp. olive oil
3 tbsp. vinegar
1 tbsp. mustard
salt and pepper to taste

Combine the olive oil and vinegar and mix well. Add the minced garlic and mustard. Season with salt and pepper. Shake well in a small bottle until all ingredients are combined. Pour over the salad just before serving.

Začin od Kiselog Vrhnja
Sour Cream Dressing

1 c. sour cream
1 egg yolk
1 tbsp. mustard
1 tsp. lemon juice
1 tsp. ground parsley
salt and pepper to taste

Mix the first three ingredients in a deep bowl. Season with salt and pepper. Add the lemon juice and whip until very smooth and creamy. If necessary, dilute with a few drops of milk. Stir in the ground parsley just before serving. Do not allow this dressing to sit on the salad.

Začin od Ulja i Octa
Oil and Vinegar Dressing

½ c. salad oil
2 tbsp. vinegar
2 tbsp. lemon juice
½ tsp. salt
½ tsp. minced garlic

Combine all the ingredients in a small bottle. Shake well before using.

Motički Začin
Bacon Dressing

¼ c. smoked bacon, diced
2 tbsp. vinegar
salt and pepper to taste

Fry the bacon in its own fat until it becomes crisp. Do not drain. Add the vinegar. Season with salt and pepper. Mix well. Serve with leafy salads, but do not allow the dressing to sit on the salad before serving.

Začin od Bijelog Vina
White Wine Dressing

3 tbsp. olive oil
3 tbsp. dry white wine
1 tsp. lemon juice
½ tsp. paprika
salt and pepper to taste

Combine the seasonings. Add them to the oil. Add the wine and mix well. Add the lemon juice drop by drop stirring constantly. Use with any green salad.

Salata od Cikle
Beet Salad

2 lbs. red beets
6 tbsp. wine vinegar
3 tbsp. water
2 tsp. sugar
1 bay leaf
1 medium onion
1 ½ tbsp. oil
1 clove garlic, thinly sliced
salt to taste

Clean the beets well and cook in boiling water until tender. Boil the vinegar, water, sugar, bay leaf and salt together for about five minutes. Peel the beets and cut them into strips or slices. Slice the onion and separate into rings. Add the onion and garlic to the beets. Pour the oil and cooked vinegar over the vegetables. Pickle the beets in this marinade for several hours before serving.

Salata od Rajčice i Paprike
Pepper and Tomato Salad

3-4 firm ripe tomatoes
3 green peppers
1 small onion
1 tsp. chopped parsley
2 tbsp. olive oil
1 tbsp. vinegar
salt and pepper to taste

Scald the tomatoes and peppers with boiling water. Allow them to sit for a few minutes until the skins come off easily. Cut each pepper into four sections, removing the seeds and ribs. Slice them into thin strips. Slice the onion and tomatoes. Combine the vegetables in a serving bowl. Season with salt and pepper. Add the oil and vinegar and toss well. Sprinkle with parsley before serving.

Salata od Paprike
Pepper Salad

2 sweet green peppers
2 sweet red peppers
2 yellow peppers
2 onions, cut into strips
3 tbsp. olive oil
1 tbsp. lemon juice
salt, pepper and paprika to taste

Place the whole peppers in a deep bowl. Scald with boiling water and allow to sit in the water for about a minute. Drain the water. Remove the seeds and ribs and cut the peppers into strips. Make a dressing from the olive oil, lemon juice, salt, pepper and paprika. Shake well. Place the peppers and onions in a serving bowl. Pour the dressing over them. Mix well. Refrigerate for several hours before serving.

Kupus Salata
Cabbage Salad

1 head cabbage (red or white)
1 carrot
2 tbsp. vinegar
2 tbsp. oil
1 tsp. minced garlic
salt to taste

Finely shred the cabbage and grate the carrot. Season with salt and allow to sit for at least half an hour. Combine the vinegar, oil and garlic. Shake well. Pour this dressing over the salted cabbage and carrot. Allow the cabbage to marinate in this dressing for at least one hour, refrigerated.

Dalmatinska Morska Salata
Dalmatian Seafood Salad

12 oz. cooked crab
12 oz. cooked shrimp
12 oz. cooked squid
1 small red pepper
1 small green pepper
½ c. black olives
6 tbsp. olive oil
4 tbsp. lemon juice
2 tbsp. capers
3 tbsp. chopped parsley
2 cloves garlic, minced
black olives to garnish
lemon slices

Cut the squid into rings approximately three eighths of an inch wide. Combine the squid, crab and shrimp in a large bowl. Add the finely diced peppers and olives. Make a dressing of the oil, lemon juice, capers, parsley and garlic. Season with salt and pepper. Mix well in a small bottle. Pour this dressing over the seafood. Mix lightly. Refrigerate for at least an hour. Garnish with parsley, black olives and lemon slices.

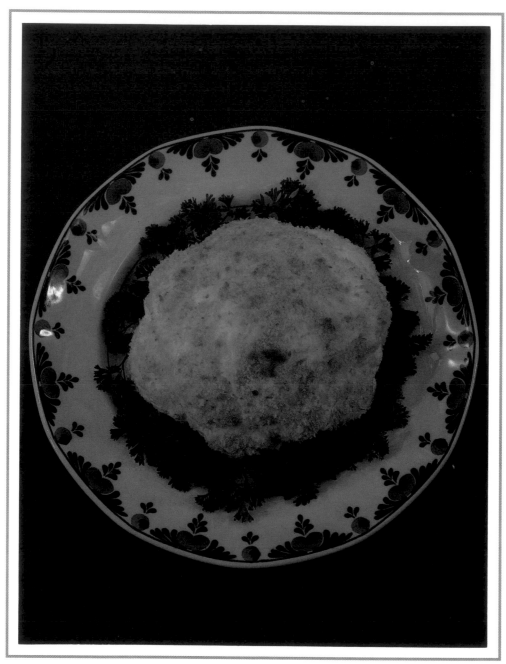

Cvjetača s Vrhnjem
Cauliflower with Sour Cream

Vegetables

Vegetables are frequently served in their natural state in a variety of crisp salads or they may be sautéed in hot butter, stewed, served with a compatible sauce, or simply covered with warm sour cream. They can also be prepared in various combinations as meatless casseroles.

Tomatoes and peppers may be fried, sautéed, baked, stuffed or served in combination with other vegetables. The methods of preparation vary considerably and they can often be quite elaborate. Tomatoes with Eggplant, Green Pepper Satarash and Onions in Tomato Sauce are all popular combinations.

Mushrooms abound in Croatia, growing wild in many regions. Long stretches of richly-wooded forests provide countless varieties. The countless edible species are firmly rooted in the cooking of Croatia and are used in a variety of ways. They are breaded, deep fried, stuffed, baked, sautéed and served with a wide variety of other foods. Mushrooms are added to many dishes to flavor meats, sauces, soups, stews and casseroles. Their rich flavor makes them an excellent condiment in any dish.

Cabbage is a staple in many parts of Croatia, especially in the north. It is served both fresh and pickled as sauerkraut. All types of cabbage are found in the country, including savoy, milan, red and green cabbage and kale. These are prepared in layered casseroles, sautéed in lard or served with smoked meat. They are also deep fried, served with sour cream or used in salads. Sauerkraut often adds zest to casseroles, meat dishes and soups.

Eggplant, asparagus and zucchini are especially popular in Southern Croatia. These vegetables are well suited for stuffing and are often baked with olive oil or sour cream.

Potatoes are an important side dish and are prepared in many ways. Boiled, stuffed, sautéed, baked with cottage cheese, mashed or breaded and fried as croquettes, they provide a fine addition to a well planned meal. They may be served with sour cream, smoked bacon, tomato sauce or smothered in butter.

Croatian cuisine uses diverse vegetables in a variety of enticing, nutritious and often unique dishes which accompany other courses, or which are served as the main course.

Pečene Gljive
Baked Mushrooms

1¾ lb. mushrooms
1 c. sour cream
1 tbsp. chopped parsley
4 small onions, finely chopped
2 tbsp. lemon juice
salt and pepper to taste

Clean the mushrooms well. Place in a well-greased baking dish with the tops upward. Cover with sour cream. Sprinkle with onion, parsley and lemon juice. Season with salt and pepper. Bake at 350° for approximately half an hour.

Pohane Prokule
Deep Fried Sprouts

2 lbs. Brussels sprouts
½ c. flour
2 eggs, well beaten
½ c. bread crumbs
1 tbsp. vinegar
oil for deep frying
salt and pepper to taste

Wash the sprouts. Place them in a large pot. Cover with water and add the vinegar. Season with salt and cook for approximately half an hour until tender. Drain. When the sprouts have cooled, roll in flour seasoned with salt and pepper, dip in the egg and roll in bread crumbs. Fry in hot oil until crisp and golden.

Cvjetača s Vrhnjem
Cauliflower with Sour Cream

1 large head cauliflower
¾ tbsp. salt
2 tbsp. butter
1 tbsp. bread crumbs
1 c. sour cream

Wash the cauliflower and cook it in salted water until tender, but do not overcook. Drain. Place the cauliflower in a buttered dish. Pour the sour cream over it. Sprinkle with bread crumbs. Bake in a moderate oven (350°) for about fifteen minutes.

Pohani Kupus
Fried Cabbage

3 small heads cabbage
½ c. butter or shortening
½ c. flour
2 eggs, slightly beaten
1 c. bread crumbs
salt and pepper to taste

Cut the cabbages in half. Hollow out the centers. Place in enough salted boiling water to cover. Cook for about twenty minutes. Squeeze dry and flatten like cutlets. Sprinkle with salt and pepper. Roll in flour, dip in egg and roll in bread crumbs. Fry in hot butter or shortening until golden brown.

Posavski Krumpir
Potatoes à la Posavina

2 lbs. potatoes
½ c. corn meal
½ c. oil or butter
1 tbsp. chopped parsley
salt and pepper to taste

Peel and quarter the potatoes. Season with salt and pepper and cook in salted boiling water until tender. Drain the cooked potatoes. Roll in corn meal seasoned with salt and pepper. Place the potatoes in a well greased baking dish. Cover with oil or melted butter. Sprinkle with chopped parsley. Bake in a hot oven (425°) until the potatoes begin to turn golden brown. Serve immediately.

Patlidani s Rajčicama
Eggplant with Tomatoes

2 large eggplants, diced
2-3 firm ripe tomatoes
¾ c. butter
1 onion, finely chopped
salt and pepper to taste

Melt the butter over low heat. Increase the heat and fry the eggplant in the hot butter. Add the tomatoes and onion. Stir well. Season with salt and pepper. Cover and allow to simmer for about 20-25 minutes.

Mrkva s Maslacem
Buttered Carrots

5 large carrots
¼ c. butter
1 ¾ tbsp. flour
1 c. water
salt and pepper to taste

Peel the carrots and slice them thinly. Melt the butter in a large skillet over medium heat. Reduce the heat, add the sliced carrots and sauté for five minutes. Season with salt and pepper. Stir in the flour and add water. Cover the skillet and simmer gently for about twenty minutes. Serves 4.

Šparga s Vrhnjem
Sour Cream Asparagus

2 lbs. asparagus
1 tsp. sugar
1 tsp. salt
3 tbsp. butter
1 c. sour cream
¼ c. fine bread crumbs

Peel the asparagus and cook it in salted water to which the sugar and salt have been added. When the asparagus becomes tender, drain. Grease a deep baking dish with the butter and sprinkle with bread crumbs. Place the asparagus in the dish. Cover with the sour cream and sprinkle with the bread crumbs. Bake at 325° for 25-30 minutes.

Rajčice Punjene sa Gljivama
Mushroom-Stuffed Tomatoes

10 small tomatoes
1 lb. sliced mushrooms
¾ c. bread crumbs
¼ c. butter
¼ c. beef stock
2 eggs, well beaten
3 tbsp. chopped onion
2 tbsp. flour
3 tbsp. grated cheese
1 small bunch parsley
salt, pepper and paprika to taste

Hollow the tomatoes. Melt the butter over low heat. Turn up the heat and sauté the onions in the butter until slightly browned. Add the sliced mushrooms. Sprinkle with salt, pepper and paprika. Add the parsley. Simmer until the liquid is reduced. Sprinkle with flour. Dilute with a little beef stock and bring to a boil. Add the eggs. Sprinkle the inside of the hollowed tomatoes with salt and pepper. Stuff with mushrooms. Sprinkle with grated cheese and bread crumbs. Bake at 450° until the cheese is lightly browned. Serve hot as an appetizer or as a side dish.

Zelje s Rezancima
Cabbage and Noodles

1 head cabbage
6 tbsp. shortening or oil
2 tbsp. butter
1 lb. egg noodles
1 tbsp. flour
2 tbsp. sour cream
salt and pepper to taste
chopped parsley or fried bacon bits

Wash and shred the cabbage. Sauté the cabbage in the shortening until golden brown. Cook the noodles in salted water until tender. Melt the butter in a large saucepan. Stir in the flour to make a golden roux. Add the noodles, cabbage and sour cream and cook for a minute or two. Season with salt and pepper. Garnish with ground parsley or bits of fried smoked bacon.

Krumpir s Umakom od Rajčica
Potatoes in Tomato Sauce

2 lbs. cooked potatoes
2 tbsp. butter or margarine
¼ c. chopped onion
2 tbsp. tomato paste
1 tbsp. chopped parsley
1 tbsp. flour
1 c. beef stock
salt and pepper to taste

Slice the potatoes. Melt the butter over low heat. Increase the heat and brown the onion in the butter. Stir in the flour. When the flour begins to brown, add the tomato paste and chopped parsley. Gradually stir in the stock. Season with salt and pepper. Bring the mixture to a boil. Add the potatoes and cook for 3-4 minutes over medium heat. If desired, add a little sugar to the tomato paste before adding it to the roux.

Artičoka s Vinom
Artichokes in Wine

5 medium artichokes
3 tbsp. melted butter
1 c. white wine
1 tbsp. olive oil
1 tbsp. vinegar
salt and pepper to taste

Cook the whole artichokes in salted water for approximately fifteen minutes. Drain and cut into small pieces. Remove the centers and place them in a greased baking dish. Add the wine and butter. Season with salt and pepper. Bake at 450° for 25-30 minutes. Pour olive oil and vinegar over the baked artichokes before serving. Serves 5.

Sataraš od Patlidana i Paprike
Eggplant and Green Pepper Satarash

3 eggplants
9 medium green peppers
1 tsp. minced garlic
1 tsp. chopped parsley
juice of one lemon
1 tbsp. vinegar
¼ c. olive oil
salt and pepper to taste
dash of paprika

Wash the vegetables. Place them in a baking dish and bake whole at 375° for about half an hour. When tender, remove from the oven and allow to cool slightly. Core the peppers and skin the eggplant. Place in a bowl and cover with a damp towel. Allow to cool for about 10 minutes. Slice the green peppers and eggplants. Season with garlic, salt and pepper. Mix the lemon juice and vinegar. Add them to the vegetables. Pour the olive oil over the vegetable satarash. Garnish with paprika and parsley.

Loptice od Krumpira
Potato Balls

2 lbs. potatoes
¾ c. butter or shortening
salt to taste

Peel the potatoes and cut into balls with a melon ball cutter. Boil the potato balls in salted water for 4-5 minutes. Remove and dry them on paper towels. Place the butter in a baking dish and bake the potato balls in a hot oven (400°) for about 20-25 minutes until they become golden. They should look like small round French fries when done. Season with salt and serve hot.

Mahune S Vrhnjem
Green Beans with Sour Cream

1½ lb. green beans
2 tbsp. butter
1 onion, chopped
1 ½ tbsp. flour
1 clove garlic, minced
½ c. hot beef stock
½ c. sour cream
½ tsp. paprika
salt and pepper to taste

Wash the beans and cut them lengthwise. Heat half the butter in a saucepan. Add the chopped onion and sauté for 10-15 minutes. Add the green beans. Season with salt and pepper. Make a golden roux from the remaining butter and the flour. Add the paprika and garlic. Slowly stir in the stock and mix well until smooth. Add this sauce to the beans just before serving. Serve the sour cream separately.

Cvjetača sa Šunkom
Cauliflower with Ham

1 head cauliflower
¾ c. diced ham
¾ c. grated hard cheese
2 eggs, well beaten
1 tbsp. sour cream
1 tbsp. flour
salt and pepper to taste

Wash the cauliflower and cook it in salted water for 10-15 minutes until tender. Break into flowerettes. Place a layer of cauliflower in a well greased baking dish. Put a layer of ham on the cauliflower. Follow this with a layer of cheese. Season each layer with salt and pepper. Continue alternating the ingredients until they are all used up. Beat the eggs. Add the flour and sour cream. Continue beating to make a smooth sauce. Pour this over the cauliflower casserole. Sprinkle the top with grated cheese and bake in a moderate oven 350° for about 20 minutes or until the sauce has thickened.

Mahune s Rajčicama
Green Beans and Tomatoes

1 lb. green beans
4 tbsp. lard or oil
¼ c. onion, chopped
2 cloves garlic, chopped
2 tbsp. parsley, finely chopped
5 firm ripe tomatoes
2 tbsp. bread crumbs
salt and pepper to taste

Sauté the onion in hot oil or lard until it becomes clear, but does not brown. Add the garlic, parsley and green beans and stir well. Slice the tomatoes. Add the sliced tomatoes and bread crumbs to the green beans. Season with salt and pepper. Cover and allow to simmer over moderate heat until the green beans are tender. From time to time, add water as required.

Zelje s Kiselim Vrhnjem
Cabbage in Sour Cream

1 large head cabbage
5 tbsp. butter
2 tbsp. flour
¾ c. sour cream
1 diced roll
salt and pepper to taste

Wash the cabbage well. Tear off the leaves and remove the thick stalks. Cook the leaves in salted water about ten minutes until tender. Remove from water, drain and chop coarsely. Melt the butter over low heat. Stir in the flour slowly, so that lumps do not form. When a golden roux has been made, add the cabbage and season with salt and pepper. Allow to cook for a few minutes. Add the sour cream and cook for a minute or two longer. Melt a little butter and fry the diced roll in it to make croutons. Sprinkle the croutons over the cabbage and serve immediately.

Luk u Umaku od Rajčica
Onion in Tomato Sauce

2 lbs. small onions
2 tbsp. oil
1 c. beef stock
3 tbsp. tomato paste
3 tbsp. water
2 tbsp. butter
1 tbsp. ground parsley
salt and pepper to taste

Peel the onions. Soak them in cold water for about half an hour. Cut the onions into quarters. Fry in hot oil. Melt the butter. Mix the tomato paste with the water and add to the butter with the onions, salt, pepper and parsley. Cook over medium heat until the onions are very tender. Add the beef stock, as required, while cooking so that the sauce does not become too thick.

Grašak u Gnjezdu
Peas in a Nest

6-8 cooked potatoes
2 c. cooked peas
¼ c. milk
2 tbsp. butter or oil
¼ c. smoked bacon
dash of nutmeg
¼ c. sour cream
salt to taste

Mash the potatoes with the butter and nutmeg. Season with salt. Add the milk and mash well. Finely dice the bacon. Line the bottom of individual ovenproof glass serving dishes with it. Fill the dishes with the mashed potatoes. Leave a well in the center for the cooked peas. Add the cooked peas to the centers and dab each with a little butter. Bake at 400° for 8-10 minutes. Garnish each with a teaspoon of sour cream and serve immediately.

Krumpirača sa Sirom
Cheese Potatoes

2 lbs. potatoes
¾ lb. cottage cheese
¾ c. sour cream
¼ lb. sliced smoked bacon
salt and pepper to taste

Peel the potatoes and cook them in salted, boiling water until tender. Cover the bottom of a baking dish with bacon. Place half the cooked potatoes over the bacon. Season with salt and pepper. Combine the cheese and sour cream. Place this mixture over the potatoes. Add the remaining potatoes. Season with salt and pepper. Bake at 450° for approximately an hour. Cover the top of the potatoes with the remaining slices of smoked bacon. Return to the oven and continue to bake until the bacon is very well done. Serve immediately.

Bundevke na Dalmatinski Način
Dalmatian Zucchini

1 lb. zucchini
3 firm ripe tomatoes
1 tbsp. chopped parsley
1 tsp. minced garlic
¾ olive oil
¼ c. water
salt and pepper to taste

Wash the zucchini, but do not peel them. Chop into small cubes. Peel and slice the tomatoes. Grease a deep baking dish with part of the olive oil. Place the zucchini in this dish with part of the olive oil. Cover with the sliced tomato. Season with garlic, parsley, salt and pepper. Mix the remaining olive oil with the water. Pour this mixture over the vegetables. Cover and simmer gently until the zucchini is tender. Do not stir, but shake the saucepan occasionally so that the vegetables do not stick. Serves 4-5.

Gljive sa Špinatom
Mushrooms and Spinach

2 lbs. sliced mushrooms
1 tbsp. minced parsley
2 slices bread, cubed
½ c. milk
¾ c. sour cream
¾ lb. chopped spinach
1 onion, chopped
1 tbsp. olive oil
salt and pepper to taste

Combine the mushrooms with the bread slices which have been soaked in the milk for about 5 minutes. Add the parsley. Cook this mixture over medium heat in a little salted water for about five minutes. Add the spinach and continue to cook over low heat until the liquid evaporates. Sauté the onion in the oil until it begins to brown. Add the mushroom and spinach mixture. Stir in the sour cream. Season with salt and pepper.

Pečena Šparga
Baked Asparagus

1 ½ lb. cooked asparagus
½ c. butter
1 ½ c. water
4 tbsp. flour
¾ c. grated hard cheese
salt and pepper to taste

Melt half the butter over low heat. Increase the heat and brown the flour in the butter. Add the water gradually, stirring constantly. Season with salt and pepper. Cook over low heat for a few minutes until the sauce is smooth and creamy. Place the asparagus and the sauce in a deep baking dish in alternate layers. Sprinkle with cheese. Dot with the remaining butter. Bake at 350° for approximately half an hour. Serve immediately.

Pohane Gljive
Breaded Mushrooms

2 lbs. champignon mushrooms
3 tbsp. flour
2 eggs, well beaten
¾ c. bread crumbs
1 c. butter or oil
fresh parsley
salt and pepper to taste

Wash the mushrooms well. Remove the stems. Season the caps with salt and pepper. Roll each mushroom cap in flour, dip in egg, and roll in the bread crumbs. Be sure that the coating is thick and smooth. Heat the butter or oil in a large skillet and fry the mushrooms until golden. Fry each mushroom as it is coated with the flour, egg and bread crumbs so that the coating does not fall off. Serve the fried mushrooms on a bed of steamed rice and garnish with sprigs of fresh parsley. Breaded mushrooms may be served with a small bowl of sour cream. Breaded mushrooms make an excellent appetizer.

Rumeni Krumpiri
Paprika Potatoes

2 lbs. potatoes
3 tbsp. shortening
3 tbsp. onions, chopped
1 tsp. paprika
3 tbsp. flour
1 ¾ c. water
1 c. sour cream
2 tbsp. tomato paste
salt and pepper to taste

Peel the potatoes and cook in salted, boiling water until tender. Drain and slice the cooked potatoes. Melt the shortening. Brown the onion in the hot shortening. Stir in paprika and flour and cook for about a minute or two. Add water, sour cream, salt, pepper and tomato paste. Bring to a boil. Pour this sauce over the potatoes. Serve immediately.

Špinat u Bijelom Umaku
Creamed Spinach

1 lb. fresh spinach
1 tbsp. melted butter
3 tbsp. bread crumbs
¾ c. sour cream
salt and pepper to taste

Wash the fresh spinach carefully. Place the wet spinach in a saucepan and season with salt and pepper. If you are using frozen spinach, add one quarter cup of water. Cover and cook for ten minutes. Shake the saucepan occasionally. Drain the excess water and pass the spinach through a sieve. Combine with the melted butter. Place the spinach in a warmed serving bowl. Heat the sour cream to just below the boiling point. Pour the sour cream over the spinach. Sprinkle with bread crumbs and serve immediately. Serves 4.

Pirjani Plavi Kupus
Braised Purple Cabbage

½ medium purple cabbage
¼ c. chopped onion
2 tbsp. oil
½ tsp. vinegar
1 apple, thinly sliced
1 tsp. sugar
1 tsp. salt
1 bay leaf
¼ c. water

Wash and roughly chop the cabbage. Heat the oil. Add the chopped onion and sauté until clarified. Add the cabbage, bay leaf, vinegar, apple, sugar and salt. Mix well. Add the water. Cover and simmer for approximately half an hour until the cabbage becomes tender. If necessary, add a little more water. Serve with sausages, pork chops or pork roast.

Punjeni Patliđani
Bosnian Baked Eggplant

5 medium eggplants
1 c. chopped onion
½ c. oil
1 c. chopped green pepper
½ c. chopped tomato
1 tbsp. paprika
2 tbsp. chopped parsley
salt and pepper to taste

Make several slits in each eggplant, but do not cut all the way through. Season with salt. Heat half the oil and fry the chopped onion until it clarifies. Add the chopped green pepper and tomato. Stir in the paprika. When the vegetables have softened, add the chopped parsley and season with salt and pepper. Stuff the eggplants with this mixture by filling the slits. Pour a little oil into a baking dish. Place the stuffed eggplant in this dish and bake for approximately 15 minutes at 350°. Add a little water and continue to bake for another 30 minutes. Pour the following sauce over the eggplant. Return to the oven and bake for another 15 minutes.

Sauce

3. tbsp. flour
3 tbsp. oil
¾ c. tomato juice

Heat the oil. Fry the flour in the hot oil until it begins to brown. Add the tomato juice and stir to make a medium sauce.

Krumpir S Vrhnjem
Potatoes in Sour Cream

1 lb. new potatoes
1 c. sour cream
3 tbsp. butter
2 oz. smoked bacon

Peel and halve the potatoes. Cook them in salted, boiling water until tender. Drain the potatoes and fry them in the hot butter until golden brown. Pour the sour cream over the potatoes and allow to simmer until the potatoes begin to crack. Fry the bacon in its own fat, drain and sprinkle over the potatoes before serving.

Grašak sa Gljivama
Mushrooms and Peas

1 lb. peas
3 tbsp. butter or margarine
2 tbsp. chopped parsley
2 c. sliced mushrooms
1 tbsp. flour
¾ c. onion, finely chopped
1 c. sour cream
salt and pepper to taste

Cook the peas in boiling water until tender. Drain. Fry the onion in the hot butter until it becomes clear. Reduce the heat and add the mushrooms and half the parsley. Sauté over medium heat. When the mushrooms are tender, sprinkle with flour, add a little water and stir gently. Add the peas and season with salt and pepper. Stir in the sour cream. Allow the cream to reach the boiling point. Garnish with the remaining chopped parsley.

Pečeni Kesteni
Roasted Chestnuts

2 lbs. chestnuts
3 oz. butter
1 tbsp. salt

Wash the chestnuts and cut an incision in each. This will keep them from bursting while roasting. Sprinkle a layer of salt on a baking tin and place the chestnuts on the tin. Roast at 475° for about half an hour until they become tender. Remove the chestnuts from the oven and peel off the skins. Cream the butter and serve with the chestnuts.

Patliđani na Žaru
Broiled Eggplant

2 eggplants, halved
6 tbsp. olive oil
2 tbsp. chopped garlic
salt and pepper to taste

Make slits on the sides of the eggplant. Coat them with the olive oil. Season with garlic, salt and pepper. Place the eggplant in a large baking dish and broil for half an hour until tender. Baste frequently with the remaining olive oil while the eggplants are broiling.

Gljive s Maslacem
Buttered Mushrooms

1 lb. mushrooms
4 tbsp. butter
1 onion, chopped
salt and pepper to taste

Wash and thinly slice the mushrooms. Combine the onion and mushrooms and allow them to cook gently over low heat in their own juices. Stir frequently to avoid burning. When the mushrooms are half cooked, add the butter and continue to simmer until they become tender. Season with salt and pepper.

Pirjane Gljive
Stewed Mushrooms

2 lbs. mushrooms, sliced
1 onion, finely chopped
3 tbsp. butter
3 tbsp. flour
1 ¼ c. sour cream
1 tbsp. chopped parsley
salt and pepper to taste

Melt the butter over low heat. Add the mushrooms and chopped onion. Allow to sauté over a mild heat, stirring constantly. When the mushrooms and onions have turned a golden brown, stir in the flour. Add the sour cream. Season with salt and pepper. Simmer slowly for another 20-25 minutes. Sprinkle with parsley before serving. Serves 4-5.

Crnac u Košulji
Black and White Steamed Pudding

Desserts

Dessert after a hearty Croatian meal frequently consists of fresh fruits, a fresh fruit salad, a sweet omelette, *palachinke* or a soufflé. Pastries and enticing cakes are generally served with after dinner coffee at formal meals or on special occasions. There is no need to prepare elaborate desserts for meals in the summer. The abundance and variety of fruits that Croatia produces offer many options for natural desserts.

Many desserts are based on fruit preparations. Fruits find their way into fruit salads which may be spiced with rum or *šljivovica* and and garnished with whipped cream. A more spirited winter dessert is produced by preserving fruit in brandy. Fruits and berries are also made into compotes, jams and preserves. *Fruit Slatko*, fresh fruit preserved in a rich crystalline syrup, can be prepared from almost any fruit, including green walnuts and watermelon rind. In Moslem homes, *slatko* is promptly served to visitors in small glass serving dishes with tiny silver or golden spoons, accompanied by ice water or rose water. It can also be served as a dessert with lightly sweetened whipped cream.

Palačinke are a favorite throughout Croatia. The fillings for these delicate pancakes are even more varied than those used to prepare *savijače*. They vary from fruit jams and preserves to sweetened ground walnuts and whipped or chocolate cream. *Palačinke s Orasima, crêpes* with ground walnuts are often served with a rich wine sauce. *Palačinke* filled with cottage cheese may be spiced with raisins which have been soaked in rum. The *Krempalačinka* may be served plain or spread with one or several fillings. These dainty *crêpes* are piled on top of each other, baked lightly, then cut into wedges and served like a cake.

Alva and *Ratluk* are sinfully sweet Bosnian creations made from honey, walnuts and almonds. These dainty desserts are so sweet that they are usually savored only in small samplings. Although they may be too sweet as an ending to a meal, they provide a delightful accompaniment to Turkish coffee which is traditionally served with a small sweet or with *slatko*.

The desserts offered in this section represent a cross-section of some of the desserts that may be served in Croatia. There are many regional and family variations to these sweets which provide an enjoyable ending to a special meal.

Crnac u Košulji
Black and White Steamed Pudding

¼ c. butter, softened
5 egg yolks
½ c. sugar
3 squares chocolate, grated
5 egg whites
¼ tsp. cream of tartar
1 ½ c. ground almonds
2 tbsp. rum
1 c. whipping cream, sweetened
3 tbsp. confectioner's sugar
1 tsp. vanilla
candied violets or piped icing flowers for garnish
[optional]

Grease a 3½ c. steaming mold and sprinkle it with granulated sugar. Cream the butter. When the butter is fluffy, add the egg yolks, one at a time, beating well after each addition. Add the chocolate, almonds and sugar into the butter mixture gradually, beating constantly. Beat the egg whites until foamy. Add the cream of tartar and continue beating until very stiff. Fold egg whites into the chocolate batter. Spoon into the mold. Cover the mold with greased foil and tie securely with string. Place the mold in a pot of hot water. The water should come no more that two thirds of the way up the sides of the mold.

Cover the pot, turn the heat down to low and steam the pudding for one hour. Turn the steamed pudding over onto a serving platter immediately and allow to cool.

Boil the sugar in the water for fifteen minutes until it reaches 225° or a small amount dropped into cold water forms a large thread. Pour the hot syrup into the egg whites, beating continuously. The mixture will begin to thicken. Add the rum and continue beating until the egg whites are very stiff. Spread the egg whites over the pudding. Allow to cool, then refrigerate for at least three hours.

Whip the cream with the powdered sugar and vanilla. Garnish the pudding with whipped cream just before serving. Decorate with the candied violets or with piped frosting flowers.

Pržene Trešnje
Fried Cherries

1 lb. ripe cherries, pitted
3 tbsp. sugar
¼ c. milk
¾ c. flour
¼ c. wine
2 eggs, slightly beaten
¼ tsp. salt
hot oil for frying
confectioner's sugar

Combine the flour, salt and granulated sugar with the milk and wine. Beat well to form a smooth pancake batter. Add the eggs and beat well. Wash the cherries and roll them in the flour. Coat with the batter and fry in hot oil until golden brown. Remove from the oil, drain on paper towels and sprinkle with confectioner's sugar. Serve hot or cold.

Rolada od Kestena
Chestnut Roll

3 lbs. chestnuts
2/3 c. sugar
1 ¼ c. butter
7 squares semi-sweet chocolate
whipped cream

Shell and boil the chestnuts. Mince them. Beat ¾ c. melted butter and the sugar until fluffy. Add the chestnuts and mix until you obtain a smooth dough. Shape the dough into a loaf and roll out on a sheet of wax paper. Melt the remaining butter in the top of a double boiler. Add the chocolate. Mix well until smooth. Remove from heat and allow to cool slightly. When the chocolate has thickened, spread half the mixture over the chestnut dough. Warm the remaining chocolate mixture and pour it over the log. Refrigerate for at least two hours. Slice and serve with whipped cream.

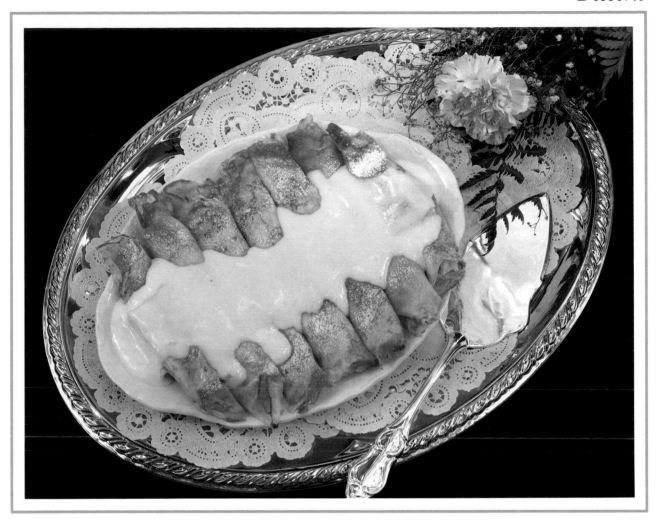

Palačinke sa Sirom
Cheese Palacinke

3 eggs
1½ c. milk
1½ c. flour
2 tbsp. sugar
6 tbsp. butter, melted
½ c. water
½ c. sour cream
3 tbsp. powdered sugar
ground walnuts for garnish

Whisk the eggs, granulated sugar, salt, flour and half the milk in a bowl. By adding just enough liquid to make a thick batter, you eliminate the possibility of lumps. When the mixture is smooth, add the remaining ingredients and stir well. You will have a batter that is like a light syrup. Heat a 6" skillet on medium heat. Grease the skillet only for the first palachinka. Pour approximately three tablespoons batter into the skillet. Tilt so that the bottom will be evenly coated. The thinner the coating, the better the palachinka. Cook over medium heat for approximately 45 seconds. Bang the pan on a pot holder to release the pancake and flip the palachinka, or use a spatula to turn the palachinka to the other side. Place the cooked palachinke on a warmed plate while you make the balance of the palachinke.

Continued on next page.

Spread with filling and roll the palachinka up into a cylinder. Place it in a shallow baking dish and place in a warm oven until the other palachinke are cooked. Continue making palachinke until all the batter is used up.

Cheese filling:

1 lb. cottage cheese
2 tbsp. sugar
2 egg yolks
1 tsp. vanilla
½ c. heavy cream [optional]

Beat the egg yolk slightly. Add the remaining ingredients and mix well. Fill the palachinke. Mix two tablespoons powdered sugar into the heavy cream. Pour over the palachinke and return to the oven at 350° for ten minutes, or sprinkle with confectioner's sugar and, if desired, with ground walnuts. Serve hot.

Palačinke s Orasima
Palachinke with Walnuts

1 c. ground walnuts
½ c. sugar

Prepare the palachinke as for Palachinke with Cheese, but do not fill them. Combine the ground walnuts and the sugar. Spread each pancake with one tablespoon of sweetened waltnuts. Fold each palachinka in half, then fold over again to make a pie-shaped wedge. Place the folded palachinke on a serving platter. If desired, pour a little Wine Sauce over them serve Wine Sauce on the side.

Preljev od Vina
Wine Sauce

3 eggs
3 tbsp. flour
½ c. sugar
3 c. white wine

Beat all the ingredients with a wire whisk in the top of a double boiler. Place over boiling water and continue beating until the mixture thickens. This sauce can be served with *palacinke*, simple vanilla cakes, or other dry desserts.

Palačinke s Vrhnjem
Cream-Filled Palachinke

1 c. whipped cream
½ tsp. salt
1 c. milk
¼ c. chocolate sauce
¼ c . ground walnuts
vanilla
confectioner's sugar

Prepare the palachinke as for Cheese Palachinke. Allow the pancakes to cool for about five minutes after they are fried. Whip the cream. Mix the cream, walnuts, and vanilla together. Fill the palachinke with this mixture and roll them. Arrange the filled palachinke on a serving platter. Pour the chocolate sauce over them. Sprinkle with confectioner's sugar and ground walnuts.

Drobljenac
Drobljenac

6 egg yolks, well beaten
6 egg whites, stiffly beaten
3 tbsp. butter
1 c. milk
5 tbsp. sugar
5 tbsp. flour
¼ tsp. salt

Sift the flour and the salt together twice. Add the sugar. Gradually add the milk and stir well. Add the egg yolks and beat well. Fold in the stiffly beaten egg whites. Melt the butter in a large skillet over low heat. Increase the heat and fry the batter in the hot butter until golden brown. Turn and lightly brown the other side. You will have a thick, light pancake. Tear into pieces with two forks.

If preferred, pour the batter into a well greased and heated baking pan and bake at 400° for a few minutes until the pancake is golden, then tear into pieces with a fork.

Serve the pancake plain, with powdered sugar or garnished with sweetened cream.

Krempalačinke
Cream Crepes

5 tbsp. soft butter
5 egg yolks, well beaten
1 tbsp. sugar
5 tbsp. sifted cake flour
5 egg whites, stiffly beaten
5 tbsp. warm milk
vanilla sugar

Cream the soft butter until it becomes frothy. Add the well beaten egg yolks and beat well. Add the flour, sugar, and milk, a tablespoon at a time, beating well after each addition. Fold in the stiffly beaten egg whites. Heat a pancake skillet, well greased with oil. Spoon out three tablespoons of the palachinka batter and fry until the bottom is golden brown. The palachinka will expand like an omelette. Leave the top of the palachinka slightly undercooked-do not turn it over. Place the palachinke on a warm plate with the soft side up. Sprinkle with vanilla sugar. Allow to sit in a warm place while the other palachinke are cooking. Place the palachinke on top of one another so that they end up looking like a cake. Continue cooking until all the batter is used up. Serve either hot or cold and slice like a cake. If preferred, the krempalachinke can be filled with any of the fillings used for rolled palachinke.

Continued on next page.

Lemon Sauce:

2 tbsp. lemon juice
½ c. sugar
2 tbsp. butter
¼ tsp. salt
1 tbsp. corn starch
1 c. water

Combine the sugar and corn starch. Add a little water and mix to make a smooth paste. Boil the water and add the sugar paste to the boiling water. And the salt and cook in a double boiler for about half an hour. Remove from heat. Cream the butter. Beat in the thick clear sugar sauce and the lemon juice. Continue beating until very thick and creamy.

Pržene Kuglice od Riže
Fried Rice Balls

1 c. rice
2 c. milk
1 tsp. vanilla
½ c. butter
½ c. sugar
1 egg
¼ c. fine bread crumbs
oil for deep frying
maraschino cherries
flour

Combine the butter, vanilla, milk and sugar in the top of a double boiler and cook until the sugar is dissolved. Wash the rice and add it to the milk mixture. Cook until the rice is soft. Allow the mixture to cool. Shape small balls from the mixture. Roll the balls in a little flour. Dip them into the well beaten egg, then roll them in bread crumbs. Fry each rice ball in the hot oil. Sprinkle with confectioner's sugar and garnish each with a maraschino cherry.

Nabujak sa Limunom
Lemon Soufflé

6 tbsp. butter
4 egg yolks
2/3 c. sugar
juice of 1 lemon
rind of 1 lemon, grated
4 egg whites, stiffly beaten
1 c. flour
¼ c. raisins

Add the egg yolks and sugar and mix well. Add the lemon juice, grated lemon rind, flour and raisins, one ingredient at a time. Beat well after each addition. Fold in the egg whites. Pour this batter into a well greased and floured mold. Steam for about 45 minutes. Pour the lemon sauce over the pudding. Allow to cool slightly. Slice and serve.

Zimska Salata od Voća
Winter Fruit Salad

3 large tart apples
3 ripe pears
¼ c. chopped walnuts
¼ c. sugar
¼ c. almonds
3 c. seedless grapes
¼ c. water
½ c. apple sauce
½ c. whipped cream

Cook the sugar in the water until dissolved. Allow to cool. Add the rum. Wash the apples and pears and dice them. Combine with the nuts and grapes. Pour the sugar mixture over the fruit and mix well. If desired, transfer to individual serving dishes and garnish with apple sauce and whipped cream.

Voćna Torta i Salata od Jagodinog Voća / Fruit Torte [page 192] and Berry Fruit Salad

Salata od Jagodinog Voća
Berry Fruit Salad

½ c. blueberries
½ c. strawberries
½ c. gooseberries
½ c. pitted cherries
½ c. sugar
¼ c. white wine
1 tbsp. lemon juice
½ c. whipped cream
¼ c. chopped walnuts [optional]

Wash and drain the fruit. Mix the sugar with the berries, being careful not to squash them. Pour the wine over the fruit. Add the lemon juice. Mix again, carefully. Refrigerate for at least an hour. Place the fruit in individual serving dishes. Garnish with whipped cream, and if desired, with ground nuts.

Pohane Trešnje u Rumu
Deep Fried Cherries

1 lb. firm ripe cherries, with stems
2 eggs
½ c. flour
vanilla sugar
½ c. oil
½ c. butter
2 tbsp. rum
1 tbsp. confectioner's sugar
dash salt

Wash the cherries, but do not remove the stems. Combine the eggs, flour, confectioner's sugar, salt and rum. Beat well. Allow the batter to sit covered for about an hour. Heat the butter and oil in a deep saucepan. Dip the cherries in the batter and place them carefully in the hot oil and butter mixture. Turn them gently by their stems to allow them to become crisp and golden on all sides. Drain on paper towels, then roll in a little confectioner's sugar. Arrange in a pyramid and sprinkle with vanilla sugar.

Sir sa Voćem
Cottage Cheese With Fruit

1 lb. cottage cheese
1 tbsp. rum
¼ c. sugar
1 tbsp. lemon juice
1 lb. fresh fruit
½ c. whipped cream
¼ c. chopped nuts

Blend the cheese in a blender. Place into a deep bowl. Add the sugar and whip until smooth and frothy. Finely chop the fresh fruit. (Leave berries whole, if used.) Combine the finely chopped fruit, lemon juice and rum with the cottage cheese mixture in tall parfait glasses. Refrigerate for at least an hour. Garnish with whipped cream, chopped nuts and a few chunks of fruit before serving.

Kuglice od Kestena
Chestnut Balls

1 ½ lbs. chestnuts
3 c. sugar
1/3 c. water
1 tbsp. lemon juice
confectioner's sugar

Place the chestnuts in boiling water and cook until tender. Peel the chestnut skins. Purée the chestnuts in a blender or food processor. Dissolve the sugar in the water over moderate heat. Lower the heat and continue cooking until a thick syrup forms. Add the chestnuts and lemon juice to the syrup. Mix well. Allow the chestnut mixture to cool until it can be handled. Shape into small balls. Roll the balls in confectioner's sugar until well coated.

Punjenje Naranče
Stuffed Oranges

10 oranges
4 egg yolks
2 whole eggs
2 tbsp. rum
½ c. sugar
1 ½ c. whipped cream
10 maraschino cherries

Cut off the tops of the oranges. Remove the juice and pulp. Strain the orange juice. Beat the eggs and egg yolks and sugar in the top of a double boiler. When very light and fluffy, beat in the orange juice and rum. Beat the mixture over boiling water until it reaches the boiling point. Remove from heat and continue beating until the mixture cools. Fold in half the whipped cream. Stuff the oranges with this filling. Garnish with the remaining whipped cream and maraschino cherries.

Salama od Suhog Voća
Dried Fruit Salami

½ lb. pitted prunes
¼ lb. diced dates
1 c. sugar
½ c. water
½ lb. diced dried figs
1 c. chopped walnuts or almonds
2 tbsp. rum
¼ c. powdered sugar

Wash the prunes and place in a medium saucepan. Add enough water to cover and cook until tender. Drain, chop finely and refrigerate. Boil the sugar in the water to the soft ball stage (225°). Add the prunes, figs, dates, nuts and rum. Mix well. Sprinkle powdered sugar over a sheet of aluminum foil. Transfer the fruit mixture to the aluminum foil and with the help of the foil, shape it into a sausage, covering the log well with powdered sugar. Refrigerate for about two hours. Slice into thin slices to look like salami. Serve over pieces of pound cake to look like salami sandwiches and make a "salad" of mint leaves and sliced strawberries.

Pjena od Jagoda
Strawberry Froth

4 c. strawberries
1 c. sugar
1 c. whipping cream

Sieve the berries, saving a few for garnish. Add the sugar and mix well. Whip the cream. Combine the fruit and ¾ c. of the whipped cream. Place in parfait glasses. Refrigerate for at least an hour. Garnish with the remaining whipped cream and the whole berries before serving.

Jabuke u Šlagu
Apples in Whipped Cream

6 large cooking apples
½ c. raisins
1 tsp. cinnamon
1 c. chopped walnuts
1 tbsp. grated lemon peel
¼ c. sugar
1 tsp. vanilla
3 tbsp. butter
1 c. heavy whipping cream

Wash and core the apples. Place them in a saucepan. Sprinkle with the sugar and the juice of one lemon. Pour enough water over the apples to cover. Cook them in this mixture for approximately ten minutes. Mix the walnuts, raisins, cinnamon, lemon peel, half the whipping cream and vanilla. Fill the apples with this mixture. Place half a tablespoon of butter on top of each apple. Carefully arrange the apples in a baking dish and add the water that the apples were cooked in. Bake in a hot oven 450° until the apples are well baked. Cool. Whip the remaining whipping cream. Garnish the apples with whipped cream and maraschino cherries and pour the syrup around them before serving.

Varenac od Riže
Steamed Rice Pudding

1 ½ c. milk
1. c. rice
½ c. butter
½ c. sugar
5 egg yolks
1 tsp. vanilla
5 egg whites
¼ tsp. cream of tartar
apricot jam or preserves

Grease a steaming mold and sprinkle with granulated sugar. Cook the rice in the milk in the top of a double boiler until tender. Allow to cool. Cream the butter and sugar together until light and frothy. Add the egg yolks, one at a time, beating well after each addition. Stir in the cooked rice and the vanilla. Beat the egg whites until frothy. Add the cream of tartar and continue beating until stiff. Fold the egg whites into the mixture. Spoon half the batter into the mold. Spread with the jam or preserves. Add the rest of the batter. Place a sheet of greased foil over the mold. Tie the foil securely to the mold with string. Place the mold into a large pot of hot water. The water should go up no more than two thirds of the sides of the mold. Cover the pot and steam for approximately an hour. Unmold unto a serving platter immediately. Serve with strawberry froth.

Jabuke u Rumu
Apples in Rum

6 medium sour apples
1 c. sugar
2 c. water
3 tbsp. rum
2 tsp. cinnamon
1 c. whipping cream
6 maraschino cherries
6 tbsp. sweet liquer
juice of one lemon
2 tbsp. confectioner's sugar

Combine the sugar and water in a large saucepan. Stir to dissolve the sugar. Simmer over low heat to the thread ball stage (225°). When a thin syrup has formed, add the rum, cinnamon and lemon juice. Continue cooking for another five minutes. Peel and core the apples. Sprinkle them with lemon juice so that they do not brown. Place the apples in the syrup and simmer in the covered pan until the apples are tender. Do not allow them to overcook. Place each apple in a serving glass. Add the syrup around the apples and allow to cool. When the apples have cooled, whip the cream with the confectioner's sugar. Fill the apples with the whipped cream. Place the remaining cream on top of the apples. Add a tablespoon of liqueur to each apple. Garnish with a maraschino cherry.

Jabuke u Košulji
Coated Apples

6 cooking apples
3 tbsp. sugar
1 ½ c. flour
2 tbsp. rum
1 c. milk
oil for deep frying
confectioner's sugar

Make a thick pancake batter from the sugar, milk and flour. Peel and slice the apples. Sprinkle them with rum. Dip the slices into the batter and deep fry in hot oil or shortening. Sprinkle with confectioner's sugar before serving. Pears, plums, peaches and apricots can be prepared in the same manner.

Loptice od Šljiva
Prune Balls

1 c. pitted prunes
½ c. confectioner's sugar
½ c. ground nuts
¼ c. raisins
2 tbsp. rum or sljivovica brandy
vanilla sugar

Mince the prunes, nuts and raisins. Combine them with the confectioner's sugar and the rum or *sljivovica*. Mix the dough well. Form little balls out of a tablespoon of dough at a time. Roll the balls in confectioner's or vanilla sugar. Serve in tiny paper candy cups as a dessert or as a sweet accompaniment to Turkish coffee.

Žličnjaci od Snijega
Snow Eggs

6 egg whites	1 ¾ c. sugar
½ tsp. salt	2 ½ c. milk
6 egg yoks	1 tsp. vanilla

Beat the egg whites with the salt until firm. Add ¾ c. sugar and continue beating for another minute. Fold in ¼ c. sugar. Heat a large skillet of water to the point where it is gently boiling. Using an ice-cream scoop, spoon the eggs into the boiling water. You may wish to round the top of the egg white with your finger to make the ball as round as possible before dropping it into the water. Cook for two to three minutes on each side. Remove with a slotted spoon to drain on waxed paper. When the "eggs" have drained, refrigerate while you prepare the custard.

Bring the milk to a boil and set aside in the pan. Place the yolks, sugar and vanilla in a bowl and whisk until the mixture is light and lemon-colored. Stir in the flour. Add half the milk and mix well. Pour the mixture into the remaining milk and mix well. Bring the mixture to a boil over low heat, stirring constantly. When the mixture begins to boil, cook for five minutes, stirring constantly so that it does not scorch. Place the custard in a serving bowl and cover with plastic wrap so that a skin will not form on the custard. Allow to cool completely. Carefully place the "eggs" on top of the custard and chill completely before serving. If desired, make a caramel sauce by cooking ¼ cup sugar with ¼ cup corn syrup until it turns to caramel. Allow to cool slightly until the mixture thickens. Using a fork, drip the hot caramel over the eggs like string. Serve cool.

Krema od Lešnjaka
Filbert Parfait

3 c. whipped cream
¼ c. sugar
1 ½ c. ground filberts
3 packets gelatine
¼ c. pistachio nuts, chopped

Melt the gelatin in a little warm water. Brown the filberts in an ungreased pan, stirring constantly. Beat the gelatin, sugar and filberts into the whipped cream. Pour this mixture into a mold or into individual parfait glasses. Refrigerate for at least two hours. Garnish with the remaining whipped cream and chopped filberts.

Salama od Čokolade
Chocolate Salami

1 ½ c. ground walnuts
¼ c. chopped almonds
1 c. sugar
1 egg white
juice of half a lemon
¼ c. cocoa powder
1 tsp. cinnamon
pulp of half a lemon, chopped
red food coloring
½ c. raisins
confectioner's sugar

Beat the egg white until it forms stiff peaks. Add the ground walnuts, sugar, cinnamon, lemon juice and lemon pulp. Beat well. Add the chopped nuts and the red food coloring. Mix until all the ingredients are well blended. Sprinkle sifted confectioner's sugar on a wooden board. Shape a salami from the dough. Coat with chocolate glaze. When the glaze begins to set, sprinkle with sifted confectioner's sugar. Refrigerate for at least two hours. Slice thinly before serving.

Chocolate glaze:

1 tbsp. water
¼ c. cocoa, sifted
½ c. sifted confectioner's sugar

Combine all the ingredients to form a smooth glaze.

Slatko od Trešanja
Cherry Slatko

2 c. ripe cherries
2 c. sugar
¼ c. water
1 tsp. lemon juice
½ c. whipped cream

Pit the cherries. Line the bottom of a thick pan with a layer of pitted cherries. Add a layer of sugar. Continue alternating cherries and sugar until both ingredients are used up. Cook over medium heat until the sugar is well dissolved. Continue cooking over low heat until the *slatko* becomes thick. Remove from the pan and allow to cool for a few minutes. Add the water and lemon juice. Cook for another few minutes until all the water is absorbed. Beat well and refrigerate in small serving bowls overnight. Garnish with whipped cream just before serving.

Alva
Alva

1 lb. sugar
6 egg whites
¾ c. warm honey
½ lb. walnuts
4 wafer sheets

Clean and halve the walnuts. Beat the egg whites in the top of a double boiler until they form stiff peaks. Beat the sugar into the egg whites. Add the warm honey, stirring constantly. Continue beating until the mixture thickens. Remove from heat. Stir in the walnut halves. Spread three wafer sheets with one third of the walnut mixture. Cover with the remaining wafer. Place a wooden board on the sheets to flatten them and allow to stand overnight. The following day, cut the alva into bite-sized squares or diamonds.

Rezanci s Makom
Noodles with Poppy Seeds

¾ c. poppy seeds
4 tbsp. honey
1 lb. egg noodles
3 tbsp. sugar
4 tbsp. butter
¾ c. raisins
¾ c. milk

Cook the noodles in boiling water until tender, but do not overcook. Grind the poppy seeds. Combine the milk, poppy seeds, sugar, honey, and raisins in a saucepan. Simmer over low heat for approximately ten minutes. Add the noodles and the butter and mix well. The noodles may be served this way. For a more dramatic dessert, place the mixture in a well-grease mold. Bake at 350° until firm and the top is golden, being careful not to dry the noodles out. May be served with Wine Sauce.

Noodles can be prepared in the same manner substituting ground nuts combined with sugar for the cooked poppy seeds.

Slatko od Ruža
Rose Slatko

1 lb. rose petals
4 c. water
2 lbs. sugar
juice of one lemon

Bring the water to a boil in a large pot. Add the washed rose petals and cook for fifteen minutes. Add the sugar and lemon juice. Continue cooking, stirring constantly, until the slatko begins to thicken. Cook for approximately fifteen minutes to the soft ball stage (225°). Do not overcook. Remove from heat and scoop off the foam. Cover and refrigerate overnight. Rose slatko is traditionally served to guests in small serving dishes with miniature silver or gold spoons. Because only very small portions of *slatko* are served at a time, it can be poured into small sterilized jars and sealed with paraffin for future use.

Red May roses are the finest for this delicacy. If they are not available, substitute white rose petals, adding a few drops of red food coloring just before the slatko *is cooked.*

Nabujak od Oraha
Walnut Steamed Pudding

¾ c. sugar
8 egg yolks
¼ tsp. cream of tartar
1 ½ c. ground walnuts
1 ¼ c. milk
1 tbsp. grated lemon rind
2 tbsp. fine bread crumbs
8 egg whites, stiffly beaten

Beat the egg yolks and sugar until light and lemon colored. Add the ground walnuts and milk, and cook in the top of a double boiler until the mixture thickens, beating constantly. Remove from heat. Beat in the grated lemon rind and the bread crumbs. Beat the egg yolks until frothy. Add the cream of tartar and continue beating until stiff. Fold into the walnut mixture. Grease a mold and sprinkle with fine cake crumbs. Spoon the batter into the mold and steam for one hour. Garnish with whipped cream or serve with a lemon sauce.

Krema od Kave
Coffee Custard

4 egg yolks
2 whole eggs
2 c. milk
½ c. sugar
1 tsp. vanilla
2 c. whipped cream
½ c. strong coffee

Beat the eggs and egg yolks and combine with the sugar in the top of a double boiler. Add the scalded milk and cook in the top of the double boiler until the mixture begins to boil, stirring constantly. Remove from heat, add the coffee and continue beating until the mixture cools. When the custard is completely cooled, fold in half the whipped cream and the vanilla. Pour into serving dishes and garnish with the remaining whipped cream.

Ratluk
Ratluk

2 c. sugar
½ c. water
2 tbsp. lemon juice
4 tbsp. cornstarch
¼ tsp. rose oil
1 c. ground almonds or pistachios

Combine the sugar and half the water and boil for about fifteen minutes to the soft ball stage (225°). Add the lemon juice and cook for about a minute longer. Add the cornstarch to the remaining water. Mix well to dissolve. Add this mixture to the hot syrup gradually, stirring constantly. Continue to cook over medium heat for another ten minutes. Remove from heat. Add the rose oil and the almonds and mix well. Cover the bottom of a large square or rectangular tray with a thin layer of cornstarch. Pour the hot *ratluk* mixture onto the tray. It should be about one inch thick. Flatten with a large knife. Allow to cool and harden overnight. The following day, cut the *ratluk* into small squares or diamonds before serving.

Voće u Rakiji
Brandied Fruit

6 lbs. fruit
6 c. sugar
4 c. water
2 ½ c. brandy or rum
20-30 cloves

Wash and slice, chop, or dice the fruit. Make a syrup of the water and sugar. Place the fruit into the syrup and cook until the fruit is tender but still firm. Drain the fruit. Pack into sterilized one pint glass jars. Return the extra syrup and boil for another fifteen minutes until well thickened. Add the brandy to the syrup and pour over the fruit. Add 3-4 cloves to each jar and seal immediately. Peaches, cherries, apricots, pears, or plums can be prepared in this way. Berries and grapes should not be cooked. Simply sprinkle with layers of sugar then pour brandy over them. Marinade for at least a week before using.

Savijače
A Selection of Savijače

Pastries

At first glance, this section may seem disproportionate in comparison to the others. However, only non-Croatians might consider it so. Croatia's culinary creativeness is best expressed in her pastries and sweets. The country's pastry tradition is as rich and varied as her musical and dance traditions. Even in today's era of fast food, Croatian housewives still practice home baking. It would not be Sunday without providing a freshly baked cake or pastry.

Many Croatian pastries are challenging and may require a little practice. Others, such as Chocolate Wafer Bars, are simple enough for children to make. The most distinctive Croatian pastries are the delicate *savijače* which can be made with innumerable fillings from a variety of fruits, poppy seeds, nuts or cheese enveloped in layers of delicate flaky pastry. Although it requires some time and practice to learn the technique, once it is mastered, making the *savijača* pastry becomes surprisingly simple. The results are certainly worth the effort.

The tender tortes baked in either thick or thin layers and filled with a variety of creams and glazes, tend to be richer and more elaborate than American cakes. Luscious cakes prepared with creamy butter and whipped eggs are flavored with rum, nuts, vanilla, chestnuts and cocoa. They rely on stiffly beaten egg whites as the only leavening agent. For that reason it is very important that the eggs used in making tortes be at room temperature and very fresh to produce the greatest volume. Less than the freshest eggs might produce disappointing results.

Another delight of Croatian pastry lovers is puff pastry made into countless shapes and filled with a variety of creams. The most popular of these is the light cream slice, *Krempita*. Layers of flaky puff pastry are filled with yellow vanilla custard or sweetened whipped cream. Don't despair if your results are less than perfect the first time. Flaky Pastry is a challenge, even for master chefs. Keep trying. You will rightfully feel a sense of pride when you have accomplished the technique!

The distinctive Croatian pastry, *pita*, is a crumbly short cake filled with savory fruits, almonds, walnuts or cheese. Because it is so versatile and easy to prepare, it is a favorite across the entire country. Methods of preparation and fillings vary regionally. Filled with meat, cheese, potatoes or other vegetables, *pita* also makes an excellent entrée or side dish.

Deep-fried pastries are especially popular on the coast, where they are known as *fritule*, *kroštule* or *pršunate*. Croatian doughnuts, *pokladnice*, are light, round, fried yeast cakes filled with jam or marmalade. These Croatian Mardi Gras cakes fried in oil and butter are served warm, sprinkled with confectioner's sugar.

Orehnjača and *Makovnjača*, the rich Croatian coffee cake rolls filled with walnuts and poppy seeds, are found on Croatian tables for every holiday and festive occasion. They are favorites with coffee or as an after-dinner dessert.

Small tea biscuits and pastries are popular with children and adults alike. They are frequently made with nuts and their shapes and sizes are limited only by the imagination of the baker. They may take the form of little crescents known as *kiflice*, rum soaked little walnut tortes or fluffy little cakes made from puff pastry .

Tjesto za Savijaču
Basic Savijaca Dough

4 c. dry bread flour
1 tsp. salt
1 egg
1 tbsp. vinegar
2 tbsp. oil
1 ¼ c. warm water, approx.
1 c. melted butter

Sift the flour and salt into a large mixing bowl twice. Make a well in the center. Drop in the egg, water, vinegar and oil and mix the ingredients well. The ingredients may be placed in a food processor and blended with the metal blade. When the dough sticks together in a ball, turn it onto a floured board and knead until it becomes elastic, no longer sticking to the board or to your hands, approximately ten minutes. Experience will help you to decide when the dough is soft enough. The dough must not be overly soft, but smooth enough not to stick to the hands.

Divide the dough into two balls. Grease a deep bowl with butter or margarine. Place the balls of dough in the bowl. Turn them around so that they will be greased on all sides. Cover the dough with a kitchen towel and allow it to rest in a warm place for approximately half an hour.

Spread a large table with a tablecloth. Dust generously with flour. Roll the dough very thin with a rolling pin. Brush the entire surface with melted butter. Begin stretching the dough by pulling from the center out with floured fists. Pull the dough in all directions. When the dough covers more than half the table and the center is very thin, begin pulling the edges with the fingertips.

Walk around the table always pulling from the center. Be sure to pull the dough evenly from all sides. When the dough is fully stretched, it should cover the whole table and should be thin enough to read newsprint through it. Allow the dough to drape over the edges of the table. Trim the edges with kitchen shears or tear the thick edges away

gently. Allow the dough to dry for approximately five minutes.

Brush the *savijača* dough generously with melted butter, then spread with the desired filling over two thirds of the dough, leaving one third without filling empty.

Now for the fun part. Gently lift the table cloth away from the table, pulling so that the savijaca will roll as the tablecloth is pulled upward toward you. As it rolls, it will make a long log.

Tuck the ends and the seam under. Place the *savijača* on the baking sheet, bending it into a U-shape so that it will fit on the sheet. Brush with more melted butter. Repeat with the other ball of dough. Bake according to the filling used. When the *savijače* are baked, slide them onto wire racks to cool, then transfer to a cutting board and cut into serving portions.

Savijača sa Trešnjama
Cherry Savijaca

2 c. pitted cherries
¼ c. water
½ c. sugar
¼ c. fine cake crumbs
¼ c. butter
¼ c. sliced almonds

Cook the cherries for a few minutes in the sugar and water. Drain. Sauté the cake crumbs in the butter. Sprinkle with almond slices. Roll the savijaca by lifting the edge of the tablecloth where two thirds of the dough has been filled. Pull the tablecloth toward you so that the savijaca will roll into a log. Fold the ends. Slice onto a greased baking sheet. Brush the rolled pastry with melted butter. Bake at 425° for ten minutes. Reduce the heat and bake at 350° until the *savijača* is golden brown. If preferred, canned pie filling may be substituted for fresh cherries. However, the filling must be well drained so that the savijaca does not become soggy. Dust with confectioner's sugar before serving. Serve either hot or cold.

Illustrated on page 176.

Savijača sa Sirom
Cheese Savijača

2 lbs. cottage cheese
3 tbsp. sweet cream
1 tbsp. melted butter
¼ c. sugar
2 eggs
¼ c. raisins (optional)

Mix the cheese with the cream. Beat the eggs well and add to the cheese mixture. Beat in the sugar and raisins. Brush the *savijača* dough with melted butter. Spread with cheese filling. Roll by lifting the tablecloth upward and toward you. Roll the pastry into a log. Fold over the edges to seal the ends. Place on a greased baking sheet. Brush with melted butter. Bake at 425° for ten minutes. Reduce the heat to 375° and bake until the *savijača* is crisp and golden. Dust with powdered sugar before serving.

Illustrated on page 176.

Savijača od Oraha
Walnut Savijača

2 c. ground walnuts
2 tbsp. breadcrumbs
2 eggs
2 tbsp. sugar
2 c. sour cream
1 tsp. vanilla
1 tsp. cinnamon
rind of ½ lemon, grated

Separate the eggs. Beat the sour cream with the egg yolks, sugar, vanilla, cinnamon and the grated lemon rind. Add the walnuts and breadcrumbs and beat well. Fold in the stiffly beaten egg whites. Spread this mixture on the stretched and buttered savijaca dough. Spread only two thirds of the dough. Carefully roll up the savijaca by gently pulling the end of the tablecloth. Place on a greased baking sheet. Brush with melted butter. Bake at 400° for about twenty minutes. Sprinkle with confectioner's sugar before serving. Serve hot or cold.

Savijača od Jabuka
Apple Savijača

Savijaca Pastry Dough
1 c. fine dry bread crumbs
¼ c. melted butter
3 c. tart apples, grated
½ c. sugar
1 tsp. cinnamon
¼ c. raisins
¼ c. sliced almonds

Sprinkle the stretched savijaca pastry with melted butter and bread crumbs. Spread the grated apple over two thirds of the dough. Sprinkle the sugar and cinnamon over the apples. Spread the raisins and almonds over the filling. Roll the *savijača* by lifting the edge of the tablecloth where the filling has been spread. The empty one third of the dough will bake to a flaky pastry surrounding the apple filling. Slide the rolled savijaca onto a greased baking. Brush with melted butter. Bake at 425° for ten minutes. Reduce the heat to 350° and bake until golden. Sprinkle with powdered sugar before serving.

Illustrated on page 176.

Savijača od Limuna
Lemon Savijača

savijaca dough
2 lemons
5 egg yolks
6 tbsp. sugar
1 tsp. vanilla
1 ½ c. ground almonds
5 egg whites
¼ tsp. cream of tartar

Cook the lemons in boiling water until tender. Blend them in a blender. Beat the egg yolks with the sugar until light and lemon colored. Add the blended lemon, vanilla, sugar and ground almonds and mix well. Beat the egg whites until frothy. Add the cream of tartar and continue beating until stiff. Gently fold the egg whites into the almond mixture. Stretch the *savijača* dough. Brush with melted butter and spread with filling, spooning a tablespoon at a time over two thirds of the dough. Roll and bake as for other *savijače.*

179

Gibanica
Gibanica

3½ c. cake flour
1 egg
2 tbsp. oil
¼ c. milk
½ tsp. salt

Preheat the oven to 350°. Grease and flour a deep 10" cake pan. Sift the flour and salt twice into a deep bowl, and make a well in the center and pour the milk and oil into it. Work the flour into the milk, adding more water or flour as required, to make a smooth stretchy dough. When the dough is smooth and glossy, break it into 20 pieces and shape the dough into balls. Roll each ball into a thin round sheet. The sheets should be almost as thin as *savijača* pastry dough when stretched. Place one sheet at the bottom of the prepared pan. Brush the dough with melted butter. Place three more sheets on top, brushing each with melted butter. Spread with some of the filling. Cover with another four rounds of pastry, brushing each with melted butter. Add more filling. Continue alternating the pastry and filling until both are used up. Leave the top few sheets of pastry plain. Brush each with butter. Bake at 350°. until the top is golden brown.

Gibanica Filling

1 ½ lbs. dry cottage cheese
1 tbsp. bread crumbs
1 tbsp. raisins
¾ c. sour cream
2 eggs
2 tbsp. sugar
1 tbsp. butter

Beat the eggs. Add the remaining ingredients and beat well until smooth and creamy. *Gibanica* may also be salted. Instead of sugar, use half a teaspoon salt.

Roščići od Oraha
Walnut Horns

¾ c. butter
3 ¼ c. flour
1 whole egg
3 egg yolks
3 tbsp. sugar
2 tbsp. sour cream
¼ tsp. salt
1 cube yeast or 1 package dry yeast
1 c. warm milk

Preheat the oven to 350°. Place one tablespoon flour and one teaspoon sugar in the warm milk. Allow to rise in a warm place for fifteen minutes. Cut the butter into the flour. Add the slightly beaten egg, egg yolks and the sugar, salt and sour cream. Add the yeast mixture. When all the ingredients are well blended, knead for about ten minutes until the dough is smooth and no longer sticks to the bowl or to your fingers. Cover with a kitchen towel and allow to rise until doubled in size. Prepare the filling.

Roll the dough into a rectangle approximately ¼ inch thick and cut it into squares. Place a tablespoon of filling on each square. Make a little horn by folding two diagonal corners toward the center. Place the horns on a greased cookie sheet and allow to rise in a warm, draft-free place for about half an hour. Brush with egg white or warm milk, then bake at 350° for approximately 35 minutes until golden.

Filling

1 ½ c. ground walnuts
¾ c. sugar
½ c. milk
2 tbsp. butter
1 tsp. cinnamon
2 tbsp. rum

Heat the milk and sugar in a saucepan until the sugar dissolves. Bring to a boil, stirring constantly. Remove from heat and add the remaining ingredients. Allow to cool before using.

Makovnjača
Poppy Seed Roll

6 c. flour
1½ c. milk
½ c. sugar
1 cake yeast
2 egg yolks
2 whole eggs
1 tbsp. lemon rind, grated
6 tbsp. melted butter
¼ tsp. salt
1 tsp. vanilla

Warm one half cup milk to approximately 110°. Add 1 tbsp. flour and 1 tsp. sugar. Stir in the yeast and allow to rise for approximately fifteen minutes. Melt the butter over low heat. Add the remaining one cup milk. Beat the eggs and egg yolks together. Stir into the milk and butter mixture with the lemon rind and vanilla. Add the yeast mixture. Beat enough of the flour into this batter, a little at a time, to obtain a smooth, soft dough. Continue beating until the dough blisters. Place the dough in a greased bowl, cover with a damp towel and allow to rise in a warm place for about an hour until doubled in bulk. Divide the dough into two sections. Roll each section out very thin, brush with melted butter and fill with poppy seed filling.

Continued on next page.

181

Roll like a *savijača* by lifting the edge of the tablecloth on which the dough was rolled out. Place the two sections of *makovnjača* on a well greased baking sheet and allow to rise in a warm, draft-free place for another half hour. Brush the rolls with a well beaten egg white and bake at 350° for about an hour until they become golden. Cool completely before slicing and serving.

Filling:

2 c. ground poppy seeds
¼ c. warm milk
½ c. sugar
4 tbsp. honey
½ tsp. cinnamon
1 egg yolk
1 tbsp. rum
1 tsp. lemon rind
juice of half a lemon
3 egg whites
½ c. raisins [optional]

Beat the egg whites with a dash of salt until stiff. Combine the remaining ingredients and fold the egg whites into the mixture. Spread this mixture over the rolled out dough. Roll the *makovnjača* up like a *savijača*.

Orehnjača
Walnut Roll

Makovnjaca dough
5 ½ c. ground walnuts
1 c. sugar
3 egg whites
1 tbsp. grated lemon peel
1 tsp. cinnamon
1 tsp. vanilla
2 tbsp. rum
½ c. raisins [optional]

Prepare the *orehnjača* in the same manner as the *makovnjača* dough. Beat the egg whites with a dash of salt until stiff. Combine the remaining ingredients and fold into the egg whites. Roll out the dough. Fill with the walnut filling. Allow to rise for another half hour until again doubled in bulk. Bake according to the directions for *makovnjača*.

Osja Gnjezda
Wasp's Nests

2 ¼ c. flour
1 cake yeast
2 tbsp. butter
1 egg yolk
¼ c. sugar
2 squares semisweet chocolate,
grated
½ c. butter, melted
½ c. sliced almonds
1/3 c. raisins
1/3 c. milk
1 tbsp. grated lemon rind
2 tbsp. minced lemon pulp
1 tsp. cinnamon
¼ tsp. salt

Allow the yeast to rise in the warm milk for approximately fifteen minutes. Cream the butter. Add the egg yolk, sugar, salt, lemon rind and lemon pulp. Add the flour and milk alternately, beating well after each addition. Continue beating until the dough no longer sticks to the bowl. It should be smooth and elastic. Cover and allow to rise in a warm, draft-free place until doubled in size.

Punch the dough down and divide into two pieces. Roll each piece out on a floured board to an 8"x10" rectangle. Brush the dough with melted butter, sprinkle with sliced almonds, grated chocolate and raisins. Roll the dough up like a *savijača*. Cut into two inch slices with a greased sharp knife. Brush each slice with melted butter and place on a greased baking sheet.

Allow to rise in a warm place until doubled in size, approximately half an hour. Bake at 350° until the wasps' nests are golden, approximately half an hour. Sprinkle with confectioner's sugar. Allow to cool. Serve with milk cream.

Kuglof
Kuglof

¾ c. raisins
2 tbsp. rum
1 cake yeast
¼ c. warm water
½ c. butter
½ c. sugar
1 tsp. lemon rind, grated
1 tsp. vanilla
½ tsp. salt
3 eggs
½ c. raisins
½ c. chopped almonds
3 c. flour
½ c. warm milk
¼ c. sliced almonds

Soak the raisins in the rum. Dissolve the yeast in the water combined with 1 tsp. sugar and 1 tbsp. flour and allow to rise for fifteen minutes. Cream the butter and the sugar until light and fluffy. Add the lemon rind, vanilla and salt and beat until well blended.

Continued on next page.

Add the flour alternately with the milk, a little at a time, and mix well after each addition. Beat for approximately five minutes until the dough no longer sticks to the bowl. Cover with a kitchen towel and allow to rise in a warm, draft-free place until doubled in bulk, approximately 45 minutes to one hour.

Generously grease a decorative tube pan or mold. Arrange the almond slices in the bottom of the mold. Beat down the dough and place it in the mold. Cover and allow to rise again until the dough almost reaches the top of the pan, approximately half an hour. Bake at 350° for 45 minutes. Allow to cool for approximately ten minutes. Invert the pan onto a rack to remove the kuglof from the pan. Allow to cool thoroughly. Sprinkle with powdered sugar before serving.

Kolači sa Sirom
Cheese Kolach

1 cake yeast
½ c. warm milk
1 ¾ c. flour
¼ tsp. salt
3 tbsp. sugar
1 egg
2 tbsp. butter, melted
1 egg white, beaten lightly
¼ c. chopped almonds

Stir the yeast in the warm milk combined with 1 tsp. sugar and 1 tbsp. flour and allow to rise for fifteen minutes until frothy. Sift the flour with the salt. Add the yeast mixture, melted butter, egg and sugar. Beat until you get a smooth, elastic dough. When the dough no longer sticks to the bowl, cover with a kitchen towel and allow to rise in a warm, draft-free place until doubled in bulk, approximately one hour.

Turn out onto a floured board. Knead until smooth and elastic. Roll out into a rectangle approximately ½" thick. Cut into 3 inch squares. Arrange the squares on greased bakings sheets, approximately 1 inch apart. Place a spoonful of filling on each square. Fold the corners towards the center and press them together to hold in the filling. Allow to rise again for another 45 minutes. Brush the kolache with the beaten egg white and sprinkle with chopped almonds. Bake at 350° for 35 minutes until the tops are golden.

Filling

2 tbsp. butter, softened
8 oz. cottage cheese
2 egg yolks
2 egg whites
¼ c. sugar
grated rind of one lemon

Combine all the ingredients except the egg whites. Blend in a blender or food processor. Beat the egg whites with a dash of salt until stiff. Fold them into the mixture.

Rolada od Germe sa Čokoladom
Chocolate Yeast Roll

1 cake yeast
½ c. warm milk
2 ½ c. flour
¼ tsp. salt
2 tbsp. sugar
½ c. butter, softened
1 egg, lightly beaten
6 tbsp. cocoa
¾ c. sugar
1 tbsp. ground cinnamon
1 c. raisins
4 tbsp. butter, melted

Stir the yeast in the warm milk combined with 1 tsp. sugar and 1 tbsp. flour and allow to rise for fifteen minutes. Sift the flour with the salt. Cream the butter and the sugar until light and fluffy. Add the flour and the yeast and work until you get a smooth, elastic dough. Beat until the dough no longer sticks to the bowl. Cover with a kitchen towel and allow to rise in a warm, draft-free place until doubled in bulk, approximately one hour.

Turn out onto a floured board. Knead until smooth and elastic. Roll out into a rectangle approximately ¼" thick. Brush with melted butter. Sprinkle with cocoa, sugar and cinnamon. Sprinkle the raisins over this mixture. Sprinkle with the remaining butter. Roll into a log. Slide onto a greased baking sheet with the seam down and allow to rise again for forty-five minutes. Brush the dough with the beaten egg. Bake at 425° for ten minutes. Reduce the heat and bake at 350° for 30 minutes until the top is golden. Cool completely before serving. Cut into slices and serve.

Bosanske Urmašice
Bosnian Mock Dates

1 c. butter
½ c. sour cream
1 tbsp. sugar
2 egg yolks
3 c. flour
1 tsp. baking powder

Cream the butter until light and fluffy. Add the sour cream and egg yolks and beat well. Sift the flour and baking powder together. Gradually stir the flour into the butter mixture. Knead the dough until smooth and glossy . Break off little chunks of dough and shape them into balls. Flatten each piece on a floured grater to give them texture. Fold the ends under and place the "dates" on a greased baking sheet and bake at 375° for about thirteen minutes. Make the syrup while the *urmašice* are baking. Remove from the oven and while the "dates" are still warm, pour a little boiling syrup over each one. Pour any remaining syrup into the pan and allow the "dates" to soak up the syrup while cooling. If necessary, drain the *urmasice*, then place on a serving platter. Garnish with lemon slices.

Continue on next page

Syrup:

2 ½ c. sugar
juice of two lemons
1 c. water
2 tsp. vanilla

Bring the sugar and water to a boil. Cook for approximately fifteen minutes, stirring occasionally. Allow the syrup to reach 235°. When the syrup spins a large thread when dropped from a spoon into water, add the lemon juice and vanilla and stir well. Pour the boiling syrup over the *urmasice*.

Vanilice
Croatian Vanilla Cookies

1 c. butter
1 whole egg
3 c. flour
1 egg yolk
1 tsp. vanilla
½ c. ground nuts
juice of half a lemon
1 egg white, stiffly beaten
vanilla sugar

Cream the butter until smooth and fluffy. Add the whole egg and the egg yolk and continue beating until the mixture becomes very creamy. Gradually add the flour, vanilla, nuts and lemon juice. Knead the dough until soft. Roll it out to about one quarter inch thickness. Cut into little circles, crescents, squares and/or diamonds with a cookie cutter. Place on a greased baking sheet. Bake at 350°. Remove from the oven, and while the cookies are still hot, dip them in the beaten egg white and roll in sugar.

Bosanski Kolač
Bosnian Cake

6 egg yolks
1 c. ground almonds
½ c. butter
1 c. cream
1 c. sugar
1 c. semolina flour
1 tbsp. grated lemon rind
6 egg whites, stiffly beaten

Beat the egg yolks and sugar until very light and lemon colored. Beat in the butter, grated lemon rind, semolina flour, almonds and cream. Mix well. Fold in the stiffly beaten egg whites. Pour into a greased and floured cake pan. Bake at 350° until the top is golden. Pour boiling lemon syrup over the cake as soon as it is removed from the oven. Cut into squares or diamonds, then sprinkle with confectioner's sugar. May also be served with Wine Sauce [page 160].

Ružice
Rosettes

2 ¼ c. flour
1 c. butter
1 c. cottage cheese
½ c. granulated sugar
¼ c. marmalade
confectioner's sugar

Combine the cheese and sugar. Beat this mixture until smooth and creamy. Cut the butter into the flour. Add the cheese and mix well to form a smooth dough. Allow to sit in a warm place for half an hour. Roll the dough to ¼" thickness and cut it into squares. Cut into each corner diagonally toward the center. Fold over every other edge in pinwheel fashion. Place the rosettes on an ungreased baking sheet and bake at 350° until they begin to turn golden. Sprinkle with confectioner's sugar and place a teaspoonful of jam or marmalade in the center of each rosette.

Mramorni Kolač
Marble Kolach

¾ c. butter
1 ½ c. sugar
3 egg yolks
½ tsp. salt
1 tsp. vanilla
1 c. milk
1 tsp. baking powder
1 tsp. ground lemon rind
2 ¼ c. flour
2 squares chocolate, grated
3 egg whites
¼ tsp. cream of tartar
¼ c. water
2 tbsp. sugar

Grease and flour a 10"x14" cake pan or a kuglof mold. Preheat the oven to 350°. Sift the flour with the baking powder. Cream the butter with one cup sugar until light and fluffy. Beat in the egg yolks and vanilla and continue beating until the mixture is light and lemon colored. Add the lemon rind and the flour and milk, alternately, beating well after each addition. Beat the egg whites until frothy.

Continued on next page.

187

Add the cream of tartar and continue beating until soft peaks form. Add the remaining ½ c. sugar and beat until very stiff peaks form. Gently fold the egg whites into the egg yolk batter. Remove one third of the dough to a separate bowl. Heat the water until it begins to boil. Remove from heat and stir in 2 tbsp. sugar and the chocolate. Allow to cool slightly. Gently add this chocolate mixture to the smaller portion of batter. Spoon half the light batter into the prepared pan. Spoon the chocolate batter over this layer, then spoon the remaining light batter over the chocolate. With a knife swirl gently through the layers to create a marbled effect, but be sure to leave distinct areas of light and dark batter. Bake at 325° for approximately an hour until the cake springs back to the touch. Invert the cake on a cooling rack. Cool in the pan for ten minutes. Remove the pan and allow to cool completely. Sprinkle the finished cakes with powdered sugar, or pour a chocolate glaze over the entire cake and garnish with almonds, walnuts or a little frosting.

Tortice od Ruma
Rum Cakes

7 egg yolks
6 egg whites
¼ tsp. cream of tartar
1 c. sugar
2 c. ground walnuts
¼ c. bread crumbs
3 tbsp. rum

Beat the egg yolks with the sugar until light and lemon colored. Add the ground walnuts and the bread crumbs which have been soaked in rum. Stir in the ground walnuts. Beat the egg whites until frothy. Add the cream of tartar and continue beating until stiff. Gently fold into the walnut mixture. Pour into a well greased and floured rectangular baking pan. Bake at 350° for about half an hour. Allow to cool. Cut into two equal pieces. Cover one of the layers with Walnut Cream frosting. Place the other layer over it and cut the torte into small pieces. Pour the rum glaze over the little cakes and garnish each with a walnut half.

Walnut Cream:

½ c. butter
1 c. confectioner's sugar
½ c. ground walnuts
2 tbsp. cream cheese
1 tsp. vanilla

Cream the butter and sugar until light and creamy. Beat in the cream cheese and vanilla. Stir in the ground walnuts and continue beating until the cream is very light.

Rum Glaze:

3 tbsp. rum
½ c. confectioner's sugar

Sift the sugar and beat with the rum until the mixture is smooth and silky. Pour over the frosted rum cakes when they have been cut. If desired, dip the sides in chopped walnuts.

Illustrated on back cover.

Zamorčići
Zamorchichi

4 egg whites
4 tbsp. sifted confectioner's sugar
1 square chocolate, grated
1 c. cooked plums
½ c. halved walnuts or
whole almonds

Beat the egg whites until stiff peaks form. Beat in the sifted sugar and the grated chocolate. Pour a tablespoon of the batter at a time onto a well-greased baking sheet. Pit the plums and replace with a whole almond or a walnut half. Place a plum in the center of each chocolate meringue peak. Bake in a slow oven (275°) for about 20 minutes until dry.

Doboš Torta
Dobosh Torte

7 egg whites
¼ tsp. cream of tartar
7 egg yolks
1/3 c. sugar
1 tsp. grated lemon rind
1/3 c. cake flour
1 tsp. vanilla
¼ tsp. salt

Preheat the oven to 350°. Beat the egg yolks. Add half the sugar and beat until the mixture is light and lemon colored. Add the lemon rind and vanilla. Mix well. Add the flour, a tablespoon at a time and beat well after each addition. Beat the egg whites until foamy. Add the cream of tartar and continue beating until they are stiff but not dry. Add the remaining sugar and continue beating for another minute. Gently fold the egg whites into the egg yolk mixture. Spread one quarter of the batter into two greased and floured cake pans. You may find it easier to grease and flour the backs of two cake pans and spread the batter over the backs of the pans. The batter should not be more than ¼ inch thick. Bake for approximately ten minutes or until the layers are golden. Allow to cool completely. Continue baking the layers until all the batter is used up. There should be a total of eight layers. While the layers are cooling, prepare the filling.

Continued on next page

Filling:

5 eggs
1/3 c. sugar
¼ c. milk
2 oz. grated chocolate
¾ c. butter, at room temperature
1 tsp. vanilla

Combine the eggs and sugar in the top of a double boiler and beat until thick and creamy. Add the chocolate and milk and cook, beating constantly, until the mixture begins to boil. Cook until the mixture coats a wooden spoon. Remove from heat and add the vanilla. Continue beating until the mixture cools. When the mixture is completely cooled, add the butter and continue beating until the filling is very rich and creamy. Save the best layer of cake for the top. Spread the remaining layers generously with chocolate cream filling, leave enough chocolate cream to frost the sides. Place the layers on top of each other. Frost the sides with chocolate filling.

Caramel Glaze

1 c. sugar
2 tbsp. water

Place the water and sugar in a saucepan and melt the sugar over medium heat, stirring constantly. Continue to cook until the sugar is a golden color. The glaze will harden very quickly, therefore the cake must be prepared before the glaze is made. Brush the crumbs off the top layer of cake. Prepare a long knife by greasing the blade with oil. Work quickly because the syrup will harden within one minute. Pour the hot syrup over the top of the cake and spread smooth with a palate knife. Immediately cut the caramel topped cake into eight or twelve pieces and allow to cool. Before serving, place the caramel sections over the cake windmill-style with a strip of whipped cream under each piece. Garnish with the remaining whipped cream.

Torta od Kave
Coffee Torte

6 egg yolks
¾ c. sugar
¾ c. ground almonds
2 tbsp. fine bread crumbs
6 stiffly beaten egg whites
2 tbsp. strong coffee

Soak the bread crumbs in coffee. Combine the egg yolks and sugar and beat well until light and lemon colored. Beat in the almonds and soaked bread crumbs. Fold in the egg whites. Pour into a well greased and floured cake pan and bake at 375° until the torte springs back to the touch. Allow to cool for about five minutes. Remove from pan and allow to cool completely on a cake rack. When the cake has completely cooled, cut it into three layers. Fill and frost with Coffee Cream Frosting [page 223] or with any other suitable frosting. Decorate with sliced almonds.

Torta od Ruma
Croatian Rum Torte

6 eggs
1 c. sugar
2 c. ground almonds or
walnuts
4 tbsp. fine dry breadcrumbs
4 tbsp. rum
1 tbsp. grated lemon rind

Whip together three egg yolks and three whole eggs. Add the sugar and beat until thick and lemon-colored. Add the nuts, the bread crumbs soaked in rum and the lemon rind. Beat well. Fold in the remaining egg whites, stiffly beaten. Pour this batter into a greased and floured 8 "cake pan. Bake at 350° for approximately half an hour. Fill and garnish with a light frosting or serve with whipped cream.

Pastries

Torta od Badema
Almond Torte

8 egg yolks
1 whole egg
8 egg whites
½ tsp. cream of tartar
1 ½ c. sugar
2 ½ c. blanched almonds, ground
¼ c. breadcrumbs
3 tbsp. rum
Butter Cream Frosting [page 223]
1 c. confectioner's sugar

Preheat the oven to 350°. Grease and flour a deep 9" cake pan. Soak the bread crumbs in rum for ten minutes. Beat the whole egg, egg yolks and 1 ½ cups of sugar until light and lemon colored. Stir in the ground almonds and bread crumbs. Beat the egg whites until frothy. Add the cream of tartar and continue beating until stiff. Fold the stiffly beaten egg whites into the egg yolk mixture.

Pour this batter into the prepared cake pan. Bake for approximately twenty-five minutes until the torte springs back to the touch. Cool for five minutes. Remove from pan and place on a cake rack. Allow the torte to cool completely.

Meringue

5 egg whites
1 tsp. lemon juice
1 c. confectioner's sugar
1 tsp. vanilla
¼ c. almonds

Beat the remaining egg whites to form stiff peaks. Beat in the lemon juice. Add one cup confectioner's sugar, gradually, beating after each addition. Continue to beat until the mixture is thick and smooth. Add the vanilla and sliced almonds. Cut two 8" circles from heavy parchment paper. Spread half the meringue on each circle.

Bake at 350° for ten minutes. Remove the paper after removing from the oven. Allow to cool until crisp. Combine two tablespoons of sugar and one tablespoon water, in a small saucepan and bring to a boil. Cool to lukewarm and add the rum.

Place the almond torte on a cake rack. Pour the rum syrup over the torte. Catch any syrup that drips in a pan under the cake rack. Spoon what has dripped onto the torte. Place a meringue circle on a cake plate and decorate with almond flavored Butter Cream Frosting.

Cover this with the almond torte and again spread the torte with frosting. Place the other meringue circle on top and frost the top and sides with the frosting. Garnish the sides with chopped or sliced almonds. Sprinkle the torte with confectioner's sugar and garnish the top with halved almonds or maraschino cherries.

Torta od Kiselog Mlijeka
Buttermilk Cake

2 eggs, whole
¾ c. sugar
¾ c. butter
2 ½ c. sifted cake flour
1 ¾ c. buttermilk
1 tsp. baking powder
1 tsp. vanilla

Cream the butter and sugar together until light and frothy. Whip the eggs. Add the eggs to the butter mixture gradually beating well after each addition. Add the baking powder, flour and buttermilk, alternately, beating well after each addition. Pour the batter into two well greased and floured 8" cake pans. Bake at 350° for approximately 35 minutes. Frost or serve with whipped cream.

Krunska Torta
Crown Torte

8 egg yolks
1 c. sugar
2 ½ c. walnuts
1 tbsp. lemon juice
8 egg whites

Beat the egg yolks and the sugar until light and lemon-colored. Beat in the lemon juice and the walnuts. Fold in the stiffly beaten egg whites. Pour into two well greased and floured 8" cake pans. Bake at 350° for about 25-30 minutes. Cool. Fill and frost with whipped cream or with any preferred frosting.

191

Vočna Torta
Fruit Torte

4 egg yolks
4 tbsp. sugar
4 tbsp. flour
4 egg whites
¼ tsp. cream of tartar
1 tsp. vanilla
seasonal fresh fruit
Orange Glaze

Preheat the oven to 350°. Grease and flour a large, ribbed flan pan. Beat the egg yolks with sugar until light and fluffy. Add the vanilla and the flour, a tablespoon at a time, beating well after each addition. Beat the egg whites until frothy. Add the cream of tartar and continue beating until the egg whites stand in stiff peaks. Gently fold the egg whites into the egg yolk mixture. Spread over the prepared flan pan. Bake for approximately twelve to fifteen minutes until the cake springs back to the touch. Cool for five minutes. Invert on a wire rack. Remove the pan and allow to cool completely.

Orange Glaze

½ c. sugar
2 tbsp. corn starch
1 c. orange juice
2 tsp. grated orange rind
1 tbsp. orange flavored liqueur
¼ tsp. salt

Mix sugar, cornstarch and salt in a small saucepan. Gradually stir in the orange juice until smooth. Bring to a boil, stirring constantly. Cook for two minutes. Remove from heat. Add the orange rind, cover and cool completely. When completely cooled, stir in the orange liqueur.

Cook the harder fruits in water with a little sugar added, or used canned fruit. Leave grapes and berries whole. Arrange the fruit of your choice on the cooled cake. Carefully spoon the cooled orange glaze over the top of the cake, covering the fruit completely. The cake should be used as soon as possible. It may be refrigerated up to 8 hours.

Illustrated on page 165.

Torta sa Sirom
Cheese Cake

4 egg yolks
4 tbsp. sugar
4 tbsp. flour
4 egg whites
¼ tsp. cream of tartar
1 tsp. vanilla
2 tbsp. rum
2 tbsp. strawberry jam

Preheat the oven to 350°. Grease and flour a 9 inch cake pan. Beat the egg yolks with sugar until light and fluffy. Add the vanilla and the flour, a tablespoon at a time, beating well after each addition. Beat the egg whites until frothy. Add the cream of tartar and continue beating until the egg whites stand in stiff peaks. Gently fold the egg whites into the egg yolk mixture. Spread into the prepared cake pan. Bake for approximately twelve to fifteen minutes until the cake springs back to the touch. Cool for five minutes. Invert on a wire rack. Remove the pan and allow to cool completely.

Cut the cake into two layers. Brush the layers of the cake with the rum. Place one layer on a serving platter. Spread the raspberry jam over this layer of cake. Place a 1 inch thick layer of the filling over the jam. Replace the second layer of cake over the filling. Cover the entire cake with the filling. Smooth the top and sides with a palate knife. Fill a pastry bag with the remaining whipped cream and make a decorative border around the top of the cake. Refrigerate for at least three hours before serving.

Filling

4 tablespoons sugar
½ c. cottage cheese, sieved
2 c. heavy cream

Mix the sugar and the cottage cheese. Whip the cream. Fold all but ¼ cup of the whipped cream into this mixture.

Torta od Jagoda i Snijega
Berry Meringue Cake

10 egg whites
¼ tsp. cream of tartar
4 c. sugar

Preheat the oven to 225°. Using an 8 inch cake pan, trace 2 circles on each of three pieces of parchment paper.

Beat eight egg whites with the cream of tartar until they form soft peaks. Beat in half the sugar and continue beating for one minute. When stiff peaks form, fold in the remaining sugar.

Put the meringue mixture into a large pastry bag fitted with a plain tube. Place a sheet of parchment paper on a baking sheet. Pipe a ring of meringue inside the edge of one of the circles on the parchment paper. Continue piping circles next to each other until you reach the center and you have a filled circle of meringue. If necessary spoon a little more meringue to fill any holes. This will be the base of the cake.

Pipe a ring inside the other circle on the same parchment paper. Pipe parallel diagonal lines in the circle, making a lattice pattern, filling the circle in completely. This will be the top of the cake.

Bake the circles for 45 minutes to dry them out. Remove from the oven and cool completely. Beat the remaining two egg whites with a dash of cream of tartar until they stand in soft peaks. Beat in the remaining sugar and continue beating until stiff.

Place the remaining parchment paper on baking sheets. Use the meringue mixture to pipe a single ring approximately ½ inch in diameter inside each of the 4 circles. Refrigerate the remaining meringue until needed. Bake the rings for 45 minutes to dry the meringue out. Cool completely.

When the meringue circles have cooled, carefully peel off the paper and set the bottom of the cake in an ovenproof serving dish. Remove the paper from the other meringue circles. Remove the reserved meringue from the refrigerator and beat again until stiff. It will have softened in the refrigerator. Use this reserved meringue to build a cake from the meringue rings. It will serve as mortar to cement the rings together.

Place the rings on top of each other over the base with a little meringue between each. Smooth the remaining meringue over the side with a palate knife. Return the cake, without the lid, to the oven and dry for another twenty minutes. Cool and reserve until ready to serve.

Before serving, prepare the filling and spoon the filling into the cake. Set the lattice lid on top, but at a slight angle so that the filling can be seen. With a star tube, pipe the remaining whipped cream around the base and the lid of the cake.

Filling

3 c. heavy cream
¼ c. confectioner's sugar
2 tbsp. marschino liqueur
1 lb. fresh berries

Hull, wash and pat the berries dry. Whip the cream with the confectioner's sugar and liqueur until very stiff. Reserve ½ cup of whipped cream for garnish. Gently fold the berries into the remaining whipped cream.

Torta od Oraha
Walnut Torte

6 egg yolks
1 c. confectioner's sugar
2 ½ c. ground walnuts
¼ c. sifted breadcrumbs
3 tbsp. rum
1 tsp. grated lemon rind
1 tsp. vanilla
6 egg whites
¼ tsp. cream of tartar
¼ c. marmalade
Walnut Butter Cream Frosting [page 223]

Preheat the oven to 350°. Grease and flour two eight inch cake pans. Soak the bread crumbs in the rum for fifteen minutes. In a deep bowl, beat the egg yolks and sugar until the mixture becomes light and lemon colored. Add the ground walnuts, lemon rind, vanilla and bread crumbs which have been soaked in rum.

Beat the egg yolks until frothy. Add the cream of tartar and continue beating until stiff. Fold the egg whites into the walnut mixture. Spread the mixture in the prepared pans. Bake for approximately half an hour. Allow the cake to cool completely.

Spread the bottom layer with marmalade. Fill with Walnut Butter Cream Frosting. Replace the top layer. Frost with the remaining frosting. Garnish with walnut halves. Pour Lemon Glaze over the frosted torte.

Lemon Glaze:

1 ½ c. confectioner's sugar
juice of one lemon

Strain the lemon juice. Sift the confectioner's sugar. Add the sugar to the strained lemon juice and beat well until smooth and slightly thickened.

Illustrated on back cover.

Torta od Kestena
Chestnut Torte

1 lb. cooked chestnuts, minced
1 c. sugar
1 c. ground walnuts, almonds
or filberts
6 eggs, separated
marmalade
1 c. whipped cream

Preheat the oven to 350°. Grease and flour two 8" cake pans. Beat the egg yolks and sugar until light and lemon-colored. When the mixture thickens, add the minced chestnuts and mix well. Fold in the stiffly beaten egg whites and ground nuts. Pour the batter into the prepared cake pans and bake for approximately half an hour. Cool the torte completely.

Spread one layer with a thin layer of marmalade, then one third of the whipped cream. Top with the other layer. Frost the top and sides with the remaining whipped cream and garnish with chestnuts and nuts.

Torta od Rogača
Carob Cake

6 egg yolks
½ c. sugar
2 c. powdered carob
2 tbsp. breadcrumbs
2 tbsp. rum
1 tsp. vanilla
¼ tsp. nutmeg
6 egg whites
¼ tsp. cream of tartar
1/3 c. milk
fruit jam or preserves for spreading
¼ c. chopped walnuts

Beat the egg yolks and sugar until light and frothy. Add the carob, bread crumbs and vanilla and mix well. Beat the egg whites until frothy. Add the cream of tartar and beat until stiff. Gently fold the egg whites into the carob batter. Pour into a greased and floured baking pan and bake at 350° for 30 minutes. Cut the cake in half and spread each half with jam or preserves. Sprinkle with chopped walnuts.

Rolada sa Marmaladom
Jelly Roll

4 eggs, separated
½ c. sugar
½ tsp. vanilla
¼ tsp. salt
1 tsp. baking powder
2/3 c. flour
1 tsp. grated lemon rind
1 c. marmalade

Preheat the oven to 350°. Line the bottom of an 11"x16" jelly roll pan with wax paper. Grease the wax paper. Beat the egg yolks until thick and lemon-colored. Gradually beat in half the sugar. Add vanilla and beat well. Sift the flour, baking powder and salt together. Stir into the egg yolk mixture and beat well. Beat the egg whites until frothy. Add the cream of tartar and continue beating until stiff. Fold the egg whites into the egg yolk mixture. Spread the batter evenly on the wax paper. Bake for ten to twelve minutes.

Turn the cake out onto a towel sprinkled with confectioner's sugar. Carefully remove the wax paper. Roll the cake into a log together with the towel. Cool for five minutes. Unroll. Spread the cake with marmalade. Roll tightly. Allow to cool. Sprinkle with confectioner's sugar and slice into 1" slices. For a more dramatic roll, allow to cool completely before spreading. Spread with jam and sweetened whipped cream. Roll tightly. Garnish with a little frosting and slice at the time of serving.

Torta od Čokolade
Croatian Chocolate Torte

9 eggs, separated
1 c. sugar
½ c. fine cake crumbs
2 tsp. baking powder
2 c. ground walnuts
¼ c. sweet white wine
2 tsp. vanilla
1 tbsp. grated lemon rind
½ c. butter, melted
7 oz semisweet chocolate, melted

Preheat the oven to 350°. Grease and flour three 8" cake pans. Beat the egg yolks with the sugar, vanilla and lemon rind until light and fluffy. Stir in the walnuts, wine and cake crumbs. Beat the melted chocolate and softened butter into the mixture. Beat the egg whites to form soft peaks. Fold in the sugar. Mix together the breadcrumbs, baking powder, ground nuts and half the chocolate. Carefully fold the egg whites into this dry mixture. Beat the egg whites until frothy. Add the cream of tartar and continue beating until stiff. Gently fold the egg whites into the chocolate mixture. Divide the batter among the pans and bake for thirty minutes. Cool on wire racks. Fill the cake with Chocolate Frosting (page 223). Spread the remaining frosting over the top and sides of the cake. Pour a chocolate glaze over the entire cake. Pipe a decorative lacy pattern of melted white chocolate around the edge of the cake.

Torta od Kiselog Vrhnja
Sour Cream Torte

6 eggs yolks
6 egg whites
¼ tsp. cream of tartar
½ c. cake flour
2 tbsp. sugar
2 c. sour cream
2 tbsp. melted butter
¼ tsp. salt

Preheat the oven to 350°. Grease and flour a 9" baking pan. Beat the cream, egg yolks, sugar and salt well. When the batter begins to thicken, add the butter and flour and beat for a few minutes longer. Beat the egg whites until frothy. Add the cream of tartar and continue beating until the whites stand in stiff peaks. Fold the stiffly beaten egg whites into the egg yolks. Pour the mixture into the prepared cake pan. Bake at 350° for about half an hour. The cake is ready when it springs back to the touch. Sprinkle with confectioner's sugar or serve garnished with sweetened whipped cream.

Proljetna Torta sa Jagodama
Strawberry Springtime Cake

5 eggs
¾ c. flour
1 tsp. baking powder
1 tsp. grated lemon rind
½ c. sugar
6 tbsp. butter, softened
1 c. strawberries for garnish

Preheat the oven to 350°. Sift the flour and baking powder. Butter and flour a 9 inch springform cake pan. Whisk the eggs, lemon rind and sugar in the top of a double boiler. Cook, beating constantly until the mixture thickens. Add the butter and the flour and continue beating until the mixture is smooth.

Pour the mixture into the prepared cake pan and bake for 25 minutes until the cake springs back to touch. Allow the torte to cool completely in the pan. Remove the sides of the pan and frost with strawberry cream. Garnish with whole or sliced strawberries and mint leaves.

Strawberry Cream

8 oz. strawberries
1 ½ c. heavy whipping cream
¼ c. powdered sugar
½ tsp. vanilla
1 tbsp. strawberry liqueur or rum

Purée the strawberries in a blender or food processor. Add the powdered sugar, vanilla and strawberry liqueur or rum. Whip the cream until stiff. Gently fold the strawberry purée into the whipped cream.

Torta od Kave i Oraha
Coffee Nut Torte

8 egg yolks
½ c. sugar
8 egg whites
¼ tsp. cream of tartar
2 c. ground walnuts
1 c. fine cake crumbs

Preheat the oven to 350°. Grease and flour two nine inch cake pans. Beat the egg yolks and sugar until light and fluffy. Stir in the walnuts and cake crumbs. Beat the egg whites until frothy. Add the cream of tartar and continue beating until stiff. Gently fold the egg whites into the walnut mixture.

Pour the batter into the prepared pans. Bake for thrity-five minutes until the cake springs back to the touch. Allow to cool in the pan for ten minutes. Invert onto a wire rack and remove the pans. Allow to cool completely.

Spread one of the layers with the Coffee Cream Frosting. Place the second layer over the first. Frost the top and sides with the remaining frosting. Pour Coffee Glaze over the entire cake and garnish with walnut halves.

Trešnje sa Sirom
Cherry Cheese Cake

2 eggs, separated
½ c. cottage cheese
1 tbsp. cream
3 tbsp. bread crumbs
1 tsp. baking powder
1 c. pitted cherries
1 tbsp. sugar
1 tbsp. grated lemon peel
1 tsp. cinnamon
¼ tsp. salt

Beat the egg yolks. Beat in the sugar. Add the cottage cheese, cream, lemon peel, cinnamon, salt, baking powder and bread crumbs. Mix well. Beat the egg whites so that they form peaks. Fold into the egg and cheese mixture. Pour the batter into a well greased and floured cake pan. Place the cherries on the batter. Bake at 375° for about an hour. Sprinkle with confectioner's sugar. Serve hot or cold.

Imotska Torta
Imotski Torte

2 c. flour
¾ c. butter
¾ c. sour cream
¼ c. sugar
1 egg

Preheat the oven to 450°. Grease and flour a deep 9" springform cake pan. Cream the butter and sugar until light and fluffy. Add the egg and sour cream and continue beating until well blended. Stir in the flour to make a medium dough. Divide the dough into two balls, one twice as large as the other. Roll the larger section of the dough into a circle ¼ inch thick and approximately 12 inches in diameter. Place the dough into the prepared pan, lining the bottom and side. Cut away any dough that may be above the edge of the pan with a sharp knife. Roll the remaining dough into a sheet ¼ inch thick and cut into ½ inch strips with a dough cutter.

Filling

6 eggs	2 tbsp. rum
1 ¼ c. sugar	1 tsp. vanilla
2 ½ c. ground walnuts	1 tsp. lemon rind

Continued on next page

Make the filling by beating the egg yolks and half the sugar until light and lemon-colored. Stir in the almonds, rum, lemon rind and vanilla. Beat the egg yolks until frothy. Add the cream of tartar and continue beating until stiff peaks form. Add the remaining sugar and beat for another thirty seconds. Gently fold into the almond mixture. Pour the filling into the pastry-lined cake pan. Make a lattice top over the filling with the strips of dough. Place a blanched almond where the dough strips meet. Bake for 45 to 50 minutes until a toothpick inserted into the center comes out clean.

Turn the oven off and allow the cake to cool in the oven for at least thirty minutes, leaving the door slightly ajar. This will keep the cake from being shocked by a sudden change in temperature and falling. Allow the cake to cool completely in the springform pan. Remove the sides of the pan and dredge with confectioner's sugar.

Torta s Makom
Poppyseed Torte

6 tbsp. butter, softened
½ c. sugar
4 egg yolks
4 egg whites
¼ tsp. cream of tartar
1 c. ground poppy seeds
1 tbsp. lemon rind
2 tbsp. rum
1/3 c. confectioner's sugar

Preheat the oven to 350°. Butter and flour a nine inch cake pan. Beat the butter and sugar together until light and fluffy. Beat in the egg yolks, one at a time, beating well after each addition. Add the poppy seeds, lemon rind and rum. Beat the egg whites until frothy. Add the cream of tartar and continue beating until stiff. Fold the egg whites into the poppy seed mixture.

Pour the batter into the prepared pan and bake for forty five minutes until the cake springs back to the touch or until a toothpick inserted into the cake comes out clean. Turn the oven off. Leave the door slightly open and allow the cake to cool

for an hour. This will prevent the cake from being shocked by a change in temperature and falling. Remove the cake from the oven. Invert onto a baking rack. Gently remove the cake pan and allow the cake to cool completely. Dredge with sifted confectioner's sugar.

Torta od Jabuka
Apple Cake

4 tbsp. butter
12 tbsp. sugar
juice of half a lemon
½ c. chopped walnuts
1 ½ lbs. cooking apples
2 tbsp. rum
3 egg yolks
6 tbsp. flour
grated rind of one lemon
3 egg whites
¼ tsp. cream of tartar
¼ c. cherry preserves
1 c. heavy whipping cream
1 tsp. vanilla
3 tbsp. powdered sugar

Peel and thinly slice the apples. Sprinkle with lemon juice so that they do not discolor. Melt the butter in a large ovenproof saucepan. Sprinkle with sugar and sauté until the sugar melts and you obtain a golden carmel syrup. Arrange the sliced apples over the caramel syrup. Bake at 400° for approximately twenty minutes.

Beat the egg yolks with the lemon rind and 6 tablespons sugar until light and fluffy. Add the flour, a tablespoon at a time, beating well after each addition. Beat the egg whites until frothy. Add the cream of tartar and continue beating until stiff. Gently fold into the egg yolk mixture.

Remove the pan from the oven and sprinkle with chopped walnuts and rum. Spread the cake batter over the apples. Return to the oven and bake at 350° for another twenty minutes. Allow to cool in the pan. Invert the pan onto a serving plate. Beat the whipping cream with the powdered sugar and vanilla. Garnish the apple cake with the cherry preserves and whipped cream.

Punč Torta
Punch Torte

8 egg yolks
8 egg whites
½ tsp. cream of tartar
1 c. sugar
¾ c. flour
2 lemons
1 orange
1 c. sugar
½ c. water
¼ c. dark rum
2 squares chocolate, melted
5 tablespoons raspberry syrup

Preheat the oven to 350°. Butter and flour two 8 inch cake pans. Beat the egg yolks with ¾ cup sugar until light and fluffly. Beat in the flour, a tablespoon at a time, beating well after each addition. Beat the egg whites until frothy. Add the cream of tartar and continue beating until stiff peaks form. Add the remaining ¼ cup sugar and beat for another thirty seconds. Fold the egg whites into the egg yolk mixture. Pour the batter into the prepared pans and bake for 30 minutes or until the cake springs back to the touch. Cool the cakes for five minutes.

Continued on next page.

Invert onto cooling racks and remove the pans. Cool completely on the wire racks.

Split one of the cakes into two layers. Set aside. Cut the center out of the other cake, leaving a two inch ring. Cut the circle that you have removed from this cake into cubes.

Squeeze the juice from the lemons and the orange. Dissolve the sugar in the water. Boil for approximately fifteen minutes until it reaches the large thread stage (235°). Add the lemon and orange juice to the sugar mixture along with the rum. Bring to a boil again and cook for one minute. Remove from heat and divide into three bowls. Allow to cool. Leave one bowl the color of the rum. Add the raspberry syrup to another and the melted chocolate to the third. Divide the spongecake cubes into three and soak one third in each syrup.

Place the jam-covered layer of the cake at the bottom of a springform pan. Place the ring over this layer. Place the syrup-soaked cubes in the center and top with the remaining layer of cake. Place wax paper or parchment paper over the top of the cake. Place another cake pan over the cake and weigh it down with some weight such as food cans. Refrigerate overnight.

The following day, remove the sides of the springform pan. Frost the cake with the following frosting and garnish with fresh raspberries and mint leaves.

Raspberry Rum Icing

1 egg white
2 c. powdered sugar, sifted
2 tbsp. rum
2 tbsp. raspberry syrup

Beat the egg white into the powdered sugar until the mixture is smooth. Add the rum and raspberry syrup and continue beating until the mixture is of spreading consistency. If necessary, add a little more powdered sugar to make the consistency just right.

Sacher Torta
Sacher Torte

4 oz. semisweet chocolate
½ c. butter, melted
8 egg yolks
10 egg whites
½ tsp. cream of tartar
¼ tsp. salt
1 tsp. vanilla
½ c. sugar
¾ c. flour
½ c. apricot jam

Preheat the oven to 350°. Grease and flour two 9 inch springform cake pans. Melt the chocolate in the top of a double boiler. Combine the butter, egg yolks, vanilla, half the sugar and the chocolate. Stir well. Beat the egg whites until frothy. Add the cream of tartar and continue beating until they form stiff peaks. Gradually beat in the remaining sugar. Gently fold the egg whites into the chocolate mixture. Fold the flour into the mixture, one tablespoon at a time, gently but thoroughly mixing after each addition. Pour the batter into the prepared pans. Bake for thirty minutes until the cake springs back to the touch. Remove from the oven. Cool for five minutes. Invert onto a wire rack and release the sides of the pans. Cool the cakes completely, then remove the pans. Spread the jam over one layer and the sides of the cake. Pour chocolate glaze over the entire cake. Smooth quickly with a greased palette knife and refrigerate for at least two hours.

Chocolate Glaze

3 oz. semisweet chocolate
1 c. heavy whipping cream
¾ c. sugar
1 tsp. vanilla
1 egg

Melt the chocolate in the top of a double boiler. Add the cream and sugar and cook until the chocolate melts. Increase the heat and cook for five minutes, stirring constantly. Beat the egg lightly and add a small amount of the chocolate mixture to the egg. Mix well. Pour back into the chocolate mixture. Return to the heat and simmer slowly until the mixture coats a wooden spoon. Do not boil. Remove from heat and cool.

Pita Mađarica i Indijaneri /Hungarian Pita and Little Indian Cakes [page 204]

Pita Mađarica
Hungarian Pita

4 c. flour
1 tsp. baking powder
¾ c. butter
2 eggs, slightly beaten
¾ c. sugar
1 c. sour cream
1 tsp. vanilla

Preheat the oven to 350°. Grease the backs of three 11"x18" cookie sheets. If you do not have three cookie sheets, you may use one at a time, washing it after each section of dough has baked. Sift the flour and baking powder. Cut in the cold butter to make pea-size morsels. Make a well in the center. Drop the eggs, sugar and sour cream into the well. Quickly work into a medium dough. Refrigerate for at least one hour. Roll the dough into layers approximately ¼ inch thick, the size of the cookie sheets. Bake the dough on the back of the cookie sheets for approximately twelve minutes. While the cake is cooling, make the filling.

Continued on next page

Filling

1½ c. sugar
3 c. milk
6 tbsp. corn starch
3 tbsp. water
¾ c. butter, softened
3 oz. unsweetened chocolate, melted
1½ c. powdered sugar
2 tbsp. rum

Melt the sugar and cook over low heat until golden. Add the milk and cook until the caramel is completely melted. Mix the corn starch with the water and add to the milk mixture. Stir well. Continue cooking over low heat until the mixture thickens. Stir in the melted chocolate and rum. Allow to cool completely. Beat the softened butter with the powdered sugar until very light and fluffy, then stir into the chocolate mixture.

When the dough has cooled, cut each sheet into 2 sections. Frost each of the sheets with chocolate filling. As each sheet is frosted, place the next one on top. Place the sixth sheet on top without filling. Cover with chocolate glaze.

Chocolate Glaze

¼ c. water
¼ c. sugar
4 oz. unsweetened chocolate
6 tbsp. unsalted butter

Heat the water, sugar and chocolate until the chocolate melts. Do not allow to boil. Drop thin slices of butter into the mixture, stirring constantly. Pour over the pita while it is still warm. Refrigerate overnight before slicing into squares or diamonds.

Indijaneri
Little Indian Cakes

4 egg yolks
6 tbsp sugar
1/3 c. flour
4 egg whites
¼ tsp. cream of tartar
1 ½ c. heavy whipping cream
1 tsp. vanilla
4 tbsp. powdered sugar
Chocolate Glaze as for Hungarian Pita

Preheat the oven to 350°. Grease and flour 12 indijaner molds or 6 cupcake tins. Beat the egg yolks with the sugar until light and lemon-colored. Add the flour, a tablespoon at a time, beating well after each addition. Beat the egg whites until frothy. Add the cream of tartar and continue beating until they form firm peaks. Gently fold into the egg yolk mixture and spoon into the prepared molds or cupcake tins. The mixture should fill no more than two thirds of the molds or tins. Bake for approximately ten minutes. Allow the cakes to cool completely.

Cut the cakes in half and remove the centers of the bottom half of each cupcake. These can be ground and used as cake crumbs in other recipes. Place the tops on wire racks and pour chocolate glaze over them. Allow to cool completely.

Just before serving, beat the cream until stiff. Add the powdered sugar and vanilla and beat for another minute. Fill the bottoms of the cupcakes with the whipped cream and replace the tops.

Illustrated on page 203

Moka Rolada
Mocha Chocolate Roll

6 egg yolks
1 c. sugar
1 tsp. vanilla
6 egg whites
¼ tsp. cream of tartar
2/3 c. sifted cake flour
1/3 c. cocoa
1 ½ tsp. baking powder
½ tsp. salt

Preheat the oven to 350°. Grease an 11"x18" cookie sheet with wax paper. Grease the wax paper. Beat the egg yolks until thick and lemon-colored. Gradually beat in half the sugar. Add the vanilla and continue beating until well mixed.

Sift together the flour, baking powder, cocoa and salt. Gradually add this mixture to the egg yolks, a little at a time and beat well after each addition. Beat the egg whites until frothy. Add the cream of tartar and continue beating until soft peaks form. Add the remaining sugar and beat for another thirty seconds. Fold the egg whites into the chocolate mixture gently.

Spread the batter over the waxed paper on the prepared sheet. Bake for approximately 15 minutes.

Immediately turn out on a towel sprinkled with sifted confectioner's sugar or cocoa. Carefully remove the wax paper. If necessary, trim any dry edges of the cake. Starting at the narrow end, roll the cake and towel together. Cool completely.

When completely cooled, unroll and spread with Mocha Filling. Save a little filling for garnishing. Roll up and place on a serving platter with the seam side down. Garnish with the remaining filling.

Mocha Filling

¾ c. sugar
½ tsp. salt
2 tbsp. cornstarch
2 c. milk
1 egg, well beaten
¾ c. butter, softened
2 tbsp. very strong coffee

Blend the sugar, cornstarch and salt in a medium saucepan. Add the milk and cook, stirring constantly over medium heat until thickened and bubbly. Cook and stir for another 2 to 3 minutes.

Remove from heat. Stir a small amount of the hot mixture into the egg. Return to the hot mixture and cook for another two minutes, stirring constantly.

Allow the mixture to cool completely, then stir in the butter and coffee. Beat at high speed for a few minutes until thick and light.

Pita s Jabukama
Apple Pita

4 c. flour
2/3 c. butter
4 egg yolks
½ c. sour cream
½ tsp. salt
1 tsp. baking powder
1 tbsp. grated lemon rind
1 tbsp. rum

Soak ½ cup raisins in 3 tablespoons rum for two hours before making the pita. Preheat the oven to 350°. Grease and flour an 11"x13" baking pan. Cream the butter with the sugar. Stir in the flour and the remaining ingredients. Mix all the ingredients well to make a medium firm dough. Refrigerate this dough for at least half an hour.

Wash, core and grate the apples. Divide the dough into two sections. Flatten each half to a rectangle the size of the baking pan. Sprinkle with half the bread crumbs. Spread the filling over the dough and sprinkle with the raisins which have been well drained. Place the second sheet of dough over the first and brush the top with melted butter.

If preferred, the top layer of dough can be cut into long strips and braided diagonally over the apple filling. Bake at 350° until the top is golden, approximately thirty-five minutes. After baking, allow the pita to cool completely. Sprinkle with powdered sugar and cut into diamonds or squares before serving.

Apple Pita Filling:

2 lbs. tart apples, grated
½ c. sugar
3 tbsp. rum
1 tsp. cinnamon
3 tbsp. fine cake crumbs
4 egg whites

Beat the egg whites with a dash of salt until they form stiff peaks. Add the sugar and beat for another thirty seconds. Stir in the apples, rum and cinnamon.

Pita sa Sirom, Pita od Visanja i Pita s Cokoladom /Cheese Pita, Cherry Pita [page 209] and Chocolate Pita [page 208].

Pita sa Sirom
Cheese Pita

Pita Dough:
2 ¾ c. flour
¾ c. butter
3 tbsp. sour cream
½ c. sugar
4 egg yolks, slightly beaten
1 tsp. baking powder
1 tbsp. grated lemon rind
¼ tsp. salt

Filling:
4 egg yolks
½ c. sugar
1 lb. cottage cheese
1 tsp. vanilla
1 tbsp. lemon juice
4 egg whites
¼ tsp. cream of tartar
¼ c. sour cream
1 egg white, slightly beaten

Refrigerate the ingredients for the dough before starting. Preheat the oven to 350°. Grease and flour an 11"x13" baking pan. Sift the flour with the baking powder. Cut the cold butter into the flour. Add the egg yolks, sugar, lemon rind, salt and sour cream. Work quickly to combine the ingredients to a smooth dough. Do not handle the dough more than necessary. Divide the dough into two sections. Refrigerate for approximately half an hour.

Continued on next page

Roll each section into a rectangle the size of the baking pan. Place one section in the bottom of the prepared pan. Bake in the preheated oven for ten minutes.

While the bottom crust is baking, make the filling. Beat the egg whites until frothy. Add the cream of tartar and continue beating until stiff peaks form. Blend the cream cheese in a blender or food processor. Beat the egg yolks and sugar until light and lemon colored. Stir in the cheese, lemon rind, salt, lemon juice, vanilla and flour.

Gently fold the egg whites into the cheese mixture. Spread this filling over the first layer of dough. Place the second sheet of dough over the filling and prick little holes in the dough with a fork to allow trapped air and steam to escape. Beat the remaining egg white with one teaspoon water and brush the egg white wash over the top of the pita.

If you prefer, cut the second layer into long strips with a pastry cutter and braid them into a lattice top over the filling.

Return to the oven for another thirty minutes and bake until the top is golden. Sprinkle with confectioner's sugar. Allow to cool. Cut into diamonds or squares before serving.

Pita s Čokoladom
Chocolate Pita

4 egg yolks
1 c. butter
4 ½ c. flour
¾ c. sugar
¼ tsp. salt
1 tbsp. grated lemon rind
juice of one lemon

Preheat the oven to 350°. Refrigerate the flour and the mixing bowl for half an hour before starting to make the dough. Grease and flour an 11"x13" baking pan. Sift the flour with the salt.

Cut the butter into the flour until you obtain crumbs the size of bread crumbs. Add the sugar, lemon rind, lemon juice and egg yolks.

Make two balls from the dough, one twice as large as the other.

Pat the larger ball of dough into the bottom of the prepared pan, making it as even as possible. Bake in the preheated oven for ten minutes.

Chocolate Pita Filling

4 egg whites
¼ tsp. cream of tartar
¾ c. sugar
2 c. ground blanched almonds
4 oz. semisweet chocolate, grated
1 tsp. vanilla
¼ c. apricot jam
1 egg white for brushing pastry

While the pita dough is baking, make the filling. Beat the egg whites until frothy. Add the cream of tartar and continue beating until they form stiff peaks. Add the sugar and beat for another thirty seconds. Gently fold in the chocolate, almonds and vanilla. Spread the jam over the partially baked dough. Spread the filling over the jam.

Roll the remaining ball of dough into a thin sheet, approximately ¼ inch thick. Cut into long strips with a pastry cutter. Make a lattice top over the filling with these strips of dough. Beat the egg white with one teaspoon water and brush this egg white wash over the lattice top. Return to the oven and bake for another thirty minutes until the top is golden. Allow to cool, then cut into squares or diamonds.

Illustrated on page 205.

Pita s Orasima
Walnut Pita

3 c. flour
1 c. butter
1 tsp. baking powder
½ c. sugar
1 egg
1 tsp. grated lemon rind
1 tbsp. milk
2 tbsp. lemon juice

Sift the flour and baking powder. Cut in the butter. Add the egg, sugar, lemon rind and lemon juice. Mix well. Divide the dough into two sections and refrigerate for half an hour. Roll the section into rectangles the size of the baking pan. Grease and flour the baking pan. Line the bottom with a section of the dough. Beat the egg yolks with the sugar until light and lemon-colored. Add walnuts, lemon rind and grated chocolate. Fold in the stiffly beaten egg whites. Beat well. Spread this filling over the first layer of dough. Place the second sheet of dough over the filling. Brush with melted butter. If you prefer, cut the second layer into long strips and braid them into a lattice top over the filling. Bake at 350° until the top is evenly colored. Sprinkle with confectioner's sugar. Allow to cool, then cut into diamonds or squares.

Filling:

5 egg yolks
1 c. sugar
2 c. ground walnuts
5 egg whites, stiffly beaten
1 tbsp. lemon rind
2 squares chocolate, grated

Pita s Višnjama
Cherry Pita

4 egg yolks
1 c. butter
4 ½ c. flour
1½ c. sugar
¼ tsp. salt
1 tbsp. grated lemon rind
2 lbs. tart cherries, pitted
4 tbsp. breadcrumbs
1 c. ground walnuts
confectioner's sugar for sprinkling

Preheat the oven to 350°. Refrigerate the flour and the mixing bowl for half an hour before starting to make the dough. Grease and flour an 11"x13" baking pan. Sift the flour with the salt. Cut the butter into the flour until you obtain crumbs the size of bread crumbs. Add the sugar, lemon rind, lemon juice and egg yolks.

Make two balls from the dough, one twice as large as the other.

Pat the larger ball of dough into the bottom of the prepared pan, making it as even as possible. Sprinkle with half the bread crumbs. Spread the cherries over the bread crumbs. Sprinkle with sugar, walnuts and remaining bread crumbs.

Roll the remaining ball of dough into a thin sheet, approximately ¼ inch thick. Cut into long strips with a pastry cutter. Make a lattice top over the filling with these strips of dough. Beat the egg white with one teaspoon water and brush this egg white wash over the lattice top. Place in the preheated oven and bake for approximately forty minutes until the top is golden. Allow to cool, then cut into squares or diamonds. Dredge in confectioner's sugar.

Illustrated on page 207

Kraljevska Pita
Royal Pita

¾ c. butter
4 egg yolks
2 squares chocolate, grated
1 c. sugar
1 tsp. lemon rind
1 ¼ c. ground almonds
2 tbsp. fine breadcrumbs
6 egg whites, stiffly beaten
½ c. powdered sugar

Preheat the oven to 350°. Grease and flour an 8"x10" baking pan. Cream the butter with the sugar. Beat the egg yolks into the mixture, one at a time. Continue beating until the mixture is light and fluffy. Add the almonds, grated lemon rind, grated chocolate and breadcrumbs. Fold in four stiffly beaten egg whites. Pour into a well greased and floured baking pan and bake until the top is golden, approximately fifteen minutes. Stiffly beat the remaining egg whites. Add the powdered sugar and beat for another thirty seconds. Spread this meringue over the baked pita. Return to the oven and continue baking until the meringue browns slightly. Cut into squares or diamonds. Serve hot or cold.

Fina Pita
Fine Pita

2 c. flour
2/3 c. butter
1 egg yolk
2 tbsp. milk
8 tbsp. sugar
¼ c. currant preserves
1 ½ lbs. cooking apples
1 tbsp. lemon juice
1 tbsp. lemon rind
1 tsp. cinnamon
1 tbsp. rum

Preheat the oven to 375°. Grease and flour and 8"x10" baking pan. Cut the butter into the flour until you obtain crumbs the size of peas. Add the egg yolk, four tablespoons sugar and milk. Quickly work into a firm dough. Refrigerate the dough for half an hour. Grate the apples and sprinkle with lemon juice so that they do not discolor. Roll the dough to the size of the pan, spread it with the preserves, then sprinkle the grated apples over the marmalade. Sprinkle the apples with the remaining four tablespoons sugar, cinnamon, lemon rind and rum. Spread the topping over the apples. Bake in the preheated oven for approximately 45 minutes until the top is golden.

Topping

3 egg yolks
3 egg whites
¼ tsp. cream of tartar
½ c. flour

Beat the egg yolks and the sugar until light and lemon-colored. Add the flour, a tablespoon at a time, beating well after each addition. Beat the egg yolks until frothy. Add the cream of tartar and continue beating until they form stiff peaks. Fold the egg whites into the egg yolk mixture.

Rajska Pita
Heavenly Pita

4 ½ c. flour
1 c. sugar
½ c. sour cream
2 whole eggs, slightly beaten
¼ c. butter
1 tsp. baking powder
confectioner's sugar

Preheat the oven to 375°. Grease and flour the back of a 11"x13" baking pan. Sift the flour with the baking powder. Cut the butter into the flour. Add the sugar, sour cream and eggs. Work quickly into a firm dough. Divide the dough into four pieces and roll each piece out to the size of the pan. Bake each piece of dough for twenty minutes or until golden. Allow to cool completely. Spread the filling over three of the sheets of dough. Place the fourth sheet on top. Place a sheet of wax paper over the pita, then place a cookie sheet on top and weigh the pita down with food cans. Refrigerate overnight. The following morning, cut into squares or diamonds and sprinkle with confectioner's sugar.

Heavenly Pita Filling

2 c. milk
½ c. sugar
2 tbsp. corn starch
2 oz. unsweetened chocolate, grated
1 c. butter, softened

Melt the sugar in the milk over boiling water in the top of a double boiler. Place a little of the milk mixture into a glass. Add the corn starch and mix well. Return this mixture to the top of the double boiler. Cook until the mixture thickens, then add the grated chocolate and allow to cool completely. Add the butter and beat until smooth and creamy.

Kolač sa Šljivama
Plum Kolach

2 c. milk
1 lb. white bread
½ c. butter
½ c. sugar
¼ tsp. salt
1 tbsp. grated lemon rind
4 egg yolks
4 egg whites, stiffly beaten
½ lb. ripe plums
1 tsp. cinnamon
sugar cubes

Remove the pits from the ripe plums. Replace each with a cube of sugar. Place them in a well greased cake pan. Fill the pan only to one third. Soak the bread in the milk. Add the melted butter, egg yolks, sugar, salt, lemon rind and cinnamon. Mix well. Beat the egg whites until stiff. Fold into the batter. Pour the batter over the plums. Bake at 350° for about an hour.

Kolač od Jabuka
Apple Kolach

6-8 sour apples
1 tsp. rum or sljivovica
1/3 c. milk
3 tbsp. sour cream
2 egg yolks
2 egg whites, stiffly beaten
1 tbsp. sugar
½ c. flour

Peel and slice the apples. Cover them with rum and allow to sit for a few minutes. Mix the milk, sour cream, egg yolks and sugar. Add the flour and beat to a batter slightly thicker than pancake batter. Fold in the stiffly beaten egg whites. Place the apple slices in a well greased and floured cake pan. Pour the batter over the apples. Bake at 375° for approximately an hour.

Zagorski Kolač
Zagorje Kolach

¾ c. butter
5 egg yolks
½ c. sugar
1 tbsp. lemon rind
5 egg whites, stiffly beaten
¾ c. sugar
1 ½ c. ground almonds
1 tbsp. sugar
¼ c. marmalade
½ c. flour

Cream the butter. Add the egg yolks, one at a time, beating well after each addition. Add ½ cup of sugar and continue beating until the mixture thickens. Gradually add the flour and lemon rind. Pour this batter into a well greased and floured cake pan. Spread with marmalade. Stiffly beat the egg whites. Add ¾ cup sugar and continue beating. Fold the egg whites into the gound almonds. Spread the almond meringue over the kolach batter. Bake at 350° for approximately an hour. Allow to cool slightly before cutting and serving.

Kolač s Ribizlima
Gooseberry Kolach

1 c. butter
3 oz. cream cheese
¾ c. sugar
2 c. fine bread crumbs
6 egg yolks
6 egg whites, stiffly beaten
¼ tsp. cream of tartar
2 ½ c. gooseberries

Preheat the oven to 350°. Grease and flour a 9"x12" baking pan. Wash and clean the gooseberries. Cream the butter and cream cheese with the sugar until light and frothy. Add the egg yolks one at a time, beating well after each addition. Stir in the breadcrumbs. Beat the egg whites until frothy. Add the cream of tartar and continue beting until stiff peaks form. Fold the stiffly beaten egg whites into the egg yolk mixture. Pour the batter into the prepared baking pan. Sprinkle with gooseberries and bake at 350° for about an hour.

Kolač s Višnjama
Sour Cherry Kolach

2 c. flour
2/3 c. butter
1 ½ c. powdered sugar
2 egg yolks
rind of one lemon, grated
1 ½ lb. pitted sour cherries

Preheat the over to 375°. Grease and flour an 8"x10" baking pan. Cut the butter into the flour. Add the sugar, egg yolks and lemon rind. Quickly work into a firm dough. Roll the dough to the size of the pan. Bake in the preheated oven for twenty minutes. Arrange the pitted cherries over the baked dough. Pour the topping over the cherries. Reduce the heat in the oven to 300°. Return the kolach to the oven and bake until the cream topping dries out and begins to brown slightly, approximately fifteen minutes.

Piškotne Ploškice
Angel Squares

4 eggs, separated
4 tbsp. sugar
5 tbsp. flour
1 tbsp. grated lemon rind
½ tsp. baking powder
2 tbsp. sugar
1 c. wine

Preheat the oven to 350°. Grease and flour and 11"x13" baking pan. Beat the egg yolks very well. Add two tablespoons sugar and continue beating until the mixture is thick and creamy. Fold in the well beaten egg whites. Add the flour, baking powder and lemon rind. Mix at low speed for about a minute. Pour the batter into a well greased and floured baking pan. Bake for about an hour. Allow the cake to cool completely. Cut into squares or diamonds and refrigerate overnight. Before serving, boil the wine. Add two tablespoons of sugar and cook until the mixture begins to thicken slightly. Pour over the squares. Cool, then sprinkle with confectioner's sugar.

Cream Topping

6 egg yolks
6 egg whites
¼ tsp. cream of tartar
¾ c. sugar
1 c. sour cream
2 tbsp. flour

Beat the egg yolks and the sugar until light and lemon-colored. Stir in the flour and sour cream and beat well. Beat the egg whites until frothy. Add the cream of tartar and continue beating until stiff peaks form. Gently fold the egg whites into the egg yolk mixture.

Roščići od Sira
Cheese Horns

2 c. flour
1 c. butter
2 eggs, separated
¼ c. sugar
1 c. cottage cheese
1 tsp. cinnamon
1 tbsp. grated lemon rind
¼ c. milk

Cream the butter and sugar until light and frothy. Add the well beaten egg yolks. Beat well. Beat in the flour and milk alternately, beating well after each addition. Allow the dough to sit for half an hour. Combine the cheese, cinnamon, lemon rind and stiffly beaten egg whites. Roll the dough to ½" thickness. Cut into triangles of equal size. Place half a teaspoon of filling onto each triangle. Roll toward the pointed end of the triangle to form little horns. Bake at 350° until golden. Roll in confectioner's sugar. Serve warm or cold.

Kolač sa Šljivama
Plum Kolach

1 c. butter, softened
4 eggs
1 c. sugar
1 tbsp. grated lemon rind
½ tsp. cinnamon
1 tsp. vanilla
1 tbsp. rum
1 ¼ c. flour
1 lb. plums
confectioner's sugar

Preheat the oven to 350°. Grease and flour a 9"x12" baking pan. Cream the butter with the eggs and sugar until light and fluffy. Add the lemon rind, cinnamon, vanilla and rum. Beat for another minute. Add the flour, a little at a time, beating constantly. Spread the batter in the prepared baking pan. Slice the plums in half and pit them. Roll each plum in sugar, then place, cut side down, over the batter. Bake for twenty minutes. Remove from oven and sprinkle generously with confectioner's sugar. Cut into slices or diamonds. May be served hot or cold.

Bijela Bazlamača
White Bazlamacha

3 tbsp. butter
3 egg yolks, well beaten
3 tbsp. powdered sugar
1 tsp. salt
1 c. sieved cottage cheese
3 c. milk
3 c. flour
½ c. sour cream
3 egg whites

Cream the butter until very light. Add the well beaten egg yolks, sugar, cheese and salt. Mix well. Add the milk and flour, alternately, beating well after each addition. Finally, fold in the stiffly beaten egg whites. Melt a little butter in a baking pan. Sprinkle with flour. Pour the bazlamaca batter into the pan and bake at 350° until golden and the cake springs back to the touch. Beat the sour cream with a tablespoon of sugar and pour over the bazlamaca. Return to the oven for 3-4 minutes. Serve hot or cold.

Karuzo Ploške
Caruso Slices

½ c. butter
½ c. sugar
4 egg yolks
1 tsp. vanilla
2 oz. unsweetened chocolate, grated
1 c. ground almonds
½ c. cake crumbs
4 egg whites
¼ tsp. cream of tartar

Preheat the oven to 350°. Grease and flour an 8"x10" baking pan. Cream the butter and sugar until light and fluffy. Add the egg yolks, one at a time, and beat well after each addition. Stir in the vanilla, chocolate and almonds. Add the cake crumbs and stir well. Beat the egg whites until frothy. Add the cream of tartar and continue beating until stiff. Gently fold into the egg yolk mixture. Pour the batter into the prepared baking pan and bake for forty-five minutes. Allow to cool completely before slicing.

Proljetna Torta
Spring Torte

2 ½ c. sugar
¼ tsp. salt
5 egg yolks, lightly beaten
2 tsp. vanilla
1 c. cream
10 egg whites
2 c. flour
1 tbsp. sugar
1 tsp. cinnamon
2 c. cherry pie filling
2 c. whipped cream

Sift the flour and salt together. Beat the egg yolks and half the sugar until light and lemon colored. Beat in the flour and five egg whites, alternately, beating well after each addition. Add the vanilla and beat well.

Pour this dough into two round greased and floured cake pans. Beat the remaining egg whites until stiff, but not dry. Add the remaining sugar gradually, and beat well. Spread this meringue mixture over the torte batter. Sprinkle one tablespoon sugar and the cinnamon. Bake at 350° for about half an hour. Allow to cool completely. Spread half the cherry filling over one layer of the torte. Spread half the whipped cream over the cherry filling. Place the other layer of torte on top. Place the remaining cherry filling in the center of this layer. Decorate the top and sides with the remaining whipped cream. For a more elaborate garnish, pipe the remaining whipped cream through a pastry tube. Fresh strawberries soaked in rum, then well drained, may be substituted for the cherry filling.

Lisnato Tjesto
Flaky Pastry Dough

2 ¼ c. unsalted cold butter
4 c. sifted pastry flour
5 tbsp. softened butter
1 c. ice water
1 tsp. salt
rum

Refrigerate all ingredients and utensils before attempting to make Flaky Pastry Dough. Throughout, the ingredients and utensils must be kept very cold for flaky pastry to be successful.

Dissolve the salt in the water. Place the flour and the softened butter in a deep bowl. Beat for 30 seconds then add the rum and the salted water. Work the dough just enough to get a smooth, homogeneous mass. Form a ball of the dough and cut the top crosswise with a knife. Refrigerate for two hours.

Place the cold butter between two sheets of wax paper and tap it several times with a rolling pin in order to flatten it. This will make it more pliable. Roll the dough. The criss-cross cut that was made earlier will divide the dough into four sections, making a large four leaf clover shape. Place the butter on top of the dough. Bring the edges of the dough (the leaves of the "clover") up over the butter. Seal the leaves well to enclose the butter completely.

Roll the dough into a thick rectangle and refrigerate for half an hour. The dough and the butter will come to the same temperature. Roll the dough gently into a long rectangle twice as long as it is wide and approximately ¼" to 3/8" thick. Roll from the center out. Be gentle. The dough is very delicate and can easily open letting butter ooze through. Frequently check to make sure that the dough is not sticking to the table. Reflour the table and rolling pin when necessary, but do so as lightly as possible each time.

Fold the dough over one third of itself, like the first fold of a letter. Roll the folded part lightly. Fold the single layer back over the dough. Now the dough has three layers. Refrigerate for half an hour. Place the folded dough with the fold facing you and roll the dough gently again until you have a rectangle twice as long as it is wide. Make two folds again and refrigerate the dough for half an hour.

Remove the dough from the refrigerator and repeat the procedure again. Roll the dough until it is twice as long as it is wide. Fold in thirds like a letter and refrigerate for half an hour. The pastry should get a total of six such folds. Refrigerate the dough again for two hours before using. The dough will keep up to four days in the refrigerator if wrapped tightly in foil or plastic. It will discolor after that time. Flaky Pastry may be frozen. Transfer from the freezer to the refrigerator 24 hours before using.

Krempita
Cream Slice

Flaky Pastry Dough
8 eggs, separated
1 c. flour
3 c. milk
1 tsp. vanilla
1 c. sugar
½ c. confectioner's sugar
1 egg white

Preheat the oven to 425°. Divide Flaky Pastry Dough into two parts. Roll each section into a rectangle. Place on an ungreased baking sheet and brush with slightly beaten egg white. Bake at 425° for ten minutes. Reduce the heat to 400° and continue baking until lightly browned on top. Allow to cool.

Bring the milk to a boil in the top of a double boiler. Beat the egg yolks with half the sugar. Add the flour and mix well. Pour a little hot milk into the egg mixture, then pour the egg mixture into the milk. Bring to a boil in the top of a double boiler. Cook, stirring constantly, until the mixture thickens and coats the back of a spoon. Beat the egg whites until very stiff. Beat the remaining sugar into the stiffly beaten egg whites. Add the egg whites to the egg yolk and milk and continue cooking for another minute.

Continued on next page.

215

Spread this cream filling over a sheet of cooled flaky pastry. The cream should be no less than 1 ½ inches thick. Cut the second pastry into 2 x 4 inch rectangles with a sharp knife. Place these rectangles over the filling to reassemble the pastry sheet. Refrigerate for at least two hours. Slice through to the bottom layer and you have cream slices. Dredge generously with confectioner's sugar. If desired, pipe sweetened whipped cream over the cream slices and drizzle with melted chocolate.

Čokoladne Ploške
Chocolate Wafer Squares

These chocolate squares are very simple to make. The wafer sheets, which are available in most European delicatessens, are called oblaten.

2 c. milk
¾ c. sugar
6 oz. semisweet chocolate, melted
1 tsp. vanilla
2 eggs
1 ½ c. ground walnuts
1 c. butter, softened
6 wafer sheets

Melt the chocolate and dissolve the sugar in the milk in the top of a double boilder. Cook over boiling water until the mixture begins to boil. Pour a little of the hot milk mixture into the eggs. Return to the top of the double boiler and continue cooking until the mixture thickens. Remove from heat and stir in the vanilla and ground walnuts. Add the butter and beat until the mixture is light and smooth and of spreading consistency. Spread the cream over five of the wafer sheets. Arrange them one on top of the other and top with the remaining wafer sheet. Pour chocolate glaze over the wafer cake and refrigerate overnight. The next day, cut into squares or diamonds.

Punjeni Tuljčići
Cream Horns

Flaky Pastry Dough
1 egg white
2 c. whipping cream
¼ c. confectioner's sugar
½ tsp. vanilla
¼ c. almonds, coarsely ground

Roll the pastry as thin as possible. Cut into long strips 15" x 1 ½" with a pastry cutter. Beat the egg white with one teaspoon of water and brush the pastry with egg white. Starting at the short end of the pastry horn tubes, wrap each tube with a strip of dough. Place the pastry horns on an ungreased baking sheet at least two inches apart. Bake at 425° for ten to twelve minutes. Carefully remove the metal tubes and allow the pastry to cool. Whip the cream with the sugar and vanilla. Fill the horns with whipped cream. Sprinkle the end with chopped almonds, if desired.

Medenjaci
Honey Cookies

3 c. flour
½ tsp. baking powder
¾ c. butter
1 c. sugar
2 eggs
1 c. ground walnuts or almonds
1 tsp. cinnamon
3 tbsp. honey
1 tbsp. lemon rind
1 egg white

Sift the flour with the baking powder. Cut the butter into the flour. When you have crumbs the size of peas, add the sugar, eggs, ground nuts, cinnamon, honey and lemon rind. Mix until the dough is firm, but smooth. Chill for an hour. Shape balls the size of walnuts from the dough. Place on a greased cookie sheet, flatten slightly, and brush with egg white. Place half a walnut on each cookie. Bake at 350° for twenty minutes.

Baklava
Baklava

Savijaca Pastry Dough
1 c. chopped walnuts
1 c. chopped almonds
½ c. raisins
1 tsp. cinnamon
½ c. melted butter
1 tsp. grated lemon rind
sugar

Preheat the oven to 400°. Butter an eleven by sixteen inch baking sheet generously . Mix the walnuts, almonds, raisins, sugar, grated lemon peel and cinnamon. Stretch the savijaca dough on a floured tablecloth. Allow to dry for about ten minutes. Cut into 12-14 sheets of equal size with a pastry cutter. Place the first sheet of dough on the baking sheet. Butter generously. Place a second sheet over the first. Repeat until four or five sheets have been used up. Spread half the filling evenly over these sheets. Place and butter two more sheets of pastry dough over the filling. Spread the remaining filling over these sheets, cover with the remaining pastry sheets, buttering each generously. Pour any remaining butter over the baklava. Cut the baklava into small diamonds. Bake at 400° until the pastry becomes golden.

Continued on next page

Drain any excess butter when the pastry is removed from the oven. Brush the tops with some of this butter to give luster to the baklava. Pour the syrup over the baklava and allow to sit for two to three hours to soak up the syrup.

Bakalava Syrup:

3 c. sugar
2 tbsp. honey
4 c. water
1 vanilla bean

In a medium saucepan, combine the sugar, honey, water and vanilla bean. Cook over moderate heat for about ten to fifteen minutes. Allow to cool, then pour over the baked Baklava.

Orahovi Štapići
Walnut Bars

1 ¾ c. flour
½ c. butter
¾ c. sugar
3 egg yolks
1 tsp. vanilla
rind of one lemon, grated
½ tsp. baking powder

Preheat the oven to 350°. Grease and flour a 9"x13" baking pan. Cream the butter and sugar until light and fluffy. Add the eggs, one at a time, beating after each addition. Add the vanilla, lemon rind and flour and beat well. Bake for ten minutes in the preheated oven. Spread the partially baked dough with strawberry jam, then spread the topping over the jam. Return to the oven for another twenty minutes until the top just begins to brown.

Topping

3 egg whites
¼ tsp. cream of tartar
¾ c. sugar
2 c. ground walnuts

Beat the egg whites until frothy. Add the cream of tartar and continue beating until they stand in soft peaks. Add the sugar and continue beating for anther minute. Gently fold in the ground walnuts.

Dalmatinske Pršunate
Dalmatian Fritters

1 cake yeast
2 tbsp. sugar
3 ½ c. flour
½ tsp. salt
1 c. raisins
2 tbsp. brandy
grated rind of 1 orange
grated rind of 1 lemon
juice of one lemon
1 ½ c. warm water
oil for deep frying
vanilla sugar

Dissolve the yeast in ½ cup warm water to which 1 tsp. sugar has been added. Allow to rise until frothy. Warm a large bowl and sift the flour with the salt in it. Add the yeast mixture, raisins, brandy, orange and lemon rind, lemon juice and enough of the remaining water to make a very soft dough. Cover and allow the dough to rise in a warm, draft-free place until doubled in bulk, approximately forty-five minutes. Drop by spoonful into hot oil (350°) until golden on all sides. Drain on paper towels. Sprinkle with vanilla sugar and serve warm.

Krostule
Fried Ribbons

3 eggs
3 tbsp. oil
3 tbsp. wine vinegar
3 tbsp. brandy
2 tbsp. sugar
½ tsp. salt
3-3½ c. flour

Beat the eggs well. Add the oil, vinegar, brandy, sugar and salt. Mix well. Add enough of the flour to make a firm dough. Knead the dough well. When smooth and glossy, roll it out to ¼ inch thickness on a well-floured pastry board. With a pastry wheel, cut ribbons, triangles or other shapes. Fry the *krostule* in hot oil (350°) until golden on both sides. Drain on paper towels and sprinkle with vanilla sugar while still warm.

Illustrated on page 219

Pokladnice i Kroštule / Croatian Mardi Gras Cakes and Fried Ribbons [page 218].

Pokladnice
Croatian Mardi Gras Cakes

1 cake yeast
4 c. sifted and warmed cake flour
1 c. warm milk
6 tbsp. softened butter
2 tbsp. sugar
4 egg yolks
¼ tsp. salt
½ c. sour cream
2 tbsp. rum
1 tbsp. grated lemon rind
3 c. oil for deep frying
confectioner's sugar
strawberry, plum or apricot marmalade

Add one tablespoon flour and one teaspoon sugar to the warm milk. Allow the yeast to rise in the warm milk for fifteen minutes. Beat the egg yolks and the sugar until light and lemon-colored. Add the butter and beat well. Stir in the salt, lemon rind, rum and sour cream. Add the yeast mixture and the flour, alternately, beating well after each addition. Beat the dough with a wooden spoon until it blisters.

Continued on next page

Cover and place in a warm, draft-free place. Allow to rise for half an hour until the dough is doubled in size. Place on a floured board and roll to ½ inch thickness.

Cut rounds out of the dough with a floured glass. Fill half the rounds with a teaspoonful of marmalade. Cover with the remaining rounds. Place each filled *pokladnica* on a floured board. Cover with a kitchen towel and allow to rise for another half hour.

Heat the oil to 350°. Fry in the hot oil, uncovered, for six minutes or until golden. Turn and fry on the other side until a golden brown color all over. As each *pokladnica* is removed from the frying pan, place it on paper towels to drain. Serve piled on a plate and sprinkled with confectioner's sugar.

Sniježne Grude
Snowballs with Apricot Cream

4 egg yolks
1 tbsp. sugar
4 tbsp. wine
2 tbsp. water
2 c. flour
1 tbsp. rum
¼ tsp. salt
½ c. oil
½ c. butter

Beat the egg yolks until very light and lemon colored. Beat in the sugar. Sift the flour and the salt. Add the flour, wine and water to the egg yolks alternately, beating well after each addition. Beat the dough well until it begins to blister. Add more flour or water as required while beating to make a firm but smooth dough. Shape a long strip about 3 inches in diameter from the dough. Cover with a kitchen towel and allow the dough to rest for about half an hour. Slice the dough into equal pieces. Make a slit in the center of each piece. Heat the oil and butter in a heavy skillet. Add the rum to the hot fat. Fry the slices of dough in the oil and butter mixture until golden brown on both sides. Sprinkle with confectioner's sugar and cover with Apricot Cream.

Uštipci
Cheese Pinches

2 eggs
2 tbsp. sugar
2 tbsp. oil
1 c. cottage cheese
1 c. lukewarm milk
2 cakes yeast
1 tsp. salt
6 c. flour
oil for deep frying

Dissolve the sugar and yeast in the milk and allow to rise in a warm place until doubled in size. Sift the flour. Add the eggs, oil, cottage cheese, salt and the yeast mixture. Mix well, then knead the dough well and allow to rise. When the dough is doubled in size, heat the oil. Drop the dough by spoonfuls into the oil. Allow the dough to become golden brown on both sides. Remove from the oil and drain. Sprinkle with confectioner's sugar.

Non-Plus Ultra
Nothing Better Than

1 ¾ c. sifted flour
1 c. butter
3 egg yolks
2 tbsp. sugar
½ tsp. vanilla
¼ c. apricot jam

Preheat the oven to 350°. Combine all the ingredients except the jam and work them into a firm dough. Knead until smooth. Roll until ¼ inch thick. Cut with a very small cookie cutter or with a shot glass. Place on a greased cookie sheet close together. Place a teaspoonful of topping on each cookie or pipe a small amount of topping with a star tube onto each cookie. Bake for twenty minutes until the cookies are a golden color and the topping is dry and begins to brown slightly. Allow the cookies to cool. Spread a little marmalade on the bottom of each cookie and place two cookies together to make a sandwich.

Topping

3 egg whites
1/3 c. sugar

Beat the egg whites until stiff. Add the sugar and beat for another minute.

Poljupci od Oraha, Non Plus Ultra, Šape, Lincer Kolači, Kolutići s Marmeladom, Čupavci i Bademovi Štapići.
Walnut Kisses [page 222], Nothing Better Than [page220], Bear Claws, Linzer Cookies [page222]
Marmalade Rounds [page 224], Shaggy Cakes [page 222] and Almond Horns [page 224].

Medvjeđe Šape
Bear Claws

3 c. ground walnuts
¼ tsp. baking powder
1 c. sugar
2 c. flour
1 c. butter, softened
1 egg, slightly beaten
2 tbsp. honey
1 tsp. vanilla
confectioner's sugar

Preheat the oven to 350°. Grease and flour madeleine molds. Combine the flour, walnuts, baking powder and sugar. Add the egg, honey, softened butter and vanilla. Mix well. Chill for half an hour. Fill the madeleine molds, but not all the way to the top. Bake for twenty minutes until they begin to brown. Remove from the molds and dredge in vanilla sugar while still warm.

Čupavci
Shaggy Cakes

6 egg yolks
6 tbsp. sugar
6 tbsp. flour
1 tsp. vanilla
6 egg whites
¼ tsp. cream of tartar
¼ tsp. salt
4 c. sweetened coconut flakes

Preheat the oven to 350°. Grease and flour an 11"x16" jelly roll pan. Beat the egg yolks with the sugar until light and lemon-colored. Add the salt and vanilla and beat well. Add the flour, a tablespoon at a time, and beat well after each addition. Beat the egg whites until frothy. Add the cream of tartar and continue beating until stiff. Gently fold the egg whites into the egg yolk mixture. Spread into the prepared pan. Bake for twelve minutes until the cake springs back to the touch. Invert the pan onto a wire rack. Remove the pan and allow the cake to cool completely. Cut the cake into bars 1½ by 3 inches. Dip the cake bars in the chocolate glaze and immediately roll in coconut. Allow the cookies to cool completely so that the chocolate can harden.

Chocolate Glaze

¼ c. water
¼ c. sugar
4 oz. unsweetened chocolate
6 tbsp. butter

Heat the water, sugar and the chocolate until the chocolate is melted. Do not allow to boil. Drop thin slices of butter into the mixture, stirring constantly. Keep the glaze warm while dipping the cake bars in it.

Poljupci od Oraha
Walnut Kisses

2 egg whites
½ c. sugar
1 tbsp. strong black coffee
2 ½ c. ground walnuts

Beat the egg whites until stiff. Add the sugar and beat until very stiff. Fold in the walnuts and coffee. Drop by spoonful onto a greased cookie sheet. Sprinkle with sugar. Bake at 300° for approximately twenty minutes until dry.

Lincer Kolači
Linzer Cookies

½ c. butter
½ c. sugar
3 c. flour
6 egg yolks

Preheat the oven to 350°. Cream the butter and the sugar until light and fluffy. Add the egg yolks, one at a time, beating well after each addition. Add the flour and work into a firm dough. When the dough is smooth, roll it to ¼ inch in thickness. Cut with flower-shaped cookie cutters. Cut the centers out of half the cookies with a thimble. Place the cookies on an ungreased cookie sheet. Brush the tops of the cookies with the holes in the center with egg white and sprinkle with ground walnuts. Bake for ten minutes. Sprinkle the cookies with the holes with confectioner's sugar. Spread the whole cookies with marmalade. Top with the cut-out cookies.

Breskve
Mock Peaches

4 eggs
2 c. sugar
2 tsp. vanilla
1 c. milk
1 c. oil
2 tsp. baking powder
6 ½ c. flour
½ tsp. salt
½ c. rum
1 c. granulated sugar

Preheat the oven to 350°. Sift the flour with the salt and baking powder. Beat the eggs and sugar until very light and fluffy. Add the vanilla and oil and half the flour and beat well. Add the remaining flour alternately with the milk, beating well after each addition. You will have a soft, but firm dough. Make small balls with floured hands, or dip a melon baller in flour and make small balls with a melon baller. Bake for approximately twelve minutes until the bottom is golden, but the tops of the balls are still white. Allow the cookies to cool. Hollow out the centers of the balls. The hollowed centers will be used to make the stuffing for the "peaches".

Continued on next page.

Stuff the hollowed balls with the filling. Join the cookie halves to make balls. Place granulated sugar in two small bowls. Add yellow food coloring to one and red food coloring to the other. Mix well. Dip the balls in rum, then roll them in the colored sugars to give the balls the color of peaches.

Stuffing for Peaches

ground centers of cookies
3 c. ground walnuts
5 tbsp. cocoa
6 tbsp. sugar
½ c. rum
¼ c. very strong coffee

Grind the centers of the cookies which were hollowed out for making mock peaches. Combine with the remaining ingredients and mix well.

Kolutići s Marmeladom
Marmalade Rounds

3 c. flour
¾ c. butter
1 egg
2 egg yolks
½ c. sugar
¼ c. gooseberry marmalade
1 tbsp. rum
confectioner's sugar

Preheat the oven to 350°. Combine the flour, butter, sugar, egg and egg yolks and work into a firm dough. Refrigerate for half an hour. Roll the dough to ¼ inch thickness. Cut the dough into circles with a cookie cutter. Cut a hole in the center of half the circles with a thimble. Place the circles on a greased cookie sheet and bake for ten minutes until they just begin to brown. Sprinkle the rounds with the holes with confectioner's sugar. Add the rum to the marmalade. Spread the marmalade over the whole circles. Place the circles with the holes over the others.

Bademovi Štapići
Almond Horns

2 c. flour
½ c. sugar
½ c . butter
3 egg yolks
1 tsp. vanilla
1 egg white
1 c. ground blanched almonds

Preheat the oven to 350°. Combine the flour, sugar, almonds, egg yolks and vanilla. Work into a firm dough. Allow the dough to rest one hour. Knead the dough again. Divide the dough in two. Roll each piece of dough into a long, thin rope. Cut the rope into pieces 3 inches long. Shape these pieces into horns. Dip the horns in slightly beaten egg white. Bake for ten minutes. Remove from heat and dip the ends of the horns in chocolate glaze.

Chocolate Glaze

2 tbsp. water
2 tbsp. sugar
2 oz. unsweetened chocolate
3 tbsp. butter

Heat the water, sugar and chocolate until the chocolate melts. Do not allow to boil. Drop thin slices of butter into the mixture, stirring constantly.

Roščići od Vanilije
Vanilla Horns

1 c. butter
1½ c. flour
2 c. ground almonds
5 tbsp. sugar

Combine all the ingredients to make a firm dough. When smooth, tear into small pieces. Roll these pieces of dough into horn shapes. Place on a greased cookie sheet and bake at 350° for fifteen minutes. Dredge in confectioner's sugar while still warm.

Frostings and Glazes

Coffee Cream Frosting:

6 egg yolks
½ c. strong black coffee
¾ c. confectioner's sugar
2 tbsp. flour
1 c. butter

Combine the egg yolks and and sugar and beat well until light and lemon colored. Add the coffee and flour and continue beating the mixture in a double boiler. When the mixture begins to thicken, remove from heat and allow to cool. Beat the butter until light and fluffy. Add the coffee cream to the butter and continue beating until the frosting is very smooth and glossy.

Krema od Oraha

Walnut Butter Cream Frosting

½ c. butter
1 c. confectioner's sugar
1 c. ground walnuts
3 tbsp. very strong black coffee

Cream the butter. Add the sugar and continue beating until light and frothy. Beat in the coffee a tablespoon at a time. Beat well after each addition. Add the walnuts and continue beating until the frosting is very smooth and light.

Krema od Badema

Almond Butter Cream Frosting

1 c. butter
¾ c. ground blanched almonds
2 c. confectioner's sugar
¼ c. strong black coffee
½ c. heavy whipping cream

Cream the butter until very light and smooth. Beat in the sugar. Add the ground walnuts and cold strong coffee. Continue beating until the mixture is thick and light. Whip the cream. Fold the whipped cream into the almond butter frosting and continue beating until the frosting is very light and creamy.

Krema od Čokolade

Chocolate Cream Frosting

½ c. heavy cream, whipped
1 c. butter
1 egg
6 squares semi-sweet chocolate
1 tsp. vanilla
2 c. confectioner's sugar

Melt the chocolate squares in a double boiler. Allow to cool completely. Whip the cream. Cream the butter. Beat in the egg and sugar and continue beating until the mixture is light and frothy. Beat in the cooled chocolate and continue beating until the frosting is very smooth and light.

Ocaklina od Čokolade

Chocolate Glaze

¼ c. water
¼ c. sugar
4 oz. unsweetened chocolate
6 tbsp. unsalted butter

Heat the water, sugar and chocolate until the chocolate melts. Do not allow to boil. Drop thin slices of butter into the mixture, stirring constantly.

Ocaklina sa Kavom

Coffee Glaze

2 c. sugar
½ c. very strong black coffee
5 oz. semisweet chocolate, melted
1 tbsp. butter

Put the sugar and coffee in a a heavy saucepan. Bring to a boil over medium heat. Boil, without stirring for 10 minutes until it reaches the large thread stage (225°). Combine the melted chocolate and the butter. Pour the hot syrup into the chocolate mixture, gradually, stirring constantly, until the glaze is thick but liquid so that it can flow freely.

A Selection of Croatian Breads

Breads

Nothing draws the family to the table more quickly than the tempting aroma of home-made bread, hot from the oven. When thickly sliced and spread with fresh butter or sour cream, warm freshly baked bread serves as an excellent appetizer for the rest of the meal.

Breads and rolls remain a major staple in the Croatian diet. They are eaten as often as three times per day and no well laid table is without a plaited bread basket containing two or more varieties of bread. Although breads are available commercially in many varieties, breads are still baked fresh for special occasion, especially Christmas and Easter.

The rich glutenous flour made from the high quality wheat of Backa and Sriem is unexcelled for baking. Europe has long had a high demand for this excellent flour for use in pastries and tortes as well as breads and rolls. Although wheat is by far the most important grain that the country consumes for baking bread, other grains are also used. This results in a large variety of breads, rolls and biscuits. The standard white breads made from rich, unbleached wheat flour are baked in unlimited shapes and designs. *Mliječni Kruh*, a popular white bread. is often plaited into a thick, golden braid which may be shaped into a ring for a special Christmas or Easter bread.

Whole wheat bread is frequently found on the Croatian table. For *marenda*, slices of brown bread are often served with *pršut* and the famous Croatian Trappist cheese. Rye, which is sown in the fields of Slavonia and Sriem is used for baking both the light and dark varieties of rye bread. *Medeni Kruh*, a special holiday bread made from honey, is a favorite with the children. They await the familiar aroma of the bread with eager appetites.

In addition to breads, Croatians frequently make little cakes called *pogačice*. These little round cakes are made in many varieties. Some are leavened with eggs, while others use yeast. They incorporate all of the readily available materials, including milk, cheese, sour cream or even pork cracklings. Easy to make, they are an excellent snack, or can be substituted for bread in sandwiches.

Kruh sa Sirom
Cheese Bread

3 c. flour
¾ tsp. salt
¾ c. hard cheese, grated
1 tbsp. sugar
½ c. lukewarm milk
1 egg
1 cake yeast

Dissolve the sugar in the warm milk. Add the yeast and allow to rise until frothy, approximately twenty minutes. Beat the egg well in the bottom of a deep bowl. Add the salt, cheese and the yeast mixture. Stir well. Add 2 ½ cups flour and work into a soft dough. Add enough of the flour to make a soft dough. Turn onto a floured board. Knead, adding enough of the remaining flour to make a smooth dough. Shape the dough into a loaf. Place it on a well greased baking pan. Cover with a kitchen towel and allow to rise in a warm place until doubled in bulk, approximately one and a half hours. Bake at 350° for about forty-five minutes.

Medeni Kruh
Sweet Honey Bread

3 c. flour
1 ½ tsp. baking soda
1 ½ tsp. cinnamon
¾ c. honey
¾ c. sugar
1 ½ c. milk
¼ tsp. salt
2 tbsp. butter

Grease and flour a bread pan. Preheat the oven to 350°. In a large bowl combine the flour, salt, sugar and cinnamon. Place the butter, milk and honey into a saucepan and heat until well mixed. Sprinkle the baking soda over the honey mixture and mix well. Stir the honey mixture into the flour. When there are no lumps in the batter, pour it into the prepared pan and bake in the preheated oven for thirty-five minutes to an hour. Be careful not to allow the bread to bake too long. Honey bread burns more easily than regular bread.

Pletenica
Braided Bread

2 ½ c. flour
3 tbsp. sugar
2 tsp. salt
1 c. butter
1 egg, well beaten
2 c. milk, lukewarm
1 cake yeast
egg whites

Melt the butter and allow it to cool. In the bottom of a deep bowl, dissolve the sugar and the salt in the milk. Add the yeast. Allow to sit in a warm place until doubled in size. Add the well beaten egg to the yeast mixture. Stir in one cup of flour and beat to form a smooth batter. Add the butter and the remaining flour alternately to form a stiff dough. Turn onto a floured board and knead well. The dough should be smooth and elastic. Place in a greased bowl and allow to rise for about half an hour in a warm place. Divide the dough into two parts. Divide each half into three parts. Braid each of these three parts into a loaf. Place the loaves onto a greased baking sheet sprinkled with cornmeal and allow to rise for another half hour. Brush with well beaten egg whites. Bake at 425° for about ten minutes. Reduce the heat to 350° and bake for another forty-five minutes.

Razljevuša
Cornmeal Bread

1 c. cornmeal
¼ c. cheddar cheese, grated
1 ½ c. dry cottage cheese
1 c. milk
4 egg yolks, well beaten
4 stiffly beaten egg whites
2 tbsp. melted butter
dash of salt

Preheat the oven to 350°. Grease and flour an 8 x 10 inch baking pan. Beat the cottage cheese and cheddar cheese until very smooth. Add milk, salt, egg yolks and butter, a little at a time, beating well after each addition. The batter should be smooth and creamy. Fold in the stiffly beaten egg whites. Pour into the prepared baking pan. Bake at 350° for half an hour. When the bread is golden brown remove from oven and serve immediately.

Krumpirski Kruh
Potato Bread

1 ½ c. grated potatoes
2 tsp. ground garlic
1 tbsp. salt
1 c. warm water
2 tbsp. sugar
3 ½ c. flour
1 cake of yeast
oil or melted butter

Combine the potato, salt, garlic, yeast, sugar and water. Stir until the yeast is dissolved. Allow to rise for about twenty minutes until foamy. Add three cups of flour. Work into a dough, adding as much of the additional flour as necessary to make a medium soft dough. Turn the dough out onto a floured board and knead the dough until all ingredients are thoroughly blended and the dough is smooth and glossy. Brush the top of the dough with oil or melted butter. Cover and allow to rise in a warm, draft-free place for about an hour until doubled in size. Punch down the dough and turn it out onto a well greased sheet. Brush the top of the bread with oil or melted butter. Allow to rise once more in a warm place for approximately half an hour. Bake at 400° until nicely browned, approximately half an hour.

Saće ili Buhtli
Sugar Buns

1 cake yeast
1 c. warm milk
3 ½ c. bread flour
½ tsp. salt
3 tbsp. sugar
2 eggs
1 c. butter, softened
¼ c. melted butter
½ c. plum jam
¼ c. confectioner's sugar

Stir the sugar into the warm milk. Crumble the yeast into the milk, stir and allow to rise until foamy, approximately twenty minutes. Sift the flour with the salt into a large bowl. Stir in the yeast mixture. Beat the egg and the softened butter. Add to the flour mixture. Work the dough until it no longer sticks to the sides of the bowl or to your hands. When the dough is smooth and elastic, cover the bowl with a kitchen towel and allow to rise in a warm place until doubled in bulk, approximately one hour.

Turn the dough out onto a floured board. Punch down and knead until smooth and elastic. Roll the dough into a rectangle approximately ½ inch thick. Cut into 2 ½ x 4 inch rectangles. Place a teaspoonful of jam over one half of each rectangle. Fold each rectangle over like a book and pinch the edges to seal them.

Place the buns on a greased and floured baking sheet and brush with the melted butter. Allow to rise again for another half hour.

Preheat the oven to 350°. Bake for thirty minutes until the tops are golden brown. Remove from the baking sheet while they are still warm and dust with confectioner's sugar. May be served warm or cold.

Kruh sa Vočem
Fruit Bread

1 lb. dried figs
¾ lb. dried dates
¾ lb. pitted prunes
¾ lb. raisins
1 c. coarsley chopped walnuts
1 c. coarsley chopped hazelnuts
1 c. coarsley chopped blanched almonds
1 tbsp. cinnamon
½ tsp. cloves
¼ c. rum
1 cake yeast
1/3 c. warm water
¾ c. bread flour
¼ tsp. salt
1 tsp. wine vinegar
1 egg white, lightly beaten
½ c. sliced almonds
½ c. confectioner's sugar

Dice the figs, chop the dates, raisins and prunes. Combine the fruit, chopped nuts and rum and allow the mixture to marinade overnight.

The following day, dissolve the yeast in the warm water and allow to rise until foamy, approximately twenty minutes.

Sift the flour with the salt and stir the yeast mixture into the flour. Add the vinegar and work into a soft dough. Allow the dough to rise in a warm, draft-free place for approximately an hour.

Preheat the oven to 325°. Knead the fruit into the dough. Shape into 3 loaves. Arrange the loaves on greased baking sheets. Brush them with the beaten egg white. Bake for two hours.

Remove from the oven. Dissolve the confectioner's sugar in two tablespoons warm water and spread this glaze over the warm fruit bread. Sprinkle with sliced almonds.

Uskrsna Pletenica
Croatian Easter Braid

4 c. sifted, unbleached flour
1 ¾ c. warm milk
2 c. granulated sugar
4 tbsp. butter
2 tbsp. active dry yeast
1/2 c. raisins
1 tsp. salt
1 tsp. lemon rind
1 egg, beaten

Melt the butter. Combine the milk, butter, sugar and yeast. Allow to stand for 20 minutes at room temperature. Stir together 3 cups of flour, salt and lemon rind, then add the yeast mixture and mix until smooth. When thoroughly mixed, add the remaining cup of flour and knead the mixture until smooth and glossy, but somewhat gummy. Knead in the raisins.

Cover and allow the dough to rise in a warm place until doubled in size. Divide the dough into 3 equal pieces and roll into ropes. Braid, then form the braid into a wreath. Place the wreath onto a greased and floured baking sheet. Allow to rise in a warm place for approximately 30 minutes. Brush the wreath with the beaten egg. Bake in a preheated 350°F oven for 45 minutes or until golden brown.

Slani Kuglof
Salty Kuglof

1 cake yeast
½ lb. smoked bacon
2 ½ c. bread flour
1 tsp. salt
1 tbsp. sugar
½ c. warm water
1 egg
3 tbsp. butter, softened
½ c. sliced almonds

Stir one tablespoon flour and the sugar into the warm water. Add the yeast and mix well. Allow to rise until the mixture becomes foamy, approximately twenty minutes. Dice the bacon and fry it in its own fat. Drain the fat and drain the fried bacon on paper towels.

Combine the flour, salt, sugar, egg and the yeast mixture. Work into a smooth, but gummy dough. Beat until the dough no longer sticks to the sides of the bowl. Add the softened butter, a little at a time, the bacon and all but two tablespoons of the sliced almonds. Cover the bowl with a kitchen towel and allow the dough to rise in a warm, draft-free place for approximately one hour until doubled in bulk.

Grease and flour the kuglof mold. Sprinkle the bottom of the mold with the remaining sliced almonds. Punch the dough down and place it in the mold. Allow to rise for another twenty to thirty minutes until the dough is just below the top of the mold.

Bake in a preheated oven at 350° for approximately thirty five minutes. Invert the mold and remove the pan. Serve hot.

Mliječni Kruh
Milk Bread

4 c. bread flour
½ c. sugar
1 cake yeast
6 tbsp. melted butter
1 ½ c. warm milk
½ tsp. salt
1 egg white, slightly beaten

Dissolve the sugar in the warm milk. Add the yeast. Stir well and set in a warm place until foamy, approximately twenty minutes.

Sift the flour with the salt into a deep bowl. Make a well in the flour and add the yeast mixture and the melted butter. Beat well to make a soft dough.

Turn out onto a well-floured board and knead well until the dough is smooth and elastic. Grease a deep bowl and place the dough in it. Turn the dough to grease the other side. Cover with a kitchen towel and allow it to rise in a warm, draft-free place for about an hour until doubled in bulk.

Knead the dough again by rolling one end onto the other. Divide the dough and shape into two loaves.

Place in a greased pan and allow to rise until doubled in size. Brush with well beaten egg white. Bake at 425° for ten minutes. Lower the heat to 350° and bake for another forty-five minutes. Cool on a wire rack.

Badnji Kruh

Christmas Eve Bread
1¼ c. whole wheat flour
2 c. bread flour
1 cake yeast
½ c. warm water
3 tbsp. honey
1 ¼ c. white wine
½ c. whole hazelnuts
½ c. whole blanched almonds
½ c. raisins
12 oz. dried figs, chopped

Grease and flour a medium bread pan. Stir the honey into the warm water. Add the yeast and mix well. Allow to rise until foamy, approximately 20 minutes. Work a firm dough from the flour, yeast and wine. Knead until smooth. Add the hazelnuts, almonds, raisins and figs. Allow to rise in a warm, draft-free place for one hour until doubled in bulk. Punch down and place in the bread pan. Allow to rise again for another half hour. Bake in a preheated oven at 375° until golden. Spread two tablespoons of honey over the warm bread as a glaze and serve warm. The bread can be refrigerated overnight. In this case, let it warm to room temperature, then allow it to rise for the time required. In the morning you will have fresh, warm bread for Christmas Eve breakfast.

Božićna Pletenica
Croatian Christmas Braid

4 c. bread flour
¾ c. warm milk
¾ c. granulated sugar
1 c. butter
2 tbsp. active dry yeast
1 c. raisins
¼ tsp. salt
¼ tsp. grated nutmeg
1 tsp. almond extract
1 tsp. lemon rind
1 egg, beaten
2 egg yolks
1 c. sliced blanched almonds
1 egg white, slightly beaten
½ c. granulated sugar
2 tbsp. water

Melt the butter. Combine the milk, butter, sugar and yeast. Allow to stand for 20 minutes at room temperature. Stir together 3 cups of flour, salt, butter, egg, egg yolks and lemon rind, then add the yeast mixture and mix until smooth. When thoroughly mixed, add the remaining cup of flour and knead the mixture until smooth and glossy, but somewhat gummy. Knead in the raisins and almonds.

Cover and allow the dough to rise in a warm place until doubled in size. Divide the dough into 3 equal pieces and roll into ropes. Braid, then form the braid into a wreath. Place the wreath onto a greased and floured baking sheet. Allow to rise in a warm place for approximately 30 minutes. Brush the wreath with the beaten egg white. Bake in a preheated 350°F oven for 45 minutes or until golden brown. Combine the confectioner's sugar with the water to make a glaze. Pour this glaze over the braid. This bread can be the centerpiece for a Christmas dinner. In the center place a candle and a glass of wheat which signifies prosperity for the coming year.

Uskrsni Kruh od Anisa
Croatian Anise Easter Bread

1 tsp. anise seeds
¼ c. white wine
1 cake yeast
5 ¾ c. flour
½ c. butter
¾ c. sugar
1 egg
3 egg yolks
1 tsp. vanilla
¼ tsp. salt
1 tsp. lemon rind
1 tsp. orange rind

Soak the anise seeds in the wine overnight. The following day, remove the seeds from the wine. Combine the yeast with one tablespoon flour, one teaspoon sugar and ¼ c. warm water. Allow to rise in a warm place until foamy, approximately twenty minutes.

In a deep bowl, cut the butter into the flour until you have crumbs the size of peas. Make a well in the center and add the wine in which the anise seeds were soaked, sugar, egg, egg yolks, vanilla, salt, lemon rind, orange rind and the yeast mixture. Mix well to make a firm dough. Work the dough until it is smooth and glossy. Allow to rise in a warm, draft-free place for approximately an hour and a half until doubled in bulk. Punch down the dough and divide it in two. Shape each half into a round loaf. Place on a greased baking sheet and allow to rise for another half hour to forty-five minutes. Make a cross on each circle and brush with egg white. Sprinkle with sugar crystals and bake in a preheated oven at 375° for about an hour.

Biskupski Kruh
Bishop's Bread

6 egg yolks
½ c. sugar
¾ c. flour
1 tsp. baking powder
½ c. sliced almonds
½ c. chopped figs
¾ c. raisins
2 tsp. grated orange rind
1 c. chocolate chips
6 egg whites
¼ tsp. cream of tartar

Preheat the oven to 350°. Grease and flour a loaf pan. Sift the flour with the baking powder. Beat the egg yolks with the sugar until light and lemon colored. Add the orange rind, figs, almonds, raisins and chocolate. Mix in the flour. Beat the egg whites until frothy. Add the cream of tartar and continue beating until the egg whites stand in stiff peaks. Gently fold the egg whites into the egg yolk mixture. Pour the mixture into the prepared pan and bake for approximately forty minutes. Allow to cool in the pan for five minutes. Invert onto a wire rack and allow to cool completely. This bread should be stored for a day or two before eating.

Pogačice sa Sirom
Cheese Biscuits

1 c. butter
2 c. flour
½ tsp. salt
8 oz. cottage cheese
1 egg yolk

Sift the flour with the salt. Cut the butter into the flour until you have small crumbs the size of bread crumbs. Blend the cheese in a blender or food processor and combine it with the flour mixture. Quickly knead into a firm dough. Roll the dough on a floured board to a thick rectangle. Fold it over twice and refrigerate for half an hour. Repeat rolling, folding and refrigerating two more times. Preheat the oven to 350°. Roll the dough to a rectangle one inch thick. Cut into rounds with a cookie cutter. Score the tops of the biscuits with a sharp knife in a lattice pattern. Beat the egg yolk slightly with one teaspoon water and brush it over the biscuits. Bake in the preheated oven for about twenty-five minutes.

Pogačice od Čvaraka
Crackling Biscuits

1 lb. finely chopped cracklings
5 c. flour
1 cake yeast
1 c. milk
4 tbsp. melted lard
2 eggs
2 tsp. salt
1 egg yolk

Crumble the yeast into the warm milk to which you have added a teaspoon sugar. When the mixture becomes foamy, combine all the ingredients and work together to make a firm smooth dough. Allow the dough to rise in a warm place until doubled in bulk. Turn it out onto a floured board and roll to about one and a half inches in thickness. Cut into circles or squares. Score the little cakes with a sharp knife to make a decorative lattice pattern. Place the cakes on a baking sheet and allow to rise for about an hour. Beat the egg yolk slightly with 1 tsp. water. Brush the biscuits with the egg yolk. Bake in a preheated oven at 350° for about half an hour. Serve warm with fresh butter.

Pogačice sa Maslacem
Butter Biscuits

½ cake yeast
¼ c. warm milk
2 tbsp. sugar
½ c. flour
2 eggs
½ c. butter
½ tsp. salt
¼ c. sour cream
1 egg yolk

Crumble the yeast into the warm milk to which the sugar has been added. Allow to rise for twenty minutes until foamy. Combine the yeast with the flour, 2 eggs, butter, salt and sour cream. Work into a smooth, medium dough. Allow to rise for half an hour. Roll the dough out on a floured board. Fold it and let is rise for another thirty minutes. Preheat the oven to 350°. Roll the dough into a rectangle, one inch thick. With a cookie cutter, cut into rounds. With a sharp knife score a lattice pattern on each biscuit. Brush with the egg yolk and bake in the preheated oven for twenty-five minutes.

Pogačice sa Kiselim Vrhnjem
Sour Cream Biscuits

1 ½ c. flour
1 c. sour cream
4 egg yolks
1 tsp. sugar
2 tsp. salt

Combine all the ingredients and work them into a medium dough. Roll the dough out to ½ inch thickness and allow it to rest for half an hour. With a sharp knife score a lattice pattern over the sheet of dough. Cut rounds out with a cookie cutter and brush with the egg white. Place the biscuits on a greased baking sheet and bake in a preheated oven at 350° for about twenty to twenty-five minutes.

Zemičke
Hard Rolls

7 c. flour
¼ c. melted butter
2 cakes yeast
1 tbsp. salt
½ c. warm water
1 tsp. sugar
1 egg white

Soften the yeast in warm water (110°) to which you have added 1 tbsp. flour and the sugar. Allow to rise until foamy. Combine yeast, butter and salt. Add 2 cups flour and beat well. Gradually add enough of the remaining flour to form a stiff dough. Knead for about ten to fifteen minutes until very smooth. Place in a greased bowl, turning the dough to grease the surface. Allow to rise for an hour in a warm, draft-free place. Punch down. Allow to rise again for another half hour. Turn out onto a floured board and allow to rest for ten minutes. Divide the dough into 20 pieces. Shape each piece into a roll and score the tops with short diagonal cuts. Place on a greased baking sheet which has been sprinkled with cornmeal. Sprinkle with poppy seeds or sesame seeds if desired. Allow to rise for another half an hour. Place a pan of water in the oven and preheat to 350°. Beat the egg white with a little warm water. Brush the rolls with the beaten egg white. Bake at 350° for about half an hour. Remove the pan of water when the rolls have been in the oven for five minutes.

Krušni Prutići
Bread Sticks

1 recipe dough for hard rolls
2 tbsp. cornmeal
1 tsp. water
1 egg white

After the second rising, divide the dough into twelve equal parts. Roll each piece of dough under your hand into pencil-like sticks, about 12 inches long and 3/8 inch in diameter. Place the sticks approximately 1 inch apart on a greased baking sheet sprikled with cornmeal. Beat the egg white lightly with the water. Brush each dough stick with a the egg white. Allow to rise in a warm place until doubled in size, approxiamtely 45 minutes. Brush again with the egg white and sprinkle with coarse salt. Bake at 400° for twelve to fifteen minutes.

Kruh sa Grožđicama
Raisin Bread

½ c. milk, scalded
1 cake yeast
¼ c. sugar
3 ½ c. sifted flour
2 egg yolks
¼ tsp. salt
½ c. raisins
6 tbsp. melted butter
1 egg white
½ c. confectioner's sugar

Cool the milk to approximately 115°. Add the yeast and the sugar to the milk in a deep bowl and set aside until foamy, approximately twenty minutes. Add two cups flour and mix well. Cover and allow to rise in a warm, draft-free place until light and bubbly.

Combine the egg yolks, raisins, salt, and butter. Beat well. Add this mixture to the dough. Add as much of the remaining flour as required, a little at a time, and make a soft, smooth dough. Knead well.

When the dough no longer sticks to the sides of the bowl, cover with a kitchen towel and allow the dough to rise in a warm, draft-free place until doubled in bulk, approximately one hour.

Punch down. Knead again until smooth and glossy. Shape into a loaf. Place on a greased baking sheet. Allow to rise again for another half hour.

Beat the egg white with a teaspoon warm water. Brush the egg white wash over the bread. Bake in a preheated oven at 350° for about forty-five minutes.

Stir the confectioner's sugar with the two tablespoons water. Pour this glaze over the bread while still warm. Allow the bread to cool slightly. May be served warm or cold.

Index

Numbers in italics indicate the page on which the recipe is illustrated.

Dobar Tek!